FOUR MILES HIGH

The US 8th Air Force 1st, 2nd and 3rd Air Divisions in World War 2

MARTIN W. BOWMAN

Patrick Stephens Limited

First published in 1992

British Library Cataloguing-in-Publication Data:
A catalogue record for this book is available
from the British Library.

ISBN 1-85260-406-9

Jacket illustrations
Front *(top left, clockwise) Sunrise at Thorpe Abbotts; B-17G-40-VE on a test flight over California before joining the 305th BG in England; Col John Driscoll posing by* Fightin' Sam *of the 389th BG at Hethel; and Lt Sam Turner and his crew after crash landing B-17* Raunchy *at Thorpe Abbotts.*
Back *(top left, clockwise) A gunner is extricated from* Liberty Lib *of the 458th BG at Horsham St Faith; B-17G of the 569th BS, 390th BG at Framlingham; 458th BG Assembly Ship* Spotted Ape *at Horsham St Faith; and sunset over Suffolk.*
Background *453rd BG Liberators in formation.*

Patrick Stephens Limited is a member of the
Haynes Publishing Group P.L.C.,
Sparkford, Nr Yeovil, Somerset, BA22 7JJ.

Printed in Great Britain by J. H. Haynes & Co. Ltd.

Contents

‘Get a load of those guys, high in the skies,
Winging to victory,
Up and at ’em in the fight for
People like you and me . . .’

People Like You and Me
By Mack Gordon and Harry Warren

Acknowledgements

I AM INDEBTED to those who kindly allowed me to quote selected passages from their books, all of which are classics in the history of the USAAF at war. Cliff Bishop's *Fortresses of the Triangle First*, is one of the most invaluable reference works I have ever come across, and it helped in the preparation of detailed photo captions and was most useful for cross-checking dates and missions. My thanks also to Paul Tibbets for passages from *The Paul Tibbets Story*; to Philip G. Day for the excerpt from *The Saga of A Reluctant Co-pilot*; to Gen Andy Low's (USAF Retd) *The Liberator Men of 'Old Buck*; *The Liberators From Wendling*, by Robert E. Vickers Jr; Gene Gaskins' *Crew Sixty-Four*; and Russell A. Strong's *First Over Germany*. I am also grateful to Ed Hicks for kindly making his researches into the early history of the 97th Bombardment Group available, and to Abe Dolim and 'Pappy' Colby for access to their war diaries. I am especially indebted to Richard E. Lewis for allowing me to quote from his gripping book, *Hell Above and Hell Below*. My good friend, artist Mike Bailey, provided his usual expertise in 8th Air Force matters.

I am no less grateful to the following: Walter Austin, the late William D. Allen, Carl L. Anderson, John Archer, Ron Batley, Ray Betcher, Stan Brett, Bob Bishop, Bob Browne, William Boutelle, the late Marvin Barnes, Frank L. Betz, Gen Harold W. Bowman, John W. Butler, Col Bill Cameron, Robert Capaldi, Bill Carleton, Claude E. Campbell, Forrest Clark; Henry C. Cordery, Frank Cotner, Hugh K. Crawford, Harry H. Crosby, Henry A. DeKeyser, Richmond Henre Dugger, Col John Driscoll, the late Gen Ira C. Eaker, Stewart Evans, Robert L. Ferrell, John C. Ford, Albert J. Filiponis, Reuben Fier, Richard E. Fitzhugh, Robert E. Foose, Lt Col Charles H. Freudenthal, Richard Gibson, Lee Gordon, Sol Greenberg, John Goldsmith, Larry Goldstein, Dan Graham, John E. Greenwood, Lee C. Gordon, Hank Gladys, Russ Harriman, Herman Hager, Cliff Hall, Frank Halm, Mike Harvey, Russ D. Hayes, the late Alan Healy, John Holden, Harry Holmes, Mike Harvey, Cliff Hatcher, Ian Hawkins, Pete Henry, the late Howard E. Hernan, John Hildebran, John Holden, Robert L. Hughes, Ed Huntzinger, John Hurd, Leonard W. Herman, Henry Heckman, the late Glenn B. Infield, the late Ben C. Isgrig, Robert A. Jacobs, Joe F. Jones Jr., Jim Kotapish, Col Myron H.

Keilman, Jake D. Krause, Ivan Johnson, Loren E. Jackson, Edwin O. Jones, the late Beirne Lay Jr., Al La Chasse, Gen Curtis E. LeMay, Richard Lewis, Rusty Lewis, Irving Lifson, Alfred R. Lea, James J. Mahoney, Floyd H. Mabee, George Matecko, William B. Menzies, Emmett J. Murphy, Anthony J. McComiskey, Gus Mencow, Frank McGlinchey, Paul Montague, Ped G. Magness, Ian McLachlan, James Kemp McLaughlin, Abe Millar, John A. Miller, Bob Maag, Raymond P. Miller, Gerald 'Bill' McClelland, Orlo G. Natvig, William Nicholls, Wiley Noble, Grady Newsom, Lt Col Harlan Oakes, Jim O'Brien, Don Olds, Malcolm 'Ossie' Osborn, John Page, Ted Parker, Ralph K. Patton, the late Col Budd J. Peaslee, the late Gen Maurice Preston, Richard Perry, Cliff Pyle, George Reynolds, Connie and Gordon Richards, Bill Robertie, Rick Rokicki, Perry Rudd, William Rose, Francis X. Sheehan, Col Albert J. Shower, Bob Shaffer, Alvin D. Skaggs, William Sterret, Paul Surbaugh, Adolph J. Lloyd B. Slimp, Ben Smith Jr., Edwin 'Ted' Smith, Robert J. Shoens, Ben Schohan, Malvern R. Sweet, William C. Stewart, W. Griswold Smith, Bob Spangler, Frank Thomas, Father G. Thuring, Ralph Trout, Leslie G. Thibodeau, Henry Tarcza, Jim Tootell, the late Ralph Tomek, Horace Varian, Geoff Ward, Joe Warth, the late Gen Charles B. Westover, Alan R. Willis, Dan Winston, 'Dusty' Worthen, Mike Wysocki, Joe Wroblewski, David M. Williams, Henry A. West, Richard J. Walsh, Peck Wilcox, Karl Wendel, Ken Wright, Sam Young and Earl Zimmerman. My grateful thanks to them all, and to any I might have missed.

Martin W. Bowman,
Norwich, England.

Chapter One

Fame's favoured few

'ACHTUNG, FEINDLICHE FLUGZEUGE!' Jagdführer (Fighter Control) Holland had spotted a number of enemy aircraft. Immediately, Luftwaffe fighter units were alerted. German radar had picked up 12 American-built Douglas Boston twin engined medium bombers thundering low across the North Sea, en route to their targets. Six of the aircraft carried RAF crews, while the others were manned by American crews of the 15th Bombardment Group (Light). All had taken off in daylight from RAF Swanton Morley in Norfolk for a strike on four German airfields in Holland. It was 4 July 1942, and the first time that American airmen had flown in American-built bombers against a German target. Although it was a small force, the 12 aircraft signalled America's recognition that, although the Japanese bombing of Pearl Harbor in the Hawaiian Islands on 7 December 1941 had brought the United States into the war, her first enemy was Germany.

Although the United States could not prevent the attack on Pearl Harbor, far-reaching decisions had been made in the event that America should become involved in the conflict with the Axis powers. Between 27 January and 27 March 1941, agreements between the United States and Great Britain were made for the provision of naval, ground and air support for the campaign against Germany. On 28 January 1942 the 8th Air Force, under Maj Gen Henry 'Hap' Arnold, had been formed at Savannah, Georgia.

Although the Independence Day raid was important historically, it was not an unqualified success. Two of the aircraft manned by Americans were shot down by what the RAF flight leader described as '. . . the worst flak barrage in my experience'. Despite the disappointing outcome of the raid, the press hailed it as the start of a 'new and gigantic air offensive'.

One of the Bostons carried Lt Boyd S. Grant of the 97th Bomb. Group (BG), which provided some of the personnel. The 97th had arrived in England in July 1942 after flying the northern Atlantic ferry route via Goose Bay, Labrador, Greenland and Reykjavik, Iceland. Brig-Gen Ira C. Eaker, the 45-year-old Commanding General of VIII Bomber Command intended to build a heavy daylight bomber force as quickly and as efficiently as possible. He would initially direct operations from RAF Bomber Command Headquarters at High

Wycombe in Buckinghamshire, where, on 22 February, his command had formerly been activated. The no-nonsense Eaker had already replaced the original 97th BG commander, Col Cornelius Cousland, with Col Frank Armstrong, one of his original staff officers, to re-impose discipline and get results – quickly. The 97th, with its four squadrons of Boeing B-17E Flying Fortresses, was based at Podington and Grafton-Underwood in Northamptonshire.

The 97th had been activated on 3 February along with the 301st, commanded by Col Ronald R. Walker, and the 303rd BG. In the USA, more heavy bombardment groups were activated for deployment to Britain. The first of the Consolidated B-24 Liberator groups activated had been the 44th, on 15 January 1941 at MacDill Field, Florida. The first B-17 group to be activated had been the 34th, at Langley Field, Virginia, also on 15 January 1941, but the group was used to train others and would remain in the USA until late March 1944. On 1 March 1942 the 92nd and 93rd Bomb Groups were activated at Barkesdale Field, Louisiana, equipped with B-17Es and B-24Ds respectively.

The 93rd BG, soon to be commanded by Col Ted Timberlake, was created using personnel from the 44th BG, whose move to England was delayed because its B-24Bs and 'Cs were needed for anti-submarine patrols in the Gulf of Mexico. One U-boat was confirmed sunk by the Group. The 44th also provided personnel for 'Killer' Kane's 98th Bomb Group, which was dispatched to North Africa, and the 90th Bomb Group, which went to the South West Pacific. Like a gigantic game of pool, the 44th was broken up and pocketed around the world, leaving only a nucleus of the original personnel who called themselves the Eightballs.

Early in August 1942 the 92nd and the 301st Bomb Groups arrived in Britain. The 92nd, commanded by Col James S. Sutton, became the first heavy bombardment group to make a successful non-stop flight from Newfoundland to Scotland. On 28 August 1942 the last of the four squadrons landed in the United Kingdom, and the 92nd set up home at Bovingdon, Hertfordshire. Meanwhile, the 301st BG dispersed to Chelveston and Podington in Northamptonshire.

Early in August Col Armstrong was able to report that 24 crews in the 97th were available for combat missions. On 10 August bombs were loaded into the bays, ammunition was checked, equipment pre-flighted and procedures checked – only to have the weather 'scrub' the mission. Two days later it was responsible for the loss of a 97th BG Fortress in Wales, when all aboard were killed. Tension mounted again with the cancellation, and the sceptics spoke louder. The RAF made every conceivable effort to help the 8th get into the war as quickly as possible, but remained sceptical about its ability to bomb in broad daylight.

On Sunday 16 August the weather reports were good. The first Fortress strike of the war was scheduled for the following morning, Monday 17 August 1942. Maj Paul Tibbets, Group Flying Executive Officer in the 97th, recalls: 'Frank Armstrong and I went to Grafton and conducted the mission briefing and elected to take Butcher's

aircraft because of its good crew and maintenance status. Frank Armstrong was not qualified in the B-17, so he elected to fly with me in the lead aircraft of the main group departing from Grafton Underwood. Twelve aircraft were designated as the main group, twelve were designated as the main force to strike at the Rouen Sotteville marshalling yards in northwestern France, and another six, from Polebrook, were to act as a diversionary force going to St. Omer.'

B-17E Yankee Doodle, *41-9023, in the 414th Bomb Squadron, 97th BG, which carried Brig Gen Ira C. Eaker to Rouen on the first B-17 mission of the war on 17 August 1942. Note RAF-style camouflage. This aircraft later served with the 92nd and 91st BGs.* (USAF.)

At 15:26 Col Armstrong and Maj Tibbets took off in *Butcher Shop*. (Tibbets was to fly an even more historic mission three years later, when he piloted the B-29 *Enola Gay*, named after his mother, over Hiroshima, Japan, during the first dropping of an atomic bomb. Spaatz had felt confident enough to allow Brig Gen Ira C. Eaker to fly on the mission. He joined the crew of *Yankee Doodle*, lead aircraft of the second flight of six. As the formation crossed the French coast the German radio proved as sceptical as the Allied critics by announcing that '12 Lancasters' were heading inland.

At Ypreville fighters began to make their appearance and Sgt Adam R. Jenkins, the tail gunner aboard *Bat Outa Hell*, flying 'tail-end Charlie', had his hands full. He later reported: 'There were eight of them in "V" formation, and the leader waggled his wings and came for us. When they were about 300 yards away I figured it was about time for me to do something. So I pulled the trigger and it looked like the ends of his wings came off. Then the other seven scattered.' One fighter was chased into the line of fire from Sgt Kent R. West, the ball turret gunner aboard *Birmingham Blitzkreig*, and he became the first American crewman to be credited with the destruction of a German aircraft.

Ten minutes before the bomb run began, Lt Frank R. Beadle, the lead bombardier, exclaimed in a sing-song voice: 'I can see the target, I can see the target!' Crew members twisted and turned, peering in all directions, probing the beautiful bright blue sky for signs of possible enemy fighter attacks; a movement which would soon become known as the 'Messerschmitt twist'. Crews were relieved that 'here was the target at last', and the tension they had been feeling began to ease. As the Initial Point (IP) was reached and the bomb run begun, Beadle again moved to the centre of the spotlight, for as he manipulated the switch to open the bomb bay doors of *Butcher Shop* he could be heard singing over the intercom: 'I don't want to set the world on fire'!

Packed into the bomb bays of the 12 Fortresses was 36,900 lb of British bombs in the form of 45 600-pounders and nine 1,100-pounders. The heavy bombs (carried by three of the B-17s) were for the locomotive repair shops, and the 600 lb bombs for the Buddicum rolling stock repair shops. RAF reconnaissance photos had revealed concentrations of more than 2,000 freight cars at Sotteville, so even if the bombs missed, any damage to what was the largest switching facility in northern France would make spectacular front page news the following morning. Bombing was made from 23,000 ft, and a few bombs hit a mile short of the target. One burst hit about a mile west in some woods, but the majority smashed into the assigned area. Anti-aircraft fire slightly damaged two B-17s, and three Bf 109s which moved in for the attack were driven off by the Spitfire escort.

At Polebrook shortly before 19:00 anxious base personnel, fellow-airmen, high-ranking American and RAF officers and about 30 Allied pressmen gathered to witness the end of an historic mission. Cheers were heard when it was realized that all of the B-17s had returned safely. Three, in complete disregard for air discipline, peeled out of formation and buzzed the control tower. Under the circumstances no-one seemed to mind. Paul Tibbets concludes: 'Once back at base we were debriefed, and then there followed a "victory celebration" at the club with the RAF fighter pilots in attendance'.

B-17E Heidi Ho*, 41-9017, in the 342nd Bomb Squadron, 97th BG, which flew the Group's first mission on 17 August 1942, displaying 'US ARMY' beneath its wings. It is painted in brown and green RAF-style camouflage with pale blue undersurfaces adopted by some 97th aircraft. In November 1942 it was transferred to the 305th BG and later served with the 92nd and 94th BGs. (USAF.)*

The first of the congratulatory messages to arrive came from Air Marshal Sir Arthur Harris, Chief of RAF Bomber Command: 'Congratulations from all ranks of Bomber Command on the highly successful completion of the first all-American raid by the big fellows on German-occupied territory in Europe. Yankee Doodle certainly went to town and can stick yet another well-deserved feather in his cap.' The *New York Times* communique describing the mission was placed on the front page.

Flushed with success, on 19 August the 97th BG despatched 24 B-17Es in support of the Allied landings at Dieppe. Their target was the airfield at Abbeville-Drucat in northern France, home of the infamous 'Abbeville Kids', whose yellow-nosed Bf 109 pilots were numbered among the Luftwaffe elite. Two of the B-17s aborted because of mechanical failures, but the rest of the group plastered the airfield, destroying a hangar and severely cratering or 'postholing' the runways. Fortunately, the Luftwaffe was heavily engaged over the Dieppe area and did not appear. British High Command reported that 16 fighters were either destroyed or damaged as a result of the bombing strike and the airfield itself put out of action for a vital two hours. In addition, the controllers of the whole of the fighter area remained out of action until that evening.

The morning of 20 August brought a hurried call from photo-reconnaissance, informing Eaker that 1,600 goods wagons and 17 locomotives were parked in the Longeau marshalling yards in Amiens. Twelve Fortresses of the 340th and 342nd Bombardment Squadrons were airborne, and 11 bombed through slight Flak. Spitfires protected the formation, and a Belgian fighter pilot who witnessed the raid reported that the bombers scored at least 15 direct hits. The bomber crews were jubilant, but senior staff officers were more reserved, well aware that so far they had flown only shallow penetration missions in predominantly fine weather. The case for daylight, high-altitude, precision bombing was as yet unproven. The indications were that the B-17s would not be able to flaunt themselves over enemy targets with impunity for very much longer.

In the early morning of 21 August 12 Fortresses were despatched to bomb the Rotterdam Wilton shipyards, the most modern in Holland. Crews still felt confident, knowing that the faithful RAF Spitfires would again be on hand to protect them, but the B-17s were slow to form up after leaving Grafton Underwood. One Fortress was barely airborne when it was forced to abort, and a replacement joined the formation. Three other B-17s suffered generator failures which caused the gun turrets to become inoperative, and they returned to base. Arriving 16 minutes late for the escort, the remaining crews knew that the fighters would not be able to accompany them all the way to the target.

The Dutch coast was in sight when the recall message came through and the Spitfires turned for home. They were immediately 'replaced' by upwards of 25 German fighters in what became a prelude to a running fight which lasted for 25 minutes. The bombers' mass fire-power was a little more than the Luftwaffe pilots could handle, and two fighters fell to the Fortresses' guns. Sgt Adam R. Jenkins, the tail-turret gunner aboard *Johnny Reb*, drew first blood. Sgt Roy Allen, the top turret gunner, fired one burst and his guns jammed. John N. Hughes, one of the waist gunners, sucked a lump of ice into the mouth of his oxygen tube in the excitement and was forced to hold the mask with one hand and fire his gun with the other, while nearing collapse from lack of oxygen.

In the nose compartment Harold Spire, the navigator, had just fired at a crossing fighter when a burst of cannon fire tore through the windshield. Donald A. Walter, the co-pilot, was raked from his legs to his chest and died instantly, and Plexiglas splinters seriously wounded Richard S. Starks, the pilot. As he struggled for breath, Starks managed to call for help and Edward Sconiers, the bombardier, and Sgt Allen, came to the cockpit. Sconiers removed the dead co-pilot and took his place at the controls, hoping that what he had learned about piloting before washing out of flying school would be useful to him now. Holding on to the wheel, the pilot began giving instructions to Sconiers, while the tail and ball turret gunners continued to blaze away at their five pursuers. *Johnny Reb* lagged behind the rest of the formation, with its number three and four engines hit. Despite this, Sconiers managed to nurse the ailing bomber back to England and land at Horsham St. Faith, near Norwich.

The Press enthusiastically credited the nine Fortresses with six fighters destroyed and praised them for beating off 25 Focke-Wulfs. Some RAF officers, however, remained sceptical, and it later transpired that only a handful of fighters had actually fired on the formation.

Eaker took advantage of the Luftwaffe's inexperience in dealing with American bomber formations, and on 24 August despatched a dozen 97th BG B-17s to the shipyard of the Ateliers et Chantiers Maritime de la Seine at Le Trait. Twelve of the 48 bombs fell within 500 yards of the aiming point, but no material damage seemed to have been done to the yards. One wayward bomb luckily hit and sank a U-boat moored in the docks, but overall it was the poorest bombing to date. Flak caused damage to the Fortresses, and two officers and three sergeants received slight wounds. On the way home the formation was jumped from above by yellow-nosed Bf 109s.

Maj Tibbets, leading the mission, was attacked by fighters from 12 o'clock. A 20 mm cannon shell ripped through the right-hand window and badly injured the co-pilot, Lt Gene Lockhart, in the left hand. Blood sprayed over what instruments were left in the shattered cabin. Tibbets struggled with the controls and managed to bring the shattered B-17 back to Grafton Underwood. Col Newton Longfellow, who was riding as an observer, bandaged Lockhart's hand and the head of the turret gunner, who was lying on the floor unconscious. Tibbets himself suffered slight injuries to the wrist and left leg.

All recovered, and an awards ceremony was arranged. This event was as much for public relations as to honour the wounded, and Gen Eaker despatched Beirne Lay, public relations officer on the staff of Gen Spaatz, to cover the ceremony. At first Lay received no

Parade for the award of Purple Hearts to wounded men of the 97th BG. Second from right is Lt Lockhart, with his hand bandaged as a result of the wounds he suffered on the mission of 24 August 1942 to Le Trait. Tibbets is on his right, facing the camera. (Tibbets.)

co-operation, but after a heated argument with Tibbets he finally got his parade. Lay recalled: 'Later we became great friends and collaborated on an MGM feature motion picture about his Hiroshima experience, called *Above and Beyond*.

With the good weather continuing to hold, bombing missions were becoming almost everyday events at Grafton Underwood and Polebrook. On 27 August nine Fortresses returned to the Wilton shipyards at Rotterdam, which was once again working to full capacity. Although only seven of the B-17s bombed the target, hits were claimed on two ships and the centre of the target was well covered. Next day the 97th BG despatched 14 B-17s to the Avions Potez factory at Meaulte in northern France. Most of the bombs from the 11 Fortresses which bombed the target fell in open fields, although some 'post-holed' the runways. The bombers returned intact, but one Spitfire was missing, along with its Canadian pilot. It was on this mission that American fighter pilots were also present for the first time.

On 29 August, for the third day running, the 97th BG was airborne and 12 of the 13 B-17s despatched bombed the German fighter base at Coutrai-Wevelghem in Belgium. The results appeared good, and even the British Press, which had at first been cautious of American claims, now openly praised them. However, Spaatz and Eaker refused to read too much into the Fortresses' success (they were claimed in some circles to have scored better than 70 per cent of hits). It was early days yet, and moves were afoot to transfer the 97th and 301st Bomb Groups to the 12th Air Force, activated in Washington DC on 20 August. Although Eaker continued to use the two groups at every available opportunity, it meant he would have to reorganise and plan for the future.

Eaker needed a Combat Crew Replacement and Training Centre (CCRC), but personnel and equipment were in such short supply that the 92nd BG, with its base at Bovingdon, was selected for the task. Bovingdon became the 11th CCRC and for a few, vital months provided the 8th with badly needed crews. Unhappily for the 92nd, their B-17Fs were transferred to the 97th BG in exchange for battered

Crew of B-17F The Red Gremlin, *41-24444, in the 340th Bomb Squadron, 97th BG, on 9 September 1942. Back Row, L-R, Paul Tibbets, Ryan, Tom Ferebee, 'Dutch' Van Kirk, Hughes and Splitt. Front Row: Peach, Quate, Fitzgerald, Gowan and Fittsworth.* (Tibbets.)

B-17Es. However, the time would come when the 92nd would fly combat missions and become known as 'Fame's Favoured Few'.

The B-17F was supposed to be an improvement on the B-17E. However, it was equipped with only two .30 calibre machine gun mountings in the nose, although it had additional .5 sockets fitted later as a field modification. Externally, the B-17F differed little from the B-17E, its most noticeable distinguishing feature being a frameless Plexiglas nose, but inwardly it incorporated over 400 major design modifications which, although making it 1,000 lb heavier than the B-17E, made it better suited for combat.

On 5 September the 97th BG despatched 25 of its newly-acquired B-17Fs together with 12 Fortresses of the 301st BG, flying its first combat mission of the war, to the marshalling yards at Rouen. Some 31 B-17s bombed, six aborting owing to mechanical problems.

Three B-17Es in the 97th BG, led by SNAFU, *taxi out at Grafton Underwood. The 97th was assigned to the 12th Air Force on 14 September 1942.* (USAF.)

Approximately only 20 per cent of the bombs fell within the target area, and some hit the city.

The next day Eaker mounted his largest bombing mission so far, to the Avions Potez factory at Meaulte. The 92nd scraped together 14 B-17Es and crews, filling in with ground personnel, and joined 22 B-17Fs of the 97th in the main strike, while the 301st BG flew a diversionary raid on St. Omer-Longueness airfield. Thirty Fortresses crossed Meaulte, but only six in the 92nd BG attacked the target. Enemy aircraft were encountered continuously from the French coast to the target, and the Americans suffered their first combat losses. Lt Clarence C. Lipsky's B-17 in the 97th BG was shot down (the Red Cross reported later that Lipsky and five of the crew were POWs), and Lt Leigh E. Stewart's B-17, from the 92nd BG was also lost.

These first losses had a deep effect on the survivors, as Paul Tibbets recalls: 'Up to this time, the war had seemed a little more than a game in the sense that we flew out in the morning and came back a few hours later after dropping our bombs and eluding enemy flak and fighter fire. We knew the flak was for real and the shells from the German attacking 'planes were dangerous, but we still had come to consider ourselves supermen whose skill in the sky would always bring us back safely. That was the state of our confidence up until the moment we saw Lipsky's airplane spin out of formation, burst into flames, and make that last grim, smoking dive to earth. Now at last the war was a bloody reality for all of us.'

Chapter Two

The eagle spreads its wings

THE 92ND BOMB Group had flown the 6 September mission only because the 8th Air Force was so desperately short of aircraft, spares and personnel. This constant drain on its resources was a direct result of the need to supply the 12th Air Force, destined for the Mediterranean theatre. Unfortunately, few in the 8th were aware that the 12th Air Force, which they nicknamed 'Junior,' was destined for Operation 'Torch' and therefore had top priority when it came to spares, personnel, B-17Fs and even training. New groups had to be trained by the 8th for eventual transfer to the 12th Air Force, a task Eaker could well have done without at such a crucial time in the 8th's history.

On 7 September 29 B-17s in the 97th and 301st BGs were despatched to the Wilton shipyards at Rotterdam again. A storm warning was flashed to the outbound Fortresses, and most of the crews received it and returned safely. However, seven Fortresses in the 97th BG formation continued to the target, where the Luftwaffe was waiting for them. The lead ship, piloted by Capt Aquilla Hughes, was badly damaged, but all B-17s returned safely after beating off heavy fighter attacks. No further raids were flown, and on 14 September the 97th and 301st were, on paper at least, assigned to the 12th Air Force. The complete break-up of VIII Bomber Command was avoided by the arrival in England of four new B-17 groups, the 91st, 303rd, 305th and

An American Red Cross clubmobile serves refreshments to ground crews of the 92nd BG working on B-17E Phyllis, *41-9020, at Bovingdon, from where it made several courier flights to North Africa in late 1942. This aircraft previously served in the 97th BG and, later, in the 303rd BG.* (Richards.)

B-17E Little Skunk Face, *41-9019, in the 414th Bomb Squadron, 97th BG, in early RAF-style camouflage. This aircraft later flew in the 305th, 92nd, 381st and 482nd BGs.* (USAF.)

306th, and two Liberator groups, the 44th and the 93rd.

Finally, on 26 September, approximately 75 B-17s were despatched to Cherbourg-Maupertus and Moriaix-Poryeau airfields, but bad weather over France forced them to return without dropping their bombs. Unable to see the coastline, the bombers flew on dead reckoning, and when they were actually over their target their plotting charts showed them still short of it. Eleven Spitfires of No. 133 Eagle Squadron ran short of fuel and were forced to land in France. The twelfth, nursing his fast-dwindling fuel supply, attempted to glide back to England but crashed on the cliffs of the Lizard. The Fortresses were able to buck the headwind and return to base.

On 2 October 30 B-17s of the 97th BG, now commanded by Col Joseph H. Atkinson (Col Armstrong having moved up to Bomber Command), and the 301st BG bombed the Avions Potez aircraft factory at Meaulte again. More than 400 fighter escorts provided cover, while the 92nd BG flew a diversionary feint along the French coast and six B-17s of the 97th attacked the airfield at St Omer.

The locomotive, carriage and wagon works of the Ateliers d'Hellemmes at Chemin de Fer du Nord at Lille had long been earmarked as a target because of its importance to an enemy which was suffering an acute shortage of rail transport. Eaker also saw it as the ideal target to demonstrate high-altitude precision bombing. He waited until 9 October before he had enough bombers capable of destroying the target in one mission. A few weeks before, VIII Bomber Command could muster only twelve aircraft, but by including the Liberators of the 93rd BG and Fortresses of the 306th BG, both of which were flying their maiden missions, Eaker was able to assemble an unprecedented 108 bombers for the raid, which would also involve an attack on the steel and engineering works of the Compagnie de Fives. A strong contingent of RAF and USAAF fighters would also fly cover for the bombers while smaller, diversionary forces attacked Coutrai-Wevelghem and St Omer airfields and the city of Roubaix.

B-17F Eager Beaver, *41-24487, in the 368th Bomb Squadron, 306th BG, was damaged on the group's first mission, to Lille on 9 October 1942, and landed at Manston.* Eager Beaver *returned to duty as a training machine and the 368th adopted the nickname 'Eager Beavers'.* (Richards.)

Crews remembered Col Ted Timberlake's address at the first briefing at Alconbury. He said: 'I know you Joes can do it'. The briefing finished, Col Timberlake in *Teggie Ann* led 24 of the Liberators and formed up behind a larger force of B-17s of the 306th, 92nd, 97th and the leading 301st. As the formation approached the French coast Lt Janic, the bombardier aboard *Shoot Luke*, reported over the intercom that the navigator had been taken ill and that to proceed could prove fatal. The pilot, Lt John H. Murphy, turned back. (*Shoot Luke* was so named because in the USA a favourite pursuit of the men was the rolling of dice, accompanied by the expression, 'Shoot Luke, you're faded'.) One of the 93rd BG's B-24s was lost over France, and *Ball of Fire Junior* made the five-hour flight only to crash-land at another airfield on its return.

Seven Fortresses in the 92nd BG formation returned early to Bovingdon. Henry A. West, the navigator in Maj Dean Byerly's Fortress in the 352nd Bomb Squadron, 301st Bomb Group formation, had no such problems: 'We picked up our fighter escort at Felixstowe, about three squadrons of Spitfires and three squadrons of P-38s. As we entered enemy territory we had some inaccurate flak, but generally we proceeded to Lille without incident. Col R.R. Walker, our CO, who was leading the entire mission, got fouled up somewhere and we just invited trouble by stooging around France for a while doing 180° turns. Finally we found the target, but just as Arthur 'Catman' Carlson, my bombardier, was sighting through his bombsight, a formation of B-17s cut in front of us and we were forced to bomb another target. This turned out to be the railway goods terminus.'

The crew of *Snoozy II* in the 367th Bomb Squadron, 306th Bomb Group, piloted by John Olsen, were on their first mission. Al La Chasse, the bombardier, recalls: 'Some smoke and dust covered the target area. As we continued the run a line of B-24s out of position were coming across the target area from the east, heading towards England. Flak hit our right inboard engine and set it on fire. Norman Gates, the co-pilot, somehow extinguished it. Flak increased. I was surprised it came in so many colours. On the bomb run Captain Olsen trimmed the ship before turning the control over to me. After our flak hit, the Norden bombsight automatically made the corrections necessary to 'right' the ship on course. I released the bomb load, not knowing there would be several malfunctions causing bomb rack problems.

'The 'plane lifted; lightened by the bomb drop. The B-24s were now behind us. It was 09:42 – time over the target as per mission plan. For *Snoozy II* the war was about to begin, and end. Bandits were everywhere. *Snoozy II* began to lag behind the rest of the formation. "Honest John" McKee's ship tried lagging back with us. Good old "Honest John". He tried.'

It was all to no avail. *Snoozy II* was too badly damaged by the fighters' actions, and the crew were ordered to bale out. La Chasse concludes: 'Our navigator, Bill Gise, got out after some trouble with the hatch. God must have opened it. The ride down was just like the book on parachutes said it would be: scary but nice. I was alive.' La Chasse, Gise, and Erwin Wissenbeck, the top-turret gunner, were the only three to bale out. La Chasse was thrown into various jails, including the infamous Napoleonic prison of Saint Giles near Brussels. At Dulag Luft he discovered he was only the 18th American POW. La Chasse finished the war at Stalag Luft III, Sagan in Silesia.

Altogether, four bombers were lost while only 69 aircraft, including just ten of the Liberators, had bombed their primary targets. To make matters worse, many of the bombs had failed to explode. The inexperienced 93rd and 306th BGs had placed many of their bombs outside the target area, killing a number of French civilians. Traffic control was bad, and some of the bombardiers never got the target in their bombsights. Liberator crews who had to jettison their bomb loads in the Channel on the way home were sardonically referred to as 'chandeliers' by their contemporaries at one B-17 base.

At the subsequent interrogations crews revealed that they had had 242 encounters with Luftwaffe fighters and put in fighter 'kills'; 48 destroyed, 18 probably destroyed, and four damaged – but the Germans admitted the loss of only one fighter. At the time the figures did much to compensate for the largely inaccurate bombing. For three months the 97th BG, and later the 301st, had pioneered American daylight bombing from England. Both groups (and four fighter groups) departed for North Africa in November 1942 and earned undying fame with raids from the desert and later from Italy.

The remaining groups in England still had to prove that high-altitude missions in daylight, often without escort, could justify further B-17 and B-24 groups being sent to the ETO. Shallow penetration missions, or 'milk-runs', as they began to be called, were not the answer, but for the time being VIII Bomber Command could not flaunt itself in force over the continent of Europe, so 'tip-and-run' missions to the U-boat pens remained the order of the day. On 21 October VIII Bomber Command flew its first mission against the U-boat bases, when a small force of bombers hit Lorient-Keroman. Just 15 B-17s bombed from as low as 17,500 ft, and three bombers were shot down in attacks by 36 Fw 190s. Eight other B-17s bombed

B-17F Delta Rebel 2, *42-5077, of the 323rd Bomb Squadron, 91st BG, in formation. This Fortress carried on into 1943 until the pilot, George Birdsong, went home to Mississippi. Veteran crews refused to fly the* Rebel, *claiming 'George had used up all her luck'. It was finally lost on 12 August 1943 on the mission to Gelsenkirchen, when it was flown by 2/Lt Robert W. Thompson.* (USAF.)

Cherbourg-Maupertus airfield.

Although they had lowered their bombing altitudes by as much as 10,000 ft, the B-17s' small high-explosive bombs barely dented the sub-pens. On 31 October Gen Spaatz told Gen Arnold that operations against the U-boat pens were proving too costly for the results achieved. He planned to send in the heavies at altitudes as low as 4,000 ft and accept the heavy casualties.

On 7 November 34 B-17s, including seven crews in the 91st BG formation, led by the CO, Col Stanley T. Wray, who were flying their inaugural mission, struck at the U-boat pens at Brest, while the 44th BG received its first baptism of fire when eight B-24s flew a diversionary sweep to Cap de la Hague in Holland.

On 9 November the Flying Eightballs flew their first bombing mission, when 12 B-24s drawn from both the 44th and 93rd BGs accompanied 31 B-17s to St Nazaire. Bombing results had been so inconsistent on earlier raids that Eaker decided to experiment with attacks at lower altitudes. The force swept out over the sea towards the mouth of the Loire in Brittany at 500 ft to avoid being tracked by enemy radar. As it neared the target the leading 91st BG formation climbed to their briefed bombing altitude of 10,000 ft, while the 306th, the last B-17 group, climbed to only 7,500 ft to drop their bombs. The Liberators climbed to their briefed altitudes of between 17,500 and 18,300 ft and followed the Fortresses. Over 50 heavy anti-aircraft guns were situated at St. Nazaire, and the Germans were in the process of installing more. Light flak, 20 mm and 37 mm, bracketed the low-flying Fortress formations, but the Liberators came through without any serious damage, although some crews reported instances of frostbite caused by the lack of protective clothing.

The heavier dual-purpose 88 mm anti-aircraft guns caused the most damage, and the Fortresses bore the brunt. Every B-17 but one in the leading 91st BG formation was peppered with flak, but all managed to return safely to base. By the time the trailing 306th BG element crossed the target, the *Flieger Abwehr Kanonen* (flak) crews had their height and speed. Their aim was so accurate that a shell was seen to make a direct hit and explode against the nose of one B-17. Altogether, the 306th lost three B-17s, and 22 B-17s in the total force were damaged. The intense flak succeeded in breaking up the formations and they flew back to England in disarray.

Thenceforth St Nazaire became known as 'Flak City', and bomber crews would not venture below four miles high. Missions to the U-boat lairs became an almost established routine, and the Germans moved in more and more anti-aircraft guns. By November there were 75 ringed around the city alone. Gradually the number was increased until it passed 100. Soon flak was so accurate that it was even dangerous well in excess of 20,000 ft. The truth of the motto 'The higher, the fewer' was established.

On 14 November 24 bombers returned to St Nazaire without suffering loss. On 17 November 35 heavies, including 16 B-17s in the 303rd BG Group from Molesworth, making their maiden mission, flew to the U-boat pens at St Nazaire. Unfortunately, cloud obscured the target and they returned to base without dropping their bombs. *Shoot Luke* in the 93rd BG formation shrugged off three flak shells which exploded under the port wing, almost turning the aircraft upside down. On the homeward flight the formation was attacked by Ju 88s for 45 minutes. *Shoot Luke's* gunners dispatched one of the fighter-bombers, which burst into flames and crashed into the sea.

On 18 November Eaker sent his small force of B-17s and B-24s to the U-boat bases at La Pallice and Lorient-Keroman. Nineteen bombers hit La Pallice and 13 bombed Lorient, but the 303rd formation, despatched to their briefed target at La Pallice, veered 100 miles off course and bombed Saint Nazaire in error. On 22 November 76 bombers attempted to hit the submarine pens at Lorient again.

Original crew of Shoot Luke. *L–R (back row): Ed Janic, bombardier; John Murphy, pilot; Frank Lown, co-pilot; Arch Rantala, navigator; L–R (front row): James Cowan, tunnel gunner; Arville D Sirmans, engineer; Paul Slankard, tail gunner; William Mercer, radio-operator; Floyd Mabee, left waist gunner; Mahlon Cressey, right waist gunner.* (Mabee.)

Eleven bombers of the 303rd BG, still smarting from their navigational error four days before, were the only B-17s to bomb the target.

The 303rd BG had been blooded. Now it was the turn of the 305th. Cliff Pyle, pilot of *We The People*, recalls: 'Col LeMay gathered us all in one of the huts and told us that we were on our own now. He further stated that he had done his best in training and he believed we would benefit from it. He said we would be face to face with the best of the German Air Force.'

The 305th came face to face with the Luftwaffe on 23 November, when Eaker sent his bombers to St Nazaire for the fifth time in two weeks. On almost every mission bombers were hitting the target, but not in large enough concentrations to damage them seriously. Experience was proving that a single bomb or even a few bombs did not have enough destructive power. LeMay was determined to alter this, and decided to try and achieve greater bombing accuracy by flying a straight course on the bomb-run instead of zig-zagging every ten seconds, a tactic which had been designed to spoil the aim of the German flak batteries. His plan was to cross the target faster, and therefore reduce the amount of time the German flak had in which to fire on the formation. It was a big step for a group commander to take on group's maiden bombing mission, and one which caused his crews great concern.

Altogether, 58 B-17s flew to Davidstowe Moor, Cornwall, to refuel before setting out for the Bay of Biscay and Saint Nazaire. Bad weather and mechanical problems forced 13 B-17s to abort, and one Fortress in the 306th BG was shot down just before the target. By the time the target was reached four of the 20 B-17s in the 305th, together with five of the ten 91st B-17s and four of the eight B-17s in the 306th, had turned back early. Only 44 B-17s remained; the 91st and 306th BGs together totalled just eight aircraft.

The 305th carried out the longest and straightest bomb run yet seen over Europe, and strike photos later revealed that the 305th had placed twice as many bombs on the target as any other outfit. Despite their fears, no crews were lost to flak, although it came close, as Cliff Pyle, in *We the People*, recalls: 'We encountered very heavy flak, accurate to altitude and range, and we received a flak hole in the left wing which burst a hydraulic line. There were no casualties in the group, but the 91st and the 303rd lost several 'planes.'

On previous missions the B-17s had been intercepted from behind, where enough guns could be brought to bear on enemy fighters. However, Luftwaffe experiments had now proved that the frontal areas of the B-17 and B-24 offered very little in defensive fire-power and, despite the dangers of very high closing speeds, a frontal attack was considered the best method of shooting them down. The B-24 normally carried two .5s in the nose, and the B-17E was equipped with four .30 calibre moveable machine gun mountings, but they had to be operated by the over-committed bombardier. Whichever mounting he used, it only offered a very poor field of fire. Fortress navigators could also operate a moveable mounted .5 Browning machine gun from enlarged windows on either side of the nose (often called cheek guns), but these suffered from the same problems as the bombardier's position. In each case a blind spot was left in front which neither the ball turret or upper turret could cover.

Oberstleutnant Egon Mayer, commander of Gruppe III of JG.2, who led the attacking fighters this day, is credited with developing the head-on attack. The new tactic worked well. The 91st lost only two bombers to head-on attacks, but the commanders of the 322nd and 323rd Bomb Squadrons, the group navigator, bombardier and gunnery officers were among the casualties. Two other B-17s were badly hit. One crashed near Leavesden, Hertfordshire, while trying to make it home to Bassingbourn, and three of the crew were killed. *Quitchurbitchin'* was the only 91st B-17 to return. *Lady Fairweather* of the 303rd BG was shot down in flames near the target.

On 27 November the 93rd's 329th Squadron transferred to Hardwick to evaluate the British Gee navigational device. A special force, consisting of selected crews from all four squadrons, was to test the device on behalf of the USAAF, which at the time was considering various RAF operational radar equipment for bombing in overcast skies. In October 1942 the 8th had agreed to spare eight valuable Liberators to help in the work. The 329th Squadron moved to Flixton airfield, near Bungay, Suffolk, after only a week at Hardwick. Flixton was still in the throes of development when the 329th arrived. Its task was of an experimental nature, involving 'intruder' or 'moling' flights over Germany in an attempt to disrupt working schedules in German factories by causing air-raid warnings to sound, upsetting civilian morale and impairing industrial output. Seven 'moling' missions were made over Germany, the last taking place on 28 March 1943. Some crews later formed the nucleus of the USAAF Pathfinder units set up to perfect blind-bombing techniques.

While the 329th was engaged in 'moling' missions Col Timberlake received orders on 5 December 1942 to lead the 328th and 409th squadrons to North Africa to participate in ten days of disruptive raids against Axis ports and shipping. One 330th Liberator crashed into a mountain south of Tafaroui, and all aboard were killed. Despite almost non-existent base facilities, first at Tafaroui, where bouts of heavy rain turned the short runways into a sea of mud, and then at Gambut Main, where the dry and dusty conditions played havoc with the B-24Ds, the 93rd flew more than a score of missions from North Africa, serving with the 12th and later the 9th Air Force. On 22 February 1943 the Travelling Circus, as they now called themselves, flew their 23rd and final mission of the first African Liberator campaign. In the three-month stint in the desert seven B-24s had been lost on missions.

During the unit's absence, the heavy bomb groups in England had continued to suffer in raids on the U-boat pens. Some, like the 44th BG at Shipdham and the 305th BG, which early in December moved from Grafton 'Undermud' to the mud at Chelveston, late home of the 301st, were still trying to come to terms with the English climate.

On Sunday 6 December the 67th Bomb Squadron in the 44th BG at last received its full quota of Liberators, and the Eightballs flew their first full group mission — a diversionary raid to the airfield at Abbeville-Drucat in Picardy. By now, crews had flown so many diversionary missions that they had painted ducks on their B-24's fuselages, each representing a decoy mission. Nineteen B-24Ds, including *Little Beaver* piloted by 1st Lt Chester 'George' Phillips and 2nd Lt Bill Cameron, flying its first mission since undergoing modifications in Northern Ireland, were dispatched, but shortly after take-off things began to go wrong. *Little Beaver* lost an engine when the supercharger controls were over-advanced during their climb to altitude. When the throttle was pulled back to slow down in formation the superchargers rammed in too much air and the engines were starved of fuel. The other B-24s continued to the target as *Little Beaver* returned to base.

As they neared the French coast an abort signal was radioed to the group after British radar tracked approaching enemy aircraft. Unfortunately only the 66th and 67th Squadrons received the signal, leaving six B-24Ds of the 68th Squadron to continue to the target alone. The small force bombed the airfield and was then bounced by 30 yellow-nosed Fw 190s, the 'Abbeville Kids'. This crack Luftwaffe fighter unit shot down Lt Dubard's Liberator in flames, and it crashed in the Channel. Five other Liberators received hits. The other crews were saved by the Germans' overestimation of the Liberators' firepower. They did not press home their attacks, and losses were not as high as they might have been.

Meanwhile, 36 B-17s struck at the Atelier d'Hellemmes locomotive factory, railroads and repair shops at Lille. Sixteen squadrons of Spitfires escorted them to the target. Cliff Pyle recalls: 'The 305th was number three in the formation, stacked up. Maj McGehee led the squadron, but he had to turn back with aircraft problems and I took over the lead. Twelve Fw 190s attacked our squadron and my tailgunner claimed two shot down and the waist gunner one. Ten minutes from the target Lt Prentice left the formation in flames and five parachutes were seen to open. We encountered very little flak in our position and there were no casualties among my crew.'

Following the Lille mission, plans were formulated for an attack on the Romilly-sur-Seine air park, south-east of Paris, but bad weather resulted in the cancellation of the mission on 10 December, and two

B-17F-25-BO Hell's *Angels, 41-24577, in the 358th Bomb Squadron, 303rd BG, was the first England-based Fortress to complete 25 combat missions. It wore out 16 engines, five sets of brakes, three landing gears, countless tyres, superchargers and oil cooling systems and outlasted two crews. After 48 missions it flew Stateside, having been autographed by members of the Group at Molesworth. Early in January 1944 it was assigned to the RAF.* (USAF.)

B-17F 42-5130, is christened Sweet Pea at Thurleigh on 20 December 1942 by Maureen, a three-year-old girl who lived in a London orphanage and was adopted by the 367th 'Clay Pigeon' Bomb Squadron, 306th BG, as their mascot after Cpl Irvin W. Combs (centre, kneeling) and fellow EM collected £101 in English pennies to pay for extras for an English orphan. On 6 March 1943 Sweet Pea, piloted by the popular Capt John L. Ryan, the 367th Squadron commander elect, failed to return from the raid on Lorient. Ryan evaded capture, was rescued by the French Underground and returned to England on 17 April, only 42 days after being shot down. (Richards.)

days later 90 bombers had already crossed the French coast before thick cloud resulted in a recall. Three B-17s were shot down. Some 17 bombers of the 303rd dropped their loads on the Rouen Sotteville marshalling yards, two B-17s being lost in the action.

Bad weather prevented a return raid until, finally on 20 December VIII, Eaker sent 101 B-17s and B-24s in a third attempt to bomb the Romilly-sur-Seine air park. Nine B-24s were forced to abort with oxygen and machine gun failures. *Little Beaver* again experienced supercharger failure and was forced to abort after flying for 3¾ hr. (Maj Donald MacDonald, CO of the 67th Squadron, refused to credit the crew with the mission because of their abort. Bill Cameron wrote: 'I began to realize that the price of a ticket back to the ZI [Zone of the Interior] might be pretty high'.) Twelve Liberators continued to the target with the Fortresses. A dozen squadrons of Spitfires flew cover, but they were soon low on fuel and had to return to England just before the heavies reached Rouen. The bombers were met at the coastline by yellow- and black-nosed Fw 190s.

For 15 minutes the bomber crews came under fire from head-on attacks, and two B-17s belonging to the 91st BG were shot down. Ralph J. Tomek was a waist gunner on board one of the victims, in the 401st Bomb Squadron. It was only his fourth mission. 'Sixty fighters ripped through our formation and made decisive hits on one Fortress flying in the rear element,' he recalled. 'The tail broke off and there was only one survivor. Salvador Dalteris, the tail gunner, was fortunate enough to be in the part that broke off and managed to bale out. Later, he told me that his pilot had told everyone that day to wear their parachutes on the mission. If he hadn't he would never have made it.

'Our ship was the next to be picked off. The fighters made head-on attacks and put two engines out of action and killed my pilot, Bob English. Our B-17 nose dived about 1,000 ft but by some miracle the top turret gunner, Sgt Mandell, scrambled out of his turret and managed to get the aircraft straightened out. The two engines were on fire, and we were losing altitude rapidly. Near Paris Mandell sounded the alarm to bale out.' Tomek was captured and admitted to hospital in Paris before being sent to POW camp for the rest of the war.

Meanwhile, as the initial Fw 190s broke off to refuel, another 50 joined the running fight and continued making attacks until shortly before 'bombs away'. Cliff Pyle, in *We The People*, saw his squadron's bombs drop short of the target. 'We were using the tactics of squadron aircraft dropping on the lead squadron aircraft,' he said. 'However, the target was hit by the mass with good results.'

The Luftwaffe fighters which had broken off to refuel reappeared on the homeward trip and made repeated attacks on the B-17 formations until the Spitfire escort showed up to cover the bomber's exit across the Channel. Altogether six B-17s, including four from the 306th, were lost and 29 damaged. The slower Forts flying below the Liberators had soaked up most of the punishment.

Gunners once again submitted high claims, and the initial score of 53 'kills' was reduced to 21, plus 31 'probably damaged'. The true figure was in fact three enemy fighters shot down and one damaged. Only 72 aircraft had bombed the target, and they had caused only minor damage to the German airfield. Despite this, Romilly had proved a turning point in the daylight aerial war in Europe. For the first time VIII Bomber Command had penetrated 100 miles into enemy territory and had successfully beaten off incessant fighter attacks without the aid of escorting fighters.

As the year drew to a close, officers and men were still working on improving the methods of bombing and aerial gunnery. At Chelveston Col Curtis E. LeMay tried 'stacked up' formations of 18 aircraft before finally deciding upon staggered three-aeroplane elements within a squadron and staggered squadrons within a group. To avoid complicated individual bombing procedures in which each aircraft would have to manoeuvre for accurate bombing, LeMay discarded individual bombing and introduced 'lead crews' comprising highly trained pilots, bombardiers and navigators. The formation bombed on the lead bombardier's signal.

On 30 December the technique was tried again over the U-boat pens at Lorient. The bomb run was made into the sun, and its glare gave the experienced Luftwaffe pilots a blind spot from which to attack the Fortresses. Making skilful head-on attacks, they succeeded in shooting down three B-17s, including a 91st BG Group aircraft which carried the 401st Bomb Squadron commander. Lt Love pulled out of the 305th BG formation to assist a loner from the 306th BG and was promptly shot down. On the return flight the 305th formation thought it was over England when, owing to a terrific headwind, it was still over France. The formation became lax and the aircraft were spread out more than usual. Fighters seized upon the lapse and badly damaged Capt Trippett's Fortress. *Boom Town*, piloted by Capt Clyde B. Walker, was also badly shot up, but managed to make it to St. Eval with one dead and two wounded aboard.

For the Americans' sixth raid on St. Nazaire, on 3 January 1943, Eaker for the first time completely abandoned individual bombing in favour of group bombing. A total of 107 bombers was despatched, but mechanical failures accounted for many aircraft returning to base early, leaving only eight B-24s and 68 Fortresses to continue to the target. The Liberators, being some 20 m.p.h. faster than the B-17s, started out behind the Fortress but had caught up with them by the time they had reached the target, and were ready to bomb at a higher altitude. Visibility was unlimited, so an unusually long bomb run was ordered. B-17s and B-24s were stacked upwards of 20,000 to 22,000 ft, but their air-speed was reduced more than half by a 115 m.p.h. gale during the run-in. The gale was so fierce that the bomb run took twice as long as briefed, and for ten minutes the bombers flew almost straight and level, taking all the flak the anti-aircraft gunners could throw at them.

Col Frank Robinson, who was leading his Liberators in the 44th formation, abandoned the bomb run and the eight B-24s headed out to sea, jettisoning their bombs as they went. They made for home at a height of 200 ft above sea level. Although the weather over the target was clear, the return over the sea was made in thick fog, and crews could see only a few feet in front of them. When the Liberators neared the Brest Peninsular, however, the fog began to clear. Unfortunately the navigators' reports were ignored, and later the Isles of Scilly were mistaken for Brest. Consequently, the small formation flew further and further up the Irish Sea. It was only when the very real threat of internment loomed before them that Col Robinson led the formation into a turn towards the Bristol Channel. Fuel was getting low, and in any case they had only allowed for landfall at Lizard Point.

Realizing they had missed Lands End, the crews searched for airfields in Wales, but there were few to be found in this part of Britain. Lt John Long, in *Texan*, discovered Talbenny airfield, only to have his last engine fail through fuel starvation just as he made his approach. Fortunately all of the crew managed to escape from the Liberator, which was destroyed in the ensuing crash. Others were not so fortunate, including two B-24s which crashed into stone walls obscured by hedges. Three crewmen were killed and three were injured. The survivors flew into nearby airfields. *Little Beaver* eventually landed at Talbenny airfield, at the time occupied by a Czech squadron, and remained there for five days, buffeted by snowstorms. Two B-17 groups were also forced to land at Talbenny. Two 305th BG B-17s were so badly shot up by flak that they were left at Talbenny.

Intelligence officers began piecing together the results of the St Nazaire raid. Men waited with bated breath, none more so than at Chelveston, where LeMay and his senior officers eagerly sought confirmation that the new tactics had paid off. Most of the 342,000 lb of bombs had fallen smack on the pens, but seven bombers had been lost over enemy territory and 47 damaged. These were the heaviest losses VIII Bomber Command had suffered so far.

The following day Col Frank Armstrong Jr took command of the battle-weary 306th BG at Thurleigh, vice Col Overcracker, although

Traditional 'smoking' of the ceiling of the 306th BG officers' club at Thurleigh with missions. Maj Harry Holt, CO 367th Bomb Squadron until 4 March 1943, far left; Capt John L. Ryan with candle; Capt John L. Lambert, 367th BS, later CO, 423rd BS, left; and Capt George Buckey, 367th CO, 19 August 1943 – 2 May 1944, right. Ryan took command of the 367th on 5 March and was shot down the next day. He evaded capture and returned to England after 42 days. This scene was used later in '12 o'clock High', which was based on the 306th. (The writer, Beirne Lay, evolved the fictional '918th Bomb Group' by multiplying 306 by three). The 367th BS, which suffered the heaviest losses in 8th Bomber Command from October 1942 – August 1943, was nicknamed 'The Clay Pigeons'. (Richards.)

his stay would be short, lasting just over a month. Crews of the 44th BG arrived back at Shipdham on 8 January to find that the well liked and respected Col Robinson had been replaced by Col Leon Johnson. Meanwhile, on 4 January the 92nd BG minus key personnel and all of the 326th Squadron, had left Bovingdon for Alconbury airfield, and bomber crews were sent to the 91st and 303rd BGs as 'temporary' replacements. Very few returned to the 92nd.

On 13 January 64 B-17s bombed the locomotive works at Fives-Lille again. The 305th BG again flew lead, with Brig Gen Hansell, Commander of the 1st Bomb Wing, flying in the lead ship, *Dry Martini II*, normally flown by Capt Allen V. Martini. Martini missed the mission because of illness, and the pilot's seat was taken by Maj T. H. Taylor, CO of the 364th Bomb Squadron. Capt Cliff Pyle was flying his seventh mission with the 305th BG this day: 'Everything went well until we reached the target area, then everything seemed to happen at once. Six Focke-Wulfs attacked us simultaneously, head-on, concentrating their fire on the third and fourth squadrons, while others attacked the second squadron. During this burst, the number two ship in the second element in the third squadron was shot down. Our ship received four cannon holes, two in the left wing, one in the right wing and the fourth went through the floor of the bomb compartment into the pilots' compartment, bursting the hydraulic lines. Hydraulic fluid spewed throughout the pilots' compartment, blinding both myself and Lt Gilbert, my co-pilot. Only moments later the windshield shattered inwardly. I believe this was caused by a hit on the side of the aircraft, and was aggravated further by the top turret guns firing forward.

'Gunfire from two other fighters entered the lower turret, wounding Sgt McCoy, the turret gunner. There were about 150 .30 calibre holes in the wings, along with the two cannon shots. There was a hole in the leading edge about the size of a bushel basket. A tracer bullet entered the radio compartment, setting fire to the upholstery.

'Luckily I managed to stay in formation. The number one engine was misfiring and spewing black smoke, and we feathered the props immediately. The number four engine was also smoking. We feathered it for a few moments at a time until we reached the coast. Then we began to lag behind, but we arrived over Chelveston in time to land with other damaged aircraft first. We had to extend the landing gear by hand. On the final approach it required both of us to hold the 'plane steady. The crippled engine was unfeathered and used on the final approach. Both tyres were flat and we landed far too short. This was lucky, because we had no braking action. We had to abandon the runway for other aircraft landing behind us, so we blasted the engines with full power and managed to swing off and clear the runway. We ended up in the ditch alongside. The aircraft landing immediately in front of us was Maj Taylor's. He had been killed by a cannon shot in the chest and his co-pilot was wounded.'

Only one Fortress in the 305th BG was lost on the raid. Two B-17s from the 306th were lost in a mid-air collision over Belgium. Gunners claimed six fighters destroyed and 13 probably destroyed. If anyone needed proof that LeMay's tactics were right, the Lille raid had provided it. The bombing was so effective that VIII Bomber Command never had need to return to Lille.

B-24D Fascinatin' Witch, *41-23811, and other Eight-ball Liberators taxi out at Shipdham. The* Witch *was lost on the Wiener Neustadt mission on 1 October 1943, while being flown by Lt Richard Bridges. The waist gunner was killed and the rest of the crew were made PoWs.* (USAF.)

On 23 January 48 Fortresses and six Liberators in the 44th BG mounted raids on the U-boat pens at Lorient and Brest. Three bombers were shot down by German fighters employing head-on attacks for the first time, and one other bomber was lost to flak. The deputy lead ship in the 44th became the fourth bomber lost when a Fw 190 pilot, who attacked head-on, failed to pull out in time and collided with the Liberator. Both aircraft crashed into the North Sea from 20,000 ft.

By the end of the month casualties exceeded replacements, with only 24 B-17 and B-24 crews arriving to replace 67 lost on missions during January. There had been talk suggesting that the small American force should be incorporated into the RAF night bombing campaign. Despite the value of daylight bombing, losses had continued to rise and many senior officers in the RAF remained unconvinced as to its ultimate success. Gen 'Hap' Arnold, Chief of the American Air Staff, was under pressure from various quarters from those who wanted to know why Eaker had been unable to mount more missions, and why French, rather than German targets, were being bombed. Once again the future of VIII Bomber Command as a separate bombing force was in question, and answers were desperately needed if it was to survive.

Chapter Three

Trial by combat

ON 14 JANUARY 1943 Ira C. Eaker, who since November 1942 had been acting Commanding-General of the 8th Air Force in the absence of General Carl Spaatz, received a cable from General 'Hap' Arnold, asking to meet him at the forthcoming Casablanca Conference in North Africa. The next day Capt Cliff Pyle and the crew of *We The People* flew the general to North Africa in a borrowed B-17F, *Boomerang*. 'Our flight en route to Marrakech was uneventful,' says Pyle, 'flying in broken clouds all the way. Gen Eaker went by car to the Conference site and we waited at the airfield for further orders.' The Conference of President Roosevelt and Prime Minister Winston Churchill and the combined heads of staff took place at the Anfa Hotel, on a hill just south of the town, overlooking the Atlantic.

Arnold warned Eaker that Churchill and Roosevelt had agreed that the 8th Air Force would cease daylight bombing and join the RAF in night bombing. Eaker was shattered, but was determined to reverse the decision. He wrote his now famous 'memorandum', less than a page long, which summarised his reasons why the daylight bombing offensive should continue. Although not fully convinced, Churchill was impressed, particularly with Eaker's 'round the clock' bombing strategy. The British Prime Minister agreed to extend the time Eaker needed to prove daylight bombing, and the conference approved additional aircraft for VIII Bomber Command.

Upon his return to England, Eaker decided that his forces were now ready to attack Germany, and the target selected for January 27 was the U-boat construction yards at Vegasack, on the Weser. Although the port had been heavily bombed by the RAF throughout 1942, it had long been earmarked as a possible target for the Americans. The RAF night bombers had caused severe damage to the town and had destroyed a large naval ammunition dump, but some of the U-boat slipways, dry docks and shipyards had escaped damage. It was an ideal opportunity for Eaker to demonstrate that daylight precision bombing could be more effective than RAF night bombing.

The mission was led by Col Frank Armstrong, CO of the 306th BG who, six months before, had led the equally momentous first American heavy bomber raid on France. Sixty-four B-17s set out over the North Sea, flying a dog-leg route to confuse the enemy, while the

Liberators flew a diversionary raid on Wilhelmshaven, but by the time the coast came into view only 55 Fortresses remained. All but two dropped their bombs blindly from 25,000 ft through a German smoke screen which drifted lazily over the shipyards, while the other two bombed Emden.

The Eightballs failed to locate their target, so crews bombed through cloud somewhere near the Dutch-German border. Navigation went uncorrected, and the 44th continued out over Friesland and encountered heavy fighter opposition. Lt Sullivan's B-24 was shot down, and Lt Cargyle's ship was destroyed in a mid-air collision when a Fw 190 careered into it after being hit by machine gun fire from another B-24. Lt Jim O'Brien barely made it home. His bombardier, Lt Reg Grant, and his assistant radio-operator, S/Sgt M. Deal, had both been killed, and his navigator, Lt Leroy Perlowin, was severely wounded by a 20 mm shell which also slightly injured one of his gunners, Sgt Guilford.

The bombing of Vegasak was described as 'fair', but the Press were ready to fete the B-17 crews. The Fortress was rapidly becoming the favourite of the American public, much to the chagrin of the Liberator crews. The Eightballs, which received barely a mention, resented being used as bait while the Boeing boys captured the headlines.

Flushed with no small measure of success, Eaker decided to crack an even bigger nut. For years RAF crews had referred to the industrial German heartland of the Ruhr as 'Happy Valley', feared and respected for its lethal concentrations of heavy flak. Twice bad weather postponed the strike, and on 2 February the heavies actually got into the air only for the mission to be aborted because of worsening weather conditions. Finally, on 4 February, 86 bombers took off and went all the way, flying a long, deceptive flight over the freezing grey waters of the North Sea before turning for Hamm. Bad weather forced the Fortresses to seek targets of opportunity at Emden and off the coast. The Fortress formation became strung out, offering an open invitation to the Luftwaffe, as Capt Cliff Pyle, who was flying *We The People*, explains. 'Everything went well until we were about 100 miles inland. There we were met by about 50 enemy fighters. They attacked us continuously to the target and until we were 30 miles out to sea.' The battle reached fever pitch, and five Fortresses were brought down as the Luftwaffe single- and twin-engined fighters tore into the depleted ranks of the bomber formation.

Bad weather grounded the 8th until 14 February, when the B-17s flew an abortive strike against Hamm. On the afternoon of the 15th 21 B-24s of the 44th BG attacked Dunkirk. Their target was the *Tojo*, a surface raider disguised as a slow freighter. The 67th Squadron, led by Major MacDonald, headed the formation. *Little Beaver* flew on his left wing in the number three position in the lead element. Just beneath them were three B-24s of the second element and six more to the left. The formation crossed the Channel to Le Havre. MacDonald's navigator, Lt 'Ben' Franklin, plotted a course to make the Germans believe that the Liberators were headed inland, but they

B-24Ds of the 44th BG bomb Dunkirk on 15 February 1943. They failed to hit the Tojo, *which was berthed in the harbour.* (USAF.)

changed direction and flew straight and level up the coast of France to Dunkirk. However, their long straight run had enabled the German gunners to determine their speed and height. From their high altitude the B-24s could release their bombs some distance out over the Channel and let their trajectory carry them in. Aboard MacDonald's Liberator the bombardier, Lt Paul D. Caldwell, called out 'target in view'. Flak enveloped the formation, and just as the bomb-release light came on, at 15:40, the B-24 took a direct hit.

When Arthur Cullen, the pilot, recovered from the shock the Liberator was in a dive, with no other ships in sight. There was no roof on the cabin, just a windshield, and the cowlings were blown off number two and three engines, which were smoking. He could not operate the rudder because his leg was broken. MacDonald, sitting in the co-pilot's seat, had a bad stomach gash but signalled to bale out. For a few moments the noseless bomber flew on, only to fall away to starboard with the port inboard engine aflame and the right inboard ripped from its mounting. Finally, the starboard wing fell off and a huge explosion scattered debris among the formation, hitting another Liberator, whose pilot managed to recross the Channel and force-land at Sandwich. MacDonald baled out in extreme pain, Cullen helping him by pushing him through the hole where the roof had been. He then followed MacDonald, hitting the tailplane and breaking his arm, and then breaking his leg a second time. MacDonald died later in a German hospital, but Cullen was eventually repatriated in September 1944 after having broken his leg a third time. Lt Oliphant's B-24 was hit by flak, exploded, and was finished off by fighters. Despite the Eightballs' endeavours the *Tojo* remained afloat.

On 16 February Howard Moore assumed command of the 67th Squadron and led them to St Nazaire. Col Leon Johnson flew Group

Liberators of the 44th BG taxi from their muddy dispersals. 41-23818 is Texan II, *which was lost in a mid-air collision with Lt Fred Billings' B-24D on the St Nazaire raid on 16 February 1943. (USAF.)*

lead. Shortly after leaving the English coast Lt Fred Billings' Liberator fell away to port, hit the port wing tip of Lt Long's *Texan II* and locked there. Seconds later they exploded, scattering debris into the Fortress formation below. Four men were amazingly thrown clear, but Air-Sea Rescue found no trace of them in the murky sea. At the target 'George' Phillips lined up *Little Beaver* for a bomb run, but the bomb bay doors refused to open. Lt 'Chubby' Hill, the bombardier, entered the bomb bay and released the bombs manually. The closed doors splintered on impact, and Hill realised they had to be tethered quickly before they broke off and damaged other B-24s in the formation. Clinging precariously to the cat-walk, 20,000 ft above the earth, Hill went to work. Using pieces of wire, he secured the remnants of the doors in what must have been the highest trapeze act of the war.

The Luftwaffe unsuccessfully tried air-to-air bombing. The 305th formation failed totally because of a bombsight malfunction in the lead aircraft. Flak enveloped the 20 B-17s in the 306th BG formation, and immediately after 'bombs away' 1st Lt Joseph A Downing's Fortress in the 367th 'Clay Pigeons' Squadron was hit in two engines. Enemy fighters knocked out a third engine after the target, and Downing had no alternative but to dive the aircraft from 10,000 to 4,000 ft and disappear into some clouds. He lost the fighters and ordered the crew to bale out. Harvey J. Ross, one of the waist gunners, was killed, but Lt Kelly, the co-pilot, and S/Sgt Allen H. Robinson, the engineer, evaded capture with the help of the French Underground.

Meanwhile, six Fw 190s attacked 1st Lt William H. Warner, in the 423rd 'Grim Reapers' Squadron, from head-on, killing Warner and Sgts Robert D. Kisling, Colin Neely and William Williams. T/Sgt Eddie Espitallier was seriously wounded in the left leg and hip by 20 mm cannon fire. Lt Arnold Carlson, the co-pilot, pulled Warner's body off the controls and put the B-17 into a rapid descent. He and Sgt Walter C Morgan, who could not be extricated from his damaged ball turret, went down with the aircraft. Altogether, eight bombers were lost, and most of the bombardiers missed their aiming point at the southwestern corner of the sub-basin.

On 25 February the number of Liberators was increased by the return of the Travelling Circus from North Africa, which flew into Hardwick. Next day the B-17s and the 44th BG headed for Bremen. A heavy undercast forced the bombers to abort the primary target and seek their secondary target at Wilhelmshaven. About 30 miles from the coast they were attacked by fighters so determined in their mission that they sustained their attacks all the way into the target. Aboard one of the two B-24s shot down was Robert B. Post, a *New York Times* reporter. He was the only one of seven journalists – the writing 69th – who chose to fly with the 44th on the mission. The rest, who flew with the B-17s, returned safely, although one B-17 was lost.

The lowest Fortress in the entire formation was piloted by Lt George E. Stallman, one of 20 pilots in the 305th BG. About 15 minutes from Bremen he came under attack from two Bf 109s. They made several passes, and the bomber took hits in the right wing and number four engine, knocking the ship out of formation. Flying in the cramped ball turret was Lee 'Shorty' Gordon, a 5 ft 2 in gunner. 'Shorty' was one of the most colourful characters in the Group, as his CO, Colonel Curtis LeMay, has written: 'He wasn't . . . in a high state of discipline. He resented being bossed. In combat he was OK. When time came for a mission, we would make him a buck sergeant, send him on the mission: then take his stripes away from him when he came home. What we were trying to do was to get better treatment for him if the airplane happened to be shot down.' 'Shorty' returned fire, but Lawrence C. Lovos, the tail gunner, was wounded in the attack.

It was fortunate that he was wearing his parachute this day, because Stallman gave the order to bale out. Gordon recalls: 'I rolled out of the turret and almost immediately opened my back pack 'chute at about 24,000 ft. The silk streamed out and I felt a terrific jerk. I had not bothered to adjust the straps. If I had not had some luck I might have slipped through my harness. The opening jolt jerked my boots right off my feet, and I came down in my stockinged feet.'

The Germans probably wished later that they had not shot down 'Shorty' Gordon, American fighting man, because after capture he was to cause them more trouble than he had caused Col LeMay! 'Shorty' attempted escape three times, including one effort disguised in

A line-up of three B-17Fs in the 423rd Bomb Squadron, 306th BG at Thurleigh. In the centre is 42-5717, the first Vega-built B-17F, which was lost on the mission to St Nazaire on 16 February 1943 when 1/Lt William H. Warner's crew were shot down. Aircraft 42-5180, left, was lost on the 25 June 1943 mission to a target of opportunity at Bremen, when Lt Thomas E. Logan's crew failed to return. The third aircraft, 41-24460, was transferred to the 482nd BG on 22 September 1943. (Richards.)

Above left *Lee 'Shorty' Gordon, who served in the 305th BG under General Curtis E. LeMay.* (Lee Gordon.)

Above right Gunners Ed Lawler and Bill Dickson pose for the camera in front of their B-17F-10-DL Oklahoma Okie, *42-29921 in the 324th Bomb Squadron, 91st Bomb Group.* Okie *was lost on 31 December 1943 when it was flown by 2/Lt Bayard T. G. Dudley.* (USAF.)

Lederhosen. The little American, with hair oiled flat and a close-shaven chin, had little difficulty passing himself off as a Bavarian youth, and obtained a bicycle and intended riding all the way to the Swiss border. He was caught, but his third escape attempt was a success, and in February 1944 he reached England via France. Gordon became the first American airman to receive the Silver Star for escaping.

The next day 65 bombers hit U-boat pens and naval facilities at Brest. Altogether, the February missions had cost 22 aircraft. On 4 March four B-17s were shot down and 34 casualties suffered during strikes by 28 and 16 B-17s respectively on Rotterdam and Hamm; the first time the bombers had attacked the Ruhr. Losses might have been higher but for the introduction of new, armoured flak vests, developed by Col Malcolm C. Grow, Chief Surgeon of the 8th Air Force, in asssociation with the Wilkinson Sword Company of Great Britain, and worn by ten crews in the 91st BG this day.

On 6 March 63 B-17s bombed the power plant, bridge and port area at Lorient while 15 Liberators made a diversionary raid on a bridge and U-boat facilities at Brest. Two days later 13 Liberators bombed the marshalling yards at Rouen in a diversionary raid to aid the B-17s attacking another marshalling yard, at Rennes. Brig Gen Hayward Hansell flew in the 305th BG formation which bombed Rennes. Fifty B-17s plastered the marshalling yards from end to end and effectively stopped any supplies reaching German bases in Brittany for up to four days. Several squadrons of RAF Spitfires and, for the first time, the 4th Fighter Group's P-47 Thunderbolts, flew interdiction strikes against airfields ahead of the bombers.

Unfortunately the fighters encountered heavy opposition and the 44th BG were left to fend for themselves. A Gruppe of Fw 190s attacked head-on. At first the B-24 crews mistook them for Thunderbolts because of their similar radial engines. All too late they realized their mistake, and Capt Clyde E. Price crashed in flames with his bombs still in their racks, and Lt Bob W. Blaine's aircraft followed. There were no survivors from Price's ship, and only two from Blaine's. Both B-24s came from the ill-fated 67th Squadron, now reduced to only three original crews and aircraft. The Spitfire escort finally appeared and prevented further losses. Even so, two B-24s barely made it back to England.

On 12 and 13 March the bombers hit marshalling yards in France and the good fighter cover helped prevent any loss to the bombers. Some 93rd BG Liberators joined the 44th BG in flying effective diversion raids for the Fortresses. With morale high, plans were laid to bomb the Vulcan shipbuilding yards at Vegasack on the Weser, a few miles north of Bremen and ranked fourth largest producer of U-boats in Germany. On 18 March Eaker ordered a maximum effort and 73 Fortresses and 24 Liberators – the highest number of heavies yet – were assembled for the raid.

Near Heligoland the bombers came under attack from the Luftwaffe, and the leading 303rd BG formation of 22 aircraft bore the brunt of most of the enemy fighters' aggression. During the bomb run the group encountered some concentrated and accurate flak. Lt Jack Mathis, the lead bombardier aboard *The Duchess*, piloted by Capt Harold Stouse, was posthumously awarded the Congressional Medal of Honor, America's highest military award, for completing his bomb run despite being mortally wounded. As lead bombardier, Mathis was

B-17F The Duchess, *41-24561, in the 359th Bomb Squadron, 303rd BG, which Jack Mathis flew on 18 March 1943 when his actions earned him a posthumous Medal of Honor.* (Via Mike Bailey.)

A tired and haggard Harold Stouse, in the 427th Bomb Squadron, 303rd Bomb Group, who piloted The Eightball *to Wilhelmshaven on 27 January 1943, the first time the 8th Air Force bombed a German target, fills out his flight report after the mission. On 18 March Stouse flew* The Duchess *home to Molesworth with the body of 1/Lt Jack Mathis, his bombardier, aboard. Mathis was awarded a posthumous Medal of Honor (the first awarded to an 8th Air Force crewmember) for his actions this day on the mission to Vegasack.* (USAF.)

doing the aiming for all the other aircraft in the 359th Squadron, using Automatic Flght Control Equipment (AFCE) for the first time. This equipment gave him lateral control of the aircraft through the Norden bombsight's connection to the auto-pilot.

Meanwhile the Liberator crews found the trip uneventful until, flying 2,000 ft below the Fortress, they reached their bombing altitude 50 miles from the German coast. It was a running fight throughout, but while the 44th encountered heavy opposition, the only B-24 shot down belonged to the 93rd BG. For almost 1¾ hrs the Liberators came under attack. However, the run into the target was good and the bombing successful. Leading the 44th BG was the 67th Squadron, led by Maj 'Pappy' Moore in *Suzy Q*. Over the target his gunners claimed six enemy fighters.

On the return leg the Luftwaffe stepped up its attacks, sometimes with as many as 30 fighters taking part. In the 93rd BG formation Frank Lown's B-24 was hit in the number four engine and a hole was blown in one of his vertical stabilizers. Next it was the turn of the twin-engined Messerschmitt Me 110s and Junkers Ju 88s. Their attacks were more nerve-wracking, taking longer to complete before they broke away. Just as the B-24 crews thought themselves safe, the German pilots would skid their fighters and fire longer bursts. When at last the fighters broke off their attacks, the crew of *Shoot Luke* saw Lown's engine beginning to smoke and vibrate badly. Lown was formerly *Luke*'s co-pilot before getting his own crew. The B-24 dropped from formation, and Lt John H. Murphy and his crew decided to help Lown home. *Shoot Luke* broke formation and took up position off the stricken Liberator's wing. Unfortunately, the stragglers attracted the attention of a lone Fw 190. Its pilot surveyed the situation and made his attack from 9 o'clock with his four machine guns and cannon blazing. Three bullets missed Lown's head by less than eighteen inches.

Shortly afterwards, *Shoot Luke* bucked with a sudden explosion in the rear section. Although hit in the eye by fragments, Sgt Floyd H. Mabee remained at his waist gun and succeeded in shooting down the fighter. Sgt Paul B. Slankard, the tail gunner, was blasted through the top of his turret by a direct hit from a 20 mm shell. Slankard flew for interminable minutes at 22,500 ft with the upper part of his body protruding from his turret. His left foot, which had caught in the gun controls, was all that had prevented him from being shot, projectile fashion, through the turret roof.

Floyd Mabee made his way back to the bomber's tail, pulled Slankard back into the aircraft and applied an oxygen-mask to his face. Lt Edmund J. Janic, the bombardier, crawled to the rear of the ship despite severe head wounds and applied sulphonamide to Slankard's wound. Together, Janic and Mabee then dragged the severely wounded tail gunner to a hole in the fuselage where the frigid air entering the aeroplane at a temperature of some 45° below zero sealed the wound. The hypodermic needles had frozen, and no amount of warming in the crew's mouths could thaw them enough to enable drugs to be administered. Slankard remained in his precarious position for 2¾ hrs while Mabee massaged his hands to maintain circulation. Janic returned to the flight deck and collapsed from loss of blood and shock. Lt Arch Rantala, the navigator, successfully navigated the two bombers home. Frank Lown landed and thanked Murphy's crew, which completely filled an ambulance, for saving him and his crew from certain destruction. (Lown was shot down on 16 April over Brest and made a POW). Slankard eventually recovered from his terrible wounds.

Vegasack was officially described as 'extremely heavily damaged'. The bombers had dropped 268 tons of high explosive smack on target, and later photographic reconnaissance revealed that seven U-boats had been severely damaged and two-thirds of the shipyards destroyed. British Prime Minister Winston Churchill and Sir Charles Portal, Chief of the Air Staff, recognised the importance of the success achieved on the mission and sent congratulatory messages to Eaker.

On 22 March the bombers attacked Wilhelmshaven. In the 44th BG formation Lt Jim O'Brien and Maj Francis McDuff, the 68th Squadron commander, led the Eightballs in *Rugged Buggy* behind five B-24s of the 93rd BG. Jim O'Brien described the mission as 'hot as my first', and later counted 29 separate holes in *Rugged Buggy*. Despite a thorough going over by Me 110s and Fw 190s, it was flak rather than fighters which claimed the sixth original 67th Squadron crew. Capt Gideon W. 'Bucky' Warne's Liberator and a 506th Squadron replacement both went down. Lt Robert Walker was the sole survivor from the two B-24s. This left *Little Beaver* and *Suzy Q* as the only remaining original Liberators in the squadron. Col Ted Timberlake, who was leading the 93rd in *Teggie Ann*, narrowly escaped death when a 20 mm shell entered the cockpit and missed him by only a few inches. Four days later Col Timberlake assumed command of the 201st Provisional Combat Wing and was replaced, on 17 May, by Lt Col Addison T. Baker.

On 31 March the bombers were sent to the E-boat pens at Rotterdam. The dock area was hit by 33 bombers, while others attacked docks at Schiedam and the city area of Bocholt. Many bombs missed the target completely and caused 300 Dutch casualties. On 4 April Eaker switched to targets in France, and that morning Fortresses throughout the Bedford area took off for a raid on the Renault factory in the Billancourt district of Paris. On the night of 3/4 March 1942 the RAF had destroyed the plant, but the Germans had rebuilt it in nine months using slave labour, and had even managed to increase production.

It took two hours for the four B-17 groups to complete assembly before a total of 97 Fortresses departed the rendevous point at Beachy Head. However, only 85 Fortresses remained when landfall was made at Dieppe, 12 having aborted through malfunctions. For once the sky was clear and blue, and many of the Spitfire escort fighters could be seen quite plainly. Others were simply vapour trails in the upper reaches of the atmosphere. From their altitude of 25,000 ft, crews could see the black mass of Paris cradled in the long, curved arm of the River Seine, 95 miles in the distance.

At 14:14 the Fortresses were over their target and 251 tons of high explosive rained down on Paris. Flak was moderate and not too accurate, and crews were able to pick out the Renault works despite the industrial haze which covered much of the city. Most of the 81 tons that landed square on the factory were released by 18 B-17s of the leading 305th formation, led by Maj McGehee in *We The People*, flown by Capt Cliff Pyle. Before the last group had left the target the whole area was blotted out by a thick pall of smoke reaching to 4,000 ft. Unfortunately the groups in the rear of the formation were not as accurate as the 305th had been, and many bombs fell outside the target area, causing a number of civilian casualties.

So far no enemy fighters had been sighted, but five minutes after the target 50–75 Luftwaffe fighters began attacks on the formation which lasted all the way to Rouen. Four B-17s were shot down in repeated frontal attacks, sometimes by four and six fighters at a time, until the Spitfire escort reappeared to provide withdrawal support. The gunners aboard *Dry Martini 4th*, piloted by Capt Allen Martini, were credited with the destruction of ten enemy fighters, a record for a bomber crew on a single mission. In all, American gunners claimed 47 enemy fighters destroyed. Pictures smuggled back to England by the French resistance after the raid showed that the Renault works had been severely damaged.

The following day the Erla aircraft factory and Erla engine works in Antwerp were bombed by 82 Fortresses and Liberators. The 306th bore the brunt of head-on attacks by Fw 190s, which shot down five of the group's B-17s. These were the only losses among the heavies this day. Another B-17, carrying Brig Gen Frank Armstrong, now commanding the 1st Bomb Wing, who was flying as an observer, was hit by cannon fire, but Maj James Wilson, the 306th Air Executive, managed to bring the Fortress home safely to Thurleigh.

After a few days' break in missions VIII Bomber Command struck at Lorient and Brest on 16 April. Flying its first mission this day, to Lorient, was Lt Claude W. Campbell's crew, in the 359th Bomb Squadron, 303rd BG. Howard E. Hernan, the top-turret gunner, recalls: 'A Fw 190 came in at about 2 o'clock high. The pilot could not have had much experience firing at a B-17 because he fired from a long way off. I gave him a burst at about 1,500 yards, a little further than I should have. About the same time he fired his 20 mm cannon and they all went off at about 400 yards ahead of us. After he fired he immediately flipped over on his back and down he went. It was the last I saw of him. We came through unscathed but the Group lost two B-17s.'

On the morning of 17 April crews throughout eastern England were alerted for a raid on the Focke-Wulf plant at Bremen, and a record 115 bombers were assembled. For the first time two large-scale combat wings, with the 91st and 306th in the first wing and the 303rd and 305th BGs making up the second, were despatched. Each wing formation consisted of three group boxes of 18–21 aircraft, flown for mutual firepower and protection. Eight bombers returned early with malfunctions, leaving the remaining 107 bombers to continue across the North Sea.

The long over-water flight was uneventful and even monotonous. William A. Boutelle, the bombardier in Lt Claude Campbell's crew, settled down and began writing, 12,000 ft above the North Sea: 'As I write this I'm on my way to Bremen, one of the hottest spots in Germany. Yesterday we flew in the leading and highest group. In that position we had a very calm and, for the most part, boring flight. The lower and rear groups caught some hell from flak and fighters while we only saw a few puffs of ack-ack and about 20 fighters. Today promises to be a very different story. We're in the highest but last group and have a grandstand view of all the other ships, of which I can count over 100 right now. We should really see a show today. I'll see it all, I hope.'

The mass formation had been spotted by a German reconnaissance aircraft shortly after leaving the English coast, and the Americans' approach was radioed to fighter controllers along the enemy coastline. The German defences did not know where the bombers were headed, but Luftwaffe fighters were vectored towards them just after they passed the Friesian Islands. However, the flak barrage was so intense that the Fw 190 pilots waited until after the bomb run before launching their attacks. Worst hit was the 306th, which lost ten bombers. One aircraft came home with a parachute harness tied to control cables which had been shot away by cannon fire. The 401st Squadron of the 91st BG, flying as the low squadron in the 1st Bomb Wing formation, lost all six aircraft.

Gunners claimed 63 fighters destroyed, but only about ten were actually shot down. Half of the Focke-Wulf factory was destroyed but Albert Speer, the German armaments minister, had issued instructions for dispersed fighter production some six months previously. Crews received a much needed boost with the news that, despite the continuing losses, the 8th Air Force was to be expanded. In February the Casablanca Conference had approved additional aircraft for VIII Bomber Command. Eaker's successful strategy meant that they were now to be used for daylight bombing.

Chapter Four

Gaining strength

DURING MID-APRIL 1943 four new Fortress groups – the 94th, 95th, 96th and 351st – were despatched to Britain, to be joined by three more B-17 groups in May. All but the 351st had B-17Fs with long-range 'Tokyo tanks' built into their wings near the tips to hold an additional 1,080 gal of fuel. Whilst the new groups continued training, Eaker scheduled another attack on St Nazaire for May Day. Thick cloud over the target curtailed bombing attempts, and the 306th flew back, unaware that it was off course through a navigational error. What was assumed to be Land's End turned out to be the Brest Peninsula, and as the formation began to descend it was bracketed by an accurate barrage of flak. Altogether, the Thurleigh group lost six aircraft.

Lt L. P. Johnson's aircraft was hit several times and caught fire. S/Sgt Maynard 'Snuffy' Smith, the ball-turret gunner, who was on his first mission, hand-cranked his turret back into the aircraft and discovered that the waist gunners and the radio operator had baled out. Smith could have baled out, but he elected to remain in the aircraft and fight the fire with a hand extinguisher. The aircraft did not show any signs of leaving formation, so Smith assumed that the pilots were still aboard and went aft to treat the badly wounded tail gunner. Then he jettisoned the oxygen bottles and ammunition in the radio compartment and manned the two waist guns during an attack by enemy fighters, stopping to dampen down the fires and treat the tail gunner. After Smith had thrown out all excess equipment, Johnson managed to bring the bomber home and put down at Predannack near Land's End. On 15 July 1943 'Snuffy' Smith received the Medal of Honor from Secretary of War Henry L. Stimson.

The raid was a special one for Capt Cliff Pyle, who was flying his 25th and final mission with the 305th BG. The 305th lost two aircraft, but Pyle and the crew of *We The People* came through safely. Within ten days of this mission he was attached to the 1st Bomb Wing with the title of 'President, Tactical Advisory Board'. The board's primary function was to advise the commanding general about combat tactics and to monitor the preparation of the Tactical Doctrine, later known as 'Standard Operations Procedures'.

Meanwhile, on 4 May Eaker despatched 79 B-17s to the Ford and

Above *S/Sgt Maynard 'Snuffy' Smith* (Richards.)

General Motors plant at Antwerp, escorted by 12 Allied fighter squadrons, including, for the first time, six squadrons of P-47s. Howard Hernan of the 303rd BG recalls: 'The Spitfires and Thunderbolts did a wonderful job of working the Focke-Wulfs over, and it was a very successful mission. We flew on Capt Calhoun's wing (CO of the squadron), and Clark Gable flew with him and handled the radio hatch gun. Claude Campbell, my pilot, could see the Hollywood film star grinning at him over enemy territory. One of our B-17s, piloted by Lt Pence, was shot up by a Fw 190 that jumped the group as we reached the English coast, and the co-pilot got shot in the leg and never flew again; the radio operator got hit over the eye and in the leg. Next morning I looked over Pence's 'plane. It had nine holes in it and I measured them. The spread was 9 ft, although they had been attacked from head-on. Capt Gable visited the co-pilot every evening at a nearby hospital to see how he was getting along.'

On the night of 12 May the 94th, 95th and 96th BG received orders to participate in a maximum effort starting at 13:00. The news came as something of a shock at Bassingbourn, Alconbury and Grafton Underwood because the ground echelons had only arrived in Britain two days before. Remarkably, the three groups managed to prepare 72 bombers for the mission, to airfields at St. Omer, but at such short notice problems were bound to occur. The 96th failed to complete assembly and aborted the mission. One B-17 got into difficulties and ditched in the Channel, where the crew were rescued by Air Sea Rescue. Some 31 B-17s in the 94th and 95th BGs continued to the target, but the bombing was 'poor'.

During the night of 13/14 May the ticker-tape machines started clattering out orders for the B-17 and B-24 bomb groups in East Anglia. At Shipdham, Lt Jim E. O'Brien had just returned from a sortie 300 miles out to sea shadowing the German battleship *Tirpitz*. (In addition to regular bombing sorties, some 44th BG Liberators were assisting RAF Coastal Command with raids on German shipping and naval forces.) O'Brien was promoted to major and given command of the 68th Bomb Squadron, replacing Maj Francis McDuff, who was rotated home. 'I had no sooner found out what a squadron commander was supposed to do,' he recalled, 'when word came recalling all crews for a maximum effort on Bordeaux. However, at 02:00 the Field Order was changed to remove the bomb bay tanks and load up with 4,000 lb of the new-type incendiary clusters for a raid on Kiel. The explanation given at the briefing on the following morning at 05:00 was that the B-17s were going to bomb the hell out of the U-boat pens, aircraft factories and seaport facilities and the B-24s were to kindle the fires. It was all very logical but it was a long trip without fighter escort.'

In the spring of 1943 it was not yet practical or possible for the 8th Air Force in East Anglia to despatch its bombers further than Bremen or Kiel, a round trip of approximately 800 miles. However, for the 14 May mission Eaker could call upon more than 200 B-17s and B-24s for the first time, with the 351st BG at Polebrook making its debut. The large number of bombers available meant that Eaker could diversify his attacks with a multiplicity of options, further improved by the debut of 12 B-26 Marauders in the 322nd BG.

Major O'Brien cancelled the recall of Lts Tom Cramer and Bud Phillips because the 68th Squadron could put up six B-24s without calling on either of them, provided that O'Brien flew with his usual co-pilot, 'Mac' Howell, to check him out as first pilot for combat flying. Lt Ralph Ernst filled in as radio operator. O'Brien adds: 'The 44th was putting up 24 ships for the mission. I showed up so much as the squadron commander but as co-pilot of *The Rugged Buggy* in a 'tail-end Charlie' slot; what a glorious way to go!'

A few of the crew members, including Bill Cameron and Maj Howard 'Pappy' Moore, who were on 48-hour passes, managed to get back to Shipdham for the briefing but were too late to be considered for the raid. *Suzy Q* was undergoing maintenance in Northern Ireland, so 'Pappy' Moore's regular crew were reassigned. Lt Robert Brown, *Suzy Q's* usual co-pilot, would take the pilot's seat aboard *Miss Delores*, and Lt Hartley 'Hap' Westbrook would fly co-pilot. Capt Bob Bishop, the navigator, plus seven others, all from the *Suzy Q*, completed the scratch crew of *Miss Delores*, or 'Q for Queenie' as she was known, because of her call letter. Gilbert 'Gibby' Wandtke, the engineer, was not happy about the change in aircraft. He had been jilted by a Delores in the States, and claimed that *Miss Delores* would probably take them over the target but would not bring them back!

Opposite *Clark Gable (centre) poses beneath his B-17F-75-BO 42-29835 in the 351st BG during a visit to Bodney, Norfolk, in 1943. In October 1942 Gable had graduated from the Officers' Candidate School in Miami as a second lieutenant and attended aerial gunnery school until February 1943. On the personal insistence of Gen Arnold, he was assigned to the 351st BG at Polebrook to make a motion picture of gunners in action. He flew a handful of combat missions and, after completing some footage for the movie* Combat America*, returned to the USA in October 1943. (USAF.)*

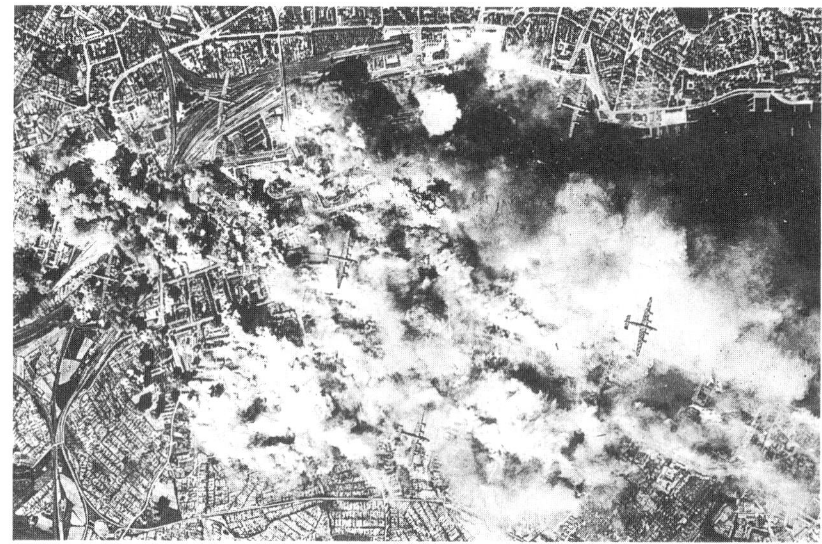

B-24Ds over Kiel on 14 May 1943. The B-17 groups at last got their wish – they flew behind and above the B-24s for the first time in the ETO. This resulted in heavy losses for the Liberators. (USAF.)

On previous missions the Liberators had bombed through the lower flying Fortress formations. To prevent this recurring, higher headquarters decreed that, on the mission to Kiel, the Liberators would have to reduce their speed and fly behind the Fortresses. It was mooted that if the B-24s tried to slow down to the speed of the B-17s they (the B-24s) 'would drop out of the sky'. The B-24D's cruising speed was 180–185 m.p.h. indicated airspeed, while the B-17s cruised at 160 m.p.h. indicated.

At 09:00 21 Liberators began taxiing out at Shipdham for the mission to Kiel. As the *Rugged Buggy* taxied out behind Lt George Jansen's ship, *Margaret Ann*, 'Mac' Howell said: 'If I get back from this trip, I'm going to get stinking drunk.' Dick Castillo, the rear gunner, commented: 'Come on, let's quit kidding, this will be just as tough as any we've ever flown.' Jim O'Brien thought, too, about Howard Moore's remark at briefing: 'I wouldn't go on this mission if I were you.' For 20 minutes the bombers circled the field and gained altitude before falling into formation. Assembly completed, they headed out over the North Sea and rendezvoused with over 100 B-17s. The B-24D pilots tried to settle down to a constant cruising speed of 180 m.p.h. while maintaining a height of only 500 ft to avoid detection by enemy raider. The task was made more difficult because they had to zig-zag continually 20 miles in one direction and 40 miles in the other to remain behind the slower Fortresses.

Meanwhile, at around 10:35 a dozen B-26Bs swooped low over the Dutch coast and continued over the outskirts of Amsterdam at roof-top height. They bombed a generating station at Ijmuiden with delayed action mines, and then departed as quickly as they had come. It was a curtain raiser for a vast armada of aircraft, the like of which had never before been seen on German radar screens during daylight hours.

About an hour after the B-26s departed, the 1st Wing formation, flying without escort, was picked up, this time approaching the

Part of Capt Claude Campbell's crew in the 303rd BG pose for the camera at Molesworth before a mission. (Howard Hernan.)

northwest coast of Germany. The German fighter controllers did not yet know where they were headed, but their target was the Germania and Deutsch Werke shipyards at Kiel. At 11:45 the formation turned south for the base of the Danish Peninsula. Five minutes later, when the Americans' destination became apparent, the German controllers scrambled their fighters.

Howard Hernan recalls: 'The fighter opposition was intense and the flak heavy. We flew at 32,000 ft in the high squadron, high group; the highest I had ever flown. Most of the 88 mm flak was below us. The Germans did shoot up some 105s but Bales, Capt Campbell's roommate, flying in *Idaho Potato Peeler*, was shot down 20 miles offshore. All of a sudden he started drifting out to the right, almost in a complete circle. With Capt Bales was Mark Mathis, whose brother Jack, had been killed over Vegasack. It was for this reason that Mark transferred from a B-26 outfit to his brother's group, and he even flew in *The Duchess*, where he used Jack's bombsight. Mathis hated the Germans, and was determined to avenge his brother and complete his 25 missions for him. Nine 'chutes came out of the *Potato Peeler*. Bales appeared to have all his engines turning over, although one or two could have been windmilling. He came around and made a water landing in the midst of all the 'chutes. We never heard anything from them again.'

Kiel was bombed at 12:05 with 'good' results. At about the same time the 96th and 351st BGs were approaching the airfield at Coutrai in France. Just over 25 minutes later they returned east over Ypres to be met by Luftwaffe fighters, which became embroiled with the bombers' escorting fighters. Fifty Fortresses won through and bombed the hangars, dispersal areas, runways and workshops at the airfield and put it out of action. The B-17s then flew north and headed for the coast between Ostend and Dunkirk. By 12:55 most of the German fighters which took part in the first attack were forced to land and refuel.

So far the overall plan seemed to be working, with the German fighter controllers at full stretch having to meet the incoming B-17 and B-26 raids. A diversionary raid on Antwerp was still to come. However, the 44th BG Liberators were having problems. The Eight-balls should have avoided the Friesian Islands, but the constant zig-zag course they had been forced to adopt caused them to stray, and they overflew the islands at 19,000 ft to be greeted by sporadic bursts of flak. Jim O'Brien recalls: 'My attention was diverted momentarily to Tom Holmes' ship, which took a burst of flak and appeared to have flames coming out of the bomb bay. [He managed to maintain height and re-cross the sea to England.] Suddenly our ship was rocked by two explosions. The manifold pressure on the two left engines dropped to 15 p.s.i., and there was a sudden drag to the left which Howell and I struggled to correct. I had thoughts of feathering the two left engines, but that would have been a sure give-away to German fighters waiting to come in for the kill.'

The interphone was put out of action in the blast, and all communication with the four men in the rear of the aircraft was lost. Unbeknown to O'Brien, flak had also blown a hole in the tail, knocking Sgt Castillo out of his rear turret and amputating his foot in the process. Three crew members in the tail came to his aid and, quickly realizing the extent of his injuries, pushed him out of the aircraft, pulling the ripcord on his parachute pack for him before they, too, baled out. Sgt Van Owen drowned in Kiel Bay although he was wearing a Mae West.

Despite the crew losses *The Rugged Buggy* and the surviving Liberators in the 44th Bomb Group continued to the target. Crews had been briefed to bomb from 21,000 ft, but the constant zig-zagging now brought them over Heligoland Bay at 18,000 ft. As they turned into the strong wind for bombing they were down to 160 m.p.h. – almost stalling speed. 'The bomb bay doors opened,' continues O'Brien, 'and the 44th let go its clusters of matchstick incendiaries. The clusters did not hold together for more than 200 ft. As soon as they hit the slipstream they were all over the sky in a negative trajectory, flying back through the formation and bouncing off wings and propellers. Nothing worked better for the Germans at this point, as the formation scattered to avoid these missiles.

'Meanwhile, we had dropped our own clusters of bombs and had plenty of trouble. The cockpit smelled of gasoline and our unspoken thoughts as Howell and I looked at each other were of fire and explosion. We had now separated from the rest of the group after leaving the target, and I noticed at least two other stragglers off to the right.' One was Capt John W. 'Swede' Swanson of the 506th Squadron in *Wicked Witch*. Flak had damaged the number two engine before the target was reached, but Swanson maintained formation and salvoed his bombs. *Wicked Witch* was finished off by enemy fighters making head-on attacks. Swanson and three others were the only survivors from the nine-man crew.

The Rugged Buggy was set on fire after incendiary bullets ignited the intense petrol fumes. Ralph Ernst, the radio operator, fought the fire.

'I managed to put out the fire temporarily between extinguishers,' he recalls, 'but I figured we would have to bale out as the 'plane would explode at any moment. There was no hydraulic pressure and the bomb bay door wouldn't open. The fire must have weakened the corrugated metal, but it was still difficult to open so I sat down on the catwalk and used my heel. I managed to get it open far enough for us to jump out.' Ernst wasted no time, and baled out of the doomed aircraft. On the way down he could see thick smoke coming from the Kiel shipyards. He landed on dry land, in a farmyard not far from a Danish village near the German border, where he was captured immediately by German soldiers.

Jim O'Brien also baled out through the open bomb bay doors, wearing a chest pack, but only after he had realized his mistake in putting on a life raft dinghy instead of his parachute. He landed in a Danish farmyard about 30 miles northwest of Kiel and was captured at about 12:30. Mac McCabe was killed when his torn parachute failed to work properly.

The 44th's cargo of incendiaries had required a shorter trajectory and a two-mile longer bomb run than the B-17s. Flying a scattered formation, the B-24s were exposed to fighter attack. Five Liberators were lost, including three belonging to the 67th Squadron, which brought up the rear of the formation. The first to go down was Lt William Roach and his replacement crew flying in *Annie Oakley*. There were only two survivors.

Miss Delores was hit by flak over the target. One burst hit 'Gibby' Wandtke, and he fell from the top turret with shrapnel wounds. John L. Susan, the radio operator, manned the turret. Unfortunately Susan's guns would not fire between the twin fins, and tail gunner Roy L. Klingler was dead. Six German fighters continued to fire at the ailing bomber from the rear. Two other gunners, George R. Millhausen and Richard Cate, were killed.

Just after Haldon R. Hayward, the bombardier, dropped his bombs, Bob Bishop spotted a fighter boring in and shouted at Hayward to duck. A shell exploded on the Plexiglas nose, and Hayward was struck in the face by fragments. Bishop had the paint stripped from his steel helmet by the blast. As *Miss Delores* fell behind, the left wing caught fire. Brown gave the bale-out order but, unknown to the crew, the flak bursts had also knocked out the intercom. Wandtke, although wounded, made his way aft via the open bomb bay at the height of the battle to warn the gunners to abandon ship. Bishop parachuted into the sea and was hauled aboard a Danish trawler. John L. Susan was pulled by his shroud lines from the sea by a fisherman after going under for about 10 ft. Brown, Westbrook, Hayward, Wandtke and August Ullrich, the assistant radio operator/gunner, were also rescued.

The third 67th Squadron Liberator lost was *Little Beaver*, piloted by Capt 'George' Phillips, which was shot down after leaving the target. Only four men from the 11-man crew survived after three explosions rocked the ship. One was caused by a 20 mm cannon shell which exploded in the nose and ignited the hydraulic fluid accumulators. The flight deck became a mass of flames, and Philips and Everett W.

Wilborn Jr, the co-pilot, were killed. The aircraft went into a flat spin. Mike Denny, the engineer, put on his parachute and then tried to extinguish the flames, but his efforts were in vain. Denny could not open the bomb bay doors, so he baled out through one of the waist windows. Tom Bartmess, the navigator, baled out of the aircraft, followed about three minutes later by 'Chubby' Hill, the bombardier. Bartmess landed in the water, but got tangled in the shrouds of his parachute and drowned. Hill landed on dry land, suffering from blows on the forehead, caused by the opening of his parachute and the landing, a bruised back, and shock. He joined Dale Glaubitz, the assistant engineer, and Charles Forehand, one of the waist gunners, as the only other survivors.

Scrappy, piloted by Lt John Y. Reed in the 66th Squadron, became the sixth and final loss to the 44th Bomb Group. The B-24 was badly damaged over the target, but Reed nursed it back to Shipdham, where ten of the crew baled out. *Scrappy* had to be shot down by RAF Spitfires. Adam Wygonik, the engineer/top-turret gunner, had been hit by 20 mm cannon fire on the bomb run and badly wounded in the head, eyes and arms. Sgt Alan Perry, the radio operator, put a parachute on Wygonik's harness and shoved him out of the aircraft while they were still over the shipyards. As he was bleeding profusely and without his oxygen supply, it is doubtful whether Wygonik would have survived the long flight back to England. He was soon picked up by German soldiers. Later, his right eye was removed at hospital in Vienna before he was eventually repatriated.

Meanwhile, at 13:00 German radar picked up the 94th and 95th BGs, led by Gen Anderson, near Ostend, heading for the Ford and General Motors plant at Antwerp. Capt Franklin 'Pappy' Colby, of the 94th BG (at 41 years of age the oldest pilot in the 8th Air Force), recalls: 'At the IP we were supposed to meet our supporting fighters, but we were 20 minutes late. Finally, we saw about 30 fighters at 2 o'clock and I heaved a sigh of relief, thinking our friends had waited for us. Suddenly they attacked, and at about the same time heavy flak started exploding dead ahead. We took violent evasive action, and then I discovered that the leading three-ship element of our low squadron had drifted left, out of the group formation. I decided to stay with the group, and it's lucky I did, because flak started exploding right behind him, where we should have been.

'I heard our guns hammering and saw little white smoke puffs just ahead of the left wingman. They were exploding cannon shells from German fighters. We dumped our load of five 1,000 lb bombs as carefully as possible and swung out over the coast for home. Flak followed us until we were out of range, but the fighters eased up. My tail gunner saw a B-17 hit the ground and explode – no parachutes. Recon' photos later showed a heavy bomb concentration on the Ford factory and the nearby canal locks, and the west end of the General Motors plant also caught it.'

In four hours VIII Bomber Command had attacked four targets, losing 11 aircraft and claiming 67 fighters shot down. Not all of the bombing was accurate, but for the first time Americans had shown that they were capable of mounting multiple attacks on a given day. The 44th BG was awarded a Distinguished Unit Citation for its part in the Kiel raid; it was the first made to an 8th Air Force Group.

On 15 May Eaker sent the 1st Wing to Wilhelmshaven while 59 B-17s of the 4th Wing were allocated Emden. Despite the unsuccessful attempt at using incendiaries at Kiel, B-17s of the 94th BG were loaded with eight 500 lb incendiary clusters for the raid. 'Pappy' Colby recalls: 'Instead of the bundles dropping like bombs, they broke open and the 4 lb sticks came fluttering back right through the formation, scaring the hell out of everybody. As we crossed the German coast, homeward bound, about 25 enemy fighters passed us on our left as if we were standing still, pulled across in front of us and then dived head-on into our formation as all hell bust loose. They hit the lead squadron mostly, and I saw at least 10–12 20 mm cannon shells explode around our ships, but everyone kept going.

'Suddenly my bombardier, Bob Gamble, let out a wild yell, and I discovered later that a shell had exploded under our nose, blowing out part of the Plexiglas window. Enough to scare anyone. Two Fw 190s started a nose attack on us, and all our gunners turned loose on them while they were still out some 800 yards, and to my great surprise they broke off the attack and turned away.' Incredibly, only one B-17, from the 95th BG was lost on the Emden mission.

Meanwhile, the 1st Wing had set a course for Wilhelmshaven. Thick cloud obscured the target, and the Fortresses were forced to seek alternative targets at Heligoland, Dune and Wangeroog Island. Heligoland was covered in only 4/10ths cloud and the flak was inaccurate. However, numerous enemy fighters put in an appearance and succeeded in shooting down five Fortresses.

On 16 May the Fortress groups were stood down while all available B-24Ds in the 44th and 93rd BGs were secretly flown to Davidstowe Moor in the West Country. Eaker planned to send the B-24s to Bordeaux while the 1st Wing bombed Kiel and the 4th Wing went to Lorient. In addition, 11 B-26 Marauders of the 322nd BG Group would fly a diversionary mission to Haarlem and Ijmuiden to bomb targets they had completely missed three days before. At 09:00 on 17 May Col Leon Johnson, Gen James Hodges and the crew of the revamped *Suzy Q* led 21 B-24s, followed closely by 18 B-24Ds of the 93rd. The Liberators flew a 700-mile arc over the Atlantic to minimize the chances of enemy detection. Four Liberators were forced to abort with mechanical troubles. Despite four new Twin Wasps, *Suzy Q* had one engine stopped when the formation started climbing to bombing altitude. To counteract the fall behind in schedule, Ed Mickolowski, the lead navigator, skilfully prepared a new course which bypassed the original curved route.

Mikolowski's alternative course brought the Liberator formation to the Bay of Biscay almost on schedule and over Bordeaux at 12:28. The city had hitherto been left untouched by the 8th Air Force, and the German defences had become complacent. The Americans could even lapse their jamming of German-controlled radio. Thirty or forty barrage balloons had been positioned over the target to prevent a low-level attack, but these did not deter the two Liberator groups bombing from 22,000 ft. 'Gentleman' Jim DeVinney, the lead bombardier, toggled his bomb release and the other bombardiers followed suit. Hits were observed on the lock gates at Basin Number One, which collapsed and was flooded by a deluge of water from a nearby river. Direct hits were observed on the Matford aeroengine factory, and the railway yards and chemical works were also hit.

The only casualties during the attack were two crewmen slightly wounded and a waist gunner who was sucked out of an open window after his parachute had accidentally opened. He was thrown against the tailplane and pitched into the sea with his parachute in shreds. One Liberator was forced to seek neutral territory after developing engine trouble shortly before the attack.

Meanwhile, 55 Fortresses in the 4th Wing had been despatched to the U-boat pens and the power station which served them at Lorient. 'Pappy' Colby recalls: 'As we came in off the sea about 30 fighters really gave us a going over. It turned out they were the famous yellow-nose fighters who defended the St Nazaire-Lorient area. To my amazement I saw one come right through the middle of the group formation in front of us. What a pilot! We made a fair bomb run and turn out, but the fighters worked us over clear out over the sea. In the middle of the fight my entire left windshield suddenly showed a million cracks, and I could barely see through it. A machine gun bullet hit it, but luckily at an acute angle, so that while it shattered the inch-thick armour glass it only put a small hole clear through. Lt Winnesheik (our Indian Chief), lost an engine but made it back. This was the roughest raid we had yet experienced.'

The B-17 groups pounded Lorient at 15-minute intervals, and six B-17s failed to return. The bombing was described as 'excellent.' Six hours after the B-24 raid on Bordeaux a photo-reconnaissance aircraft brought back pictures revealing that the 480-yard-long pier and two U-boats, which had been in the port during the attack, had vanished. The Liberator crews were jubilant, attributing much of their success to the fact that they had not had to fly behind the slower Fortresses. Sadly, the heavies' successes were not repeated by the 322nd BG, all of whose 11 Marauders were shot down.

On 19 May 68 Fortresses of the 1st Wing bombed the turbine engine building at Kiel while, further north, 55 B-17s of the 4th Wing attacked U-boat pens at Flensburg on the Danish coast. Following this mission, fog and rain cloaked East Anglia and the Fens, preventing any missions being flown until 21 May, when the 1st Wing was allocated Wilhelmshaven and the 4th Wing Emden. At Wilhelmshaven weather conditions hampered the formation, and it was further disrupted by constant head-on attacks by enemy fighters. The Emden force also encountered heavy fighter opposition despite diversionary ruses at the coast. Altogether, 12 B-17s were lost on the two raids, the 1st Wing coming off worst with seven B-17s shot down. Among them was *La Mersa Lass* in the 306th BG flown by Lt Robert H. Smith. His seven gunners set a new record, downing 11 fighters before the B-17 was forced to ditch in the North Sea. All the crew were picked up by an ASR launch and returned to Thurleigh.

It had been decided that, during May, the 94th, 95th and 96th BG of the 1st Wing would transfer south to form the nucleus of the new 4th Wing in Suffolk and Essex, commanded by Brig Gen Fred L. Anderson with his headquarters at Marks Hall, near Colchester. On 23 May the 94th began moving from Thurleigh to Earls Colne in Essex, and the 96th began leaving Grafton Underwood for Andrews Field, six miles from Earls Colne. The 95th BG was also due to move, from Alconbury to Framlingham, Suffolk, but its departure was marred by a tragic accident on 27 May, when a B-17 exploded while in the process of being loaded with ten 500 lb bombs. Nineteen officers and enlisted men were killed and 20 severely injured, one of whom died later. Four B-17s parked in the vicinity of the explosion were destroyed and 11 others were damaged in the blast.

The 96th BG's former base at Grafton Underwood was taken over by the 384th BG, commanded by Col Budd J. Peaslee, which arrived in England during late May. The 351st BG remained at Polebrook, and the 1st Bomb Wing received additional 'teeth' with the arrival of the 381st BG, commanded by Col Joe J. Nazzaro, which flew into Ridgewell on 31 May, and the 379th BG, commanded by Col Maurice 'Mo' Preston, which took over a new base at Kimbolton.

Bad weather throughout the latter part of May restricted deep-penetration missions and delayed the introduction of the new groups like the 379th. Preston's group finally 'got its feet wet' on 29 May, when the target for 1st Bomb Wing crews was St. Nazaire. Heavy cloud moving across western Europe caused several stop-go decisions before the B-17s finally got the green light. Col Preston recalls the 379th BG's debut (seven YB-40s also made their debut this day): 'A diversionary force had been sent out in an effort to induce the German fighters to take off early, thus forcing them to run out of gas as, or before, the main force arrived. Well, the tactic worked perfectly. The 'Abbeville Kids' committed themselves early and soon ran out of gas, but they got back up in time to intercept us at the tail end of the

Below left *Col 'Mo' Preston, CO of the 379th BG.* (Gen Preston.)

Below *Part of the air and ground crew of* Thundermug, *which lost a rudder on the mission to Rennes on 29 May 1943. 'Pappy' Colby is far right, back row; his co-pilot, Chris Thalman, is in the cockpit.* (Colby.)

Contrary to legend, Memphis Belle *was not the first to complete an 8th Air Force tour, but its '25th mission', on 17 May 1943, to Lorient, was duly recorded (using a 'stand-in' B-17F) in 16mm colour and used to great effect in the documentary titled* Memphis Belle. *(USAF.)*

bomber column just as we passed the IP. The fighters attacked us with a vengeance, then drew off to hit us again as we departed the target and before we were able to reassemble in wing formation. We lost three aircraft and 30 crew members, including John Hall, a squadron commander. 'Swede' Carlson, another squadron commander, lost two engines near the target and suffered damage to a third, causing it to be lost later when he had to land in a brussel sprout patch in England.'

The 29 May mission proved to be the last for some time for both the 44th and 93rd BGs, which had bombed the U-boat pens at La Pallice. Both were taken off operations. They were not, as the B-17 boys thought, being stood down permanently, but were being switched to low-level training flights over East Anglia in preparation for a top secret mission from Africa.

The weather prevented missions being flown until 11 June, when 168 heavies bombed the U-boat yards at Wilhelmshaven after cloud ruled out bombing at Bremen. During the bomb run the leading 303rd BG formation in the 1st Wing was bracketed by a severe flak barrage. Col Chuck Marion, the CO, lost two engines and following aircraft had to manoeuvre violently and reduce speed dramatically to avoid a collision. Just at that moment the Luftwaffe took advantage of the now scattered formation to make repeated head-on attacks, and one B-17 was rammed by a Fw 190 that failed to pull out in time. The 379th BG, flying only its second mission, bore the brunt of the attacks and lost six aircraft. The 8th lost eight B-17s in all.

On 13 June the 1st Wing was assigned Bremen, while the 4th Wing went to Kiel for another raid on the U-boat yards. The 94th, 95th and

96th BGs took off from their bases at Earls Colne, Framlingham and Andrews Field for the last time. Heavy losses in the Marauder groups prompted their transfer further south to these three B-17 bases so that their fighter cover could be improved. When the B-17 groups returned from the raid they would touch down at the former B-26 bases at Bury St. Edmunds (Rougham), Horham and Snetterton Heath respectively.

As it turned out, the three B-17 groups' last mission from their old bases was a disaster. It had been hoped that another twin-pronged attack on the coast would split the German fighter force, but it turned out to be a total failure, almost all of the enemy fighters foresaking the 1st Wing to concentrate on the four combat boxes of the 4th. Sgt Dick Lewis, the right waist gunner in *Mr Five By Five* (named after the pilot, Capt Kee Harrison, who was short and stocky), in the 94th BG, recalls: 'Cover from the short-range Spitfires ended as we flew northeast over the North Sea. As we approached the German coast swarms of German fighters rose to defend Kiel. It seemed that most of the Luftwaffe was gathered there. The action was intense and I saw many ships going down in flames or exploding in mid-air.'

The leading 95th BG was particularly hard hit, losing ten B-17s in combat and an eleventh in a crash in England. Among the casualties was Brig Gen Nathan B. Forrest, the first American general to be lost in combat in the European Theatre of Operations. The 94th lost nine. Six fell in the combat area and the rest flew back in a semblance of formation. Dick Lewis recalls: 'I'll never know how *Mr Five By Five* came through it unscathed. It seemed like a miracle. Returning, we were flying at low level over the North Sea. German fighters passed to the side of us at very high speed and out of gun range. Several miles ahead of us they turned and came at us head-on. Lt George W. Hendershot's 'plane [*Visiting Fireman*] was on our left wing. I saw cannon fire hit the leading edge of his wing. A section peeled off. Suddenly the ship nosed up, did a complete loop and dove into the sea. It all happened in a few seconds. It was there, and then it was gone. The entire crew of ten was lost.' Hendershot had been Harrison's original co-pilot until he had been given his own crew.

An eighth B-17 was also shot down in the encounter, and Maj Lewis G. Thorup's B-17 had its left stabiliser shot away and three engines put out of action. Thorup staggered over the sea for a further 30 miles on the one remaining engine before ditching the crippled Fortress. 'Pappy' Colby's crew dropped a life raft and a radio, but both broke up as they hit the sea. Thorup's crew were finally rescued by ASR after 11 hours in the water. In all, 22 of the 26 bombers shot down belonged to the Kiel force.

The three 4th Wing groups put down at their new bases in sombre mood. The new 4th Wing CO, Col (later Brig Gen) Curtis E. LeMay, who moved into the former home of the Third Bomb Wing headquarters at Elveden Hall near Thetford, visited the 94th BG at Bury St. Edmunds. 'Pappy' Colby recalls: 'He gave us the usual welcome talk and left the impression of being a bit hard-nosed about things, but he had flown a lot of rough ones and had a good record. And he was trying to improve the poor formation flying which had been so troublesome.'

New commanders were immediately posted to the 94th and 95th BGs. Col John 'Dinty' Moore, CO of the 94th, and Col Alfred A. Kessler, CO of the 95th, were moved out, and Col Fred Castle and Col John Gerhart, respectively, took over. Gerhart had been one of the 8th's original staff officers at its activation in January 1942. Castle had been one of the original officers whom Eaker had brought to England in February 1942. Also, the 4th Wing was strengthened by the arrival, in early June, of the 100th BG (first to Podington, then to Thorpe Abbotts, Suffolk) and the imminent arrival of two more, the 385th and 388th, which would increase the 4th Wing to six groups.

If anyone needed confirmation of the need to attack the Luftwaffe where it would hurt most, the Kiel debacle had proved it beyond doubt. Decisions taken at the Casablanca Conference led to Operation 'Pointblank', which emphasized the need to reduce the German fighter force. Eaker therefore sent his bombers on the first really deep penetration of Germany, to the synthetic rubber plant at Huls, near Recklinghausen. Huls, which accounted for approximately 29 per cent of Germany's synthetic rubber and 18 per cent of its total rubber supply, was the most heavily defended target in the Reich at this time. Most of the route was to be flown without escort, so three diversionary raids were planned to draw most of the fighters from the main attacking force.

Unfortunately, the diversionary force aimed at the Ford and General Motors plant at Antwerp failed to materialize. The 100th BG was delayed by ground mists, and the 381st and 384th BGs, which were flying their maiden missions, were behind schedule and failed to make contact with the escorts which were to escort them to Antwerp. This lapse placed another, smaller diversionary force at the mercy of the Luftwaffe, which had refuelled after an earlier raid by RAF medium bombers. Head-on attacks succeeded in shooting down four B-17s, while three badly damaged survivors flew their own formation, hugging the waves all the way back to England. Two B-17s in the 384th BG were so badly damaged that they were later named *Patches* and *Salvage Queen*.

The Huls force also came in for repeated attacks, as 'Pappy' Colby, in the 94th BG in *Thundermug*, recalls: '. . . we got the works. They hit us at the Dutch coast and it got progressively worse. Col Castle rode behind me on the camp stool and took notes all through the thick of it, cool as a cucumber. We made a beautiful 55-second run and dropped our pattern square on the buildings alongside of the burning tank, which had exploded. Flak suddenly became very heavy. After dropping, the remains of the lead and low squadrons strung along with us and we caught up with the 95th Bomb Group. At Rotterdam the Spitfires met us and chased off the German fighters, but it was a rough mission and we were beginning to wonder about the invincibility of the Flying Fortress. We lost two of our aircraft in the 333rd and the group lost quite a few more.'

Mr Five By Five lost an outboard engine, and with the propeller

A B-17F of the 366th Bomb Squadron, 305th BG, over Huls on 22 June 1943. (USAF.)

feathered it became a sitting duck. Dick Lewis says: 'Capt Harrison came on the intercom, informing us that he intended to try and escape by lowering the landing gear in sign of surrender and then diving the ship. We were told to hold our fire. Enemy fighters closed in to escort us to a landing. Suddenly, the dive began! This manoeuvre had never been covered in my flight training. It was a wild ride and I wondered if the ship would hold together. It did! Capt Harrison pulled her out at about a thousand feet and then dove again to treetop level, frustrating the enemy fighters, who broke off the action and left.

'He began zig-zagging the 'plane back to England. We took a hit from a ground battery and Lt Schaefer, our navigator, was wounded in the leg. Despite his injury he stuck to his post, changing course every few minutes. And I'll never forget the sight of Dutch farmers standing in their fields, waving their arms and making the V for Victory sign as we roared overhead.

'I breathed a sigh of relief as the Channel appeared ahead of us and that mission came safely to a close. The inside of the ship was drenched with condensation from the rapid descent, − 40F to + 75F. The entire crew was grounded for several missions, recovering from related ear problems. *Mr Five By Five* went into Repair Depot for replacement of several wing spars weakened or bent from pulling out of the dive. I never saw our 'plane again.' Huls had been well hit, with smoke rising as high as 17,000 ft, and the plant was put out of action for a month. Full production was not resumed for another five months after that. However, 16 B-17s were lost, including a YB-40 which flew

The wartime caption for this photo of Capt Robert Bender of the 336th Bomb Squadron, 95th Bomb Group read: 'He used up a million dollars worth of Fortresses on 15 [sic] missions to German targets. Uncle Sam doesn't mind the expense however, because Bender has always bombed his targets, always brought his crew home alive, and 3 times brought back enough of a B-17 to call it salvage.' Spook 1 *was written off in a crash landing at Exeter.* Spook 2 *and* 3 *were so badly shot up that they were salvaged. ('Spook' was an unattractive girl in Bender's book.) On 28 June, low on fuel and with an engine shot out over St. Nazaire, Bender ditched* Spook 4 *60 miles from England. The crew were finally rescued by ASR 22 hours later. The combat fatigued pilot, on a visit to a cinema, went berserk when a newsreel showed Fw 190s attacking B-17s, and on a test flight take-off in* Spook 5, *Bender froze at the stick. Don Merton, the co-pilot, overpowered him and prevented a crash. Bender never flew* Spook 5 *again. He was hospitalised and returned to America where he died of a heart attack aged 25. (*USAF.*)*

with the 303rd BG, and another 170 bombers received varying degrees of damage.

A period of cloudy weather hampered missions, and then on 26 June the Fortresses were despatched to targets in France while the B-17s of the 4th Wing, fitted with 'Tokyo' extra-range tanks, went to St. Nazaire. 'Pappy' Colby led the 333rd Squadron, and next morning he took command of the badly 'flakked' 410th Squadron, which had lost nine out of its ten original crews, including both of its commanding officers.

On 4 July the Fortresses made a triple attack on targets in France. Altogether, 192 Fortresses of the 1st Wing were assigned the Gnome et Rhọne Aero engine factory at Le Mans and an aircraft factory at Nantes, while 83 of the longer-range B-17s of the 4th Wing went to the U-boat pens at La Pallice. Shortly after noon the two 1st Wing formations, flying parallel courses, crossed the French coast just east of the Cherbourg Peninsular, while the B-17s of the 4th Wing headed for La Pallice, on the Bay of Biscay coast. At 12:30 the 1st Wing formations crossed Laval, 80 miles inland, then split into two formations, one heading for Nantes and the other for Le Mans.

The Nantes force was attacked by hordes of German fighters all the way from the IP, and they did not break off until 35 miles after the

B-17F Spook V *42-30226 of the 336th Bomb Squadron, 95th Bomb Group in flight, the Roman numeral V is replacing the earlier 5, used for the publicity photograph on the left.* Spook Six *was the final B-17 in the series of fated Fortresses at Horham.* (USAF.)

target. The 92nd BG formation of 16 B-17s and three YB-40s came under heavy attack, and Lt John J. Campbell's B-17 was believed to have hit the sea and burned. Six parachutes were seen to open, and another partially opened. Lt Robert L. Campbell brought *Ruthie*, named in honour of his wife, home to Alconbury and ground looped with a flat tyre after repeated attacks by enemy fighters had seriously damaged the bomber. The Le Mans force encountered intense fighter opposition 15 minutes from the target, but the B-17s were able to pick up their fighter escort at Argentan and reach safety. For once the multiplicity of bomber attacks seemed to break up the Luftwaffe concentrations, and they were able to account for only 3 per cent of the attacking force.

The weather continued cloudy, and VIII Bomber Command flew several more missions to France in the hope of spotting its targets. On 14 July, Bastille Day, groups set out for Paris and the Focke-Wulf repair sub-depot at Villacoubly and Le Bourget airport. The latter was

British civilian Roy Howard points with pride to the impressive bomb log painted on the port side of B-17F-27-BO We The People, *41-24614, in the 422nd Bomb Squadron, 305th BG at Chelveston, on 10 July 1943. In more than 30 missions it never carried exactly the same crew twice, and no crewman was ever wounded. On 8 September 1943 it led the first 8th Air Force night bombing mission.* (Cliff Pyle.)

covered with clouds, and ships in the 94th could not drop their 16 300 lb bombs. Dick Lewis, flying in Capt Harrison's B-17, a replacement for *Mr Five By Five*, which was still under repair following the Huls mission: '. . . felt the ship take a forward hit. Smoke filtered back through to the rear. "What the Hell is going on up front?", I yelled to Earl Porath, back-to-back with me at his left waist gun position. Through my own open gun port I could see German fighters continuing the attack on the front of the ship, diving from above or zooming up from below like a swarm of angry hornets.

'The ship began to fall out of formation. I squeezed off a couple of ineffective bursts from my .50 calibre Browning gun as the fighters flashed by at such speed that it was nearly impossible to track them through my gunsight for more than a fraction of a second. Those German pilots were smart veterans. I could hear and feel Porath's .50 firing behind me and Jeff Polk's twin .50s blazing away from his ball turret below me. In the tail of the ship, Ossie Asiala's guns added to the racket. But I couldn't hear firing from any of our forward guns.

'The smoke was getting heavier. The ship went into an abrupt dive, then levelled again and seemed to move erratically as if the pilot was taking evasive action. I realized that the German fighter attack had ended. I listened on the intercom for some word from the cockpit. Silence! We were in deep trouble. A horrible thought came to me. Had they all been killed up front?'

Lt David H. Turner, the co-pilot, explained what happened: 'Because of the lack of oxygen and the fact that we were blinded by smoke, we had to get down in a hurry. While I was getting rid of the fire by stamping and beating the flames, Harrison was getting downstairs as quickly as he could. Those fighters were chipping us to pieces, but none of the crew was hurt. It looked hopeless, though, and Harrison gave the orders to jump.' Four men in the nose of the ship

The original crew of B-17F Mr Five By Five, *42-29717, some of whom were lost in B-17F 42-3190 on the 14 July 1943 mission to Paris. Standing, L–R: Sgt Jeff Davis Polk, Sgt Dick Lewis, Sgt Jim Curtis, Sgt Eino 'Ossie' Asiala, Sgt Earl Porath, Sgt Charlie McNemar. Kneeling: Jack Amphlett, Capt Kee Harrison, Lt Martin Stanford, Lt Robert Schaefer.* Mr Five By Five *later flew in the 384th BG, and was lost on the 25 February 1944 mission to Stüttgart when it was flown by Lt Kack K. Larsen.* (Dick Lewis/Quentin Bland.)

baled out before Sgt James H. Curtis, the top turret gunner, who had helped Turner extinguish the fire by damping it down with his parachute pack, discovered that it was now unusable. Turner, who burned his hands badly, concluded: 'We sure couldn't jump and leave Curtis in the ship, so Harrison decided to land her, bombs and all'.

Dick Lewis continues: 'The ship went into a shallow dive and it was hard for me to hold my footing. Porath yelled: "Here they come, Looie!" German fighters were closing on us – not head-on or diving, but rather parallel to us, as if in escort. I could even see the pilot of one fighter looking at us. I was amazed by this tactic, but didn't stop to think about it. My enemy was out there at practically point-blank range. Instinct took over and I began firing. So did Porath, Polk and Asiala. Parallel to us, with their fixed wing guns at right angles to us, they were totally defenceless. I saw two fighters in flames and one of them exploded as it fell. Others may have been hit, but I wasn't sure. Then all hell broke loose! Other German fighters raked the ship. Wires and control cables dangled like spaghetti. I listened for the bale-out order. Silence – again.'

The gunners in the rear never heard the order because the intercom was shot away. They did not know that Harrison had lowered the landing gear to indicate surrender, and that was why the fighters presented such an easy target; they were literally 'sitting ducks'. Harrison had taken evasive action, hoping to reach the safety of a cloud bank, but the German fighters kept heading him off. A similar event, involving a 100th BG Fortress, created the myth that, as a result of its 'surrender' action the group was 'marked', and heavy losses at the hands of the 'avenging' Luftwaffe followed.

Lewis continues: 'She went into a steep dive. I was torn loose from my gun and flipped against the bulkhead. Porath slammed against me. Polk had gotten out of the ball turret and then he, too, fell against the

This photograph of B-17F 42-3190, piloted by Capt Kee Harrison in the 94th BG, which belly landed in a field near Paris, was taken by the Luftwaffe on 14 July and used for propaganda purposes. Oberstleutnant Egon Mayer of III/JG2, on the wing, poses with German troops. (Richard Lewis.)

bulkhead. As I lay pinned there, I couldn't see out of the ship, and thought: "Oh my God, we're going straight into the ground!" I lost all hope. "This is it," I said to myself.

'Unbelievably, the steep dive angle was lessening, and I dimly wondered if the ship was still airworthy and who was at the controls. Capt Harrison, I hoped. She began to pull out and levelled off. We staggered to our feet, heading for the door to jump. I struggled to hook my 'chute buckles as I got to the door. Porath was shaking his head "No!", and pointing out the window. The ground was rushing up to meet us. We braced ourselves. We were going in!

'She nosed up gently and bellied into a wheatfield. The tail touched first and we heard a tearing, crunching sound. Someone yelled: "The bombs!" We looked toward the bulkhead. The ball turret had torn loose and was pushed up through the floor. It seemed an eternity before we slid to a halt. There was no fire. Almost no sound. We had ridden her in!' Incredibly, Harrison had got away with it. The crew scattered in all directions. Harrison was assisted by the French Underground and, barefoot, he later crossed the Pyrenees into Spain. Lewis and Ossie Asiala, also aided by the Underground, managed to evade capture until October before being betrayed and sent to a PoW camp after some uncomfortable Gestapo interrogations. At Stalag Luft VII they were reunited with Jim Curtis and Earl Porath. Later, they heard that Turner, Polk, Charlie McNemar, the radio operator and the navigator and bombardier had travelled through the Underground and returned safely to England.

Anglo-American camaraderie at Kimbolton, home of the 379th BG, on 20 July 1943. (USAF.)

On 17 July a record 332 bombers, including the 385th and 388th BGs, which were flying their first missions as part of the 4th Wing, were despatched to Hannover, but the mission was recalled owing to bad weather after the bombers had crossed the Dutch coast. The 385th had moved to Great Ashfield, Suffolk, during the first week of July, and the 388th landed at nearby Knettishall. Two days later the seventh and final group to join the 4th Wing, the 390th, flew south from Prestwick to its permanent base at Parham, near Framlingham in Suffolk. The 8th now had the means to launch an all-out air offensive. All the commanders needed was a week of fine weather for 'Blitz Week' (after the German word for 'lightning') to succeed.

Chapter Five

Blitz week and beyond

ON 23 JULY 1943 Gen Eaker was informed that clear skies could be expected over Europe for a few days; long enough to mount the long-awaited succession of attacks which would become known as 'Blitz Week'. It began in the early hours of 24 July, and at briefing crews learned that this would be no ordinary mission to an ordinary target. For the first time the 8th Air Force would bomb targets in Norway. The 1st Wing would bomb the aluminium, magnesium and nitrate plant of Nordisk Lettmetal at Heroya, which was still nearing completion. A smaller force of 4th Wing bombers equipped with 'Tokyo tanks' would bomb the dock areas at Bergen and Trondheim, the Trondheim mission necessitating a 2,000-mile round trip, the longest American mission over Europe. To save fuel there would be no assembly; the lead B-17s would go on course immediately after take-off and would cruise at reduced power and at low altitude to allow the following aircraft to take their positions in the formation as they flew out over the North Sea.

The bomb groups began taking off in overcast, but the formation proceeded on course. Well off the coast of northern Denmark the 1st Wing flew northeast up the Skagerrak and climbed to bombing altitude at 16,000 ft, while the 4th Wing groups continued up the west coast of Norway to their targets at Bergen and Trondheim, not far south of the Arctic Circle. Each wing flew with a gap of ten minutes, or about 30 miles, to allow time for the smoke from exploding bombs to clear and give the following strike forces a more precise aiming point for their bombardiers. The planners had considered this feasible because flak defences were believed to be poor that far north.

When the bombers reached their relatively low bombing altitude of 16,000 ft over the Skagerrak they began flying above an overcast that lay below them at about 10,000 ft. The cloud blotted out the countryside, and was probably instrumental in keeping the Luftwaffe grounded at their bases in northern Denmark.

The bomb bay doors swung open beneath the B-17s, and still there appeared no break in the cloud. It began to look as though the crews would have to return to England carrying their bombs, but Col William M. Reid, CO of the 92nd BG and the air commander, took the formation around for a second time and bombed through a sudden break in the cloud. (This feat earned him the Silver Star.) The groups following had difficulty in picking out the mean point of impact, so they were instructed to bomb the centre of the smoke pall which by now hung almost stationary over the entire target area.

Col Budd J. Peaslee, CO of the 384th BG, recalls: 'On the second bombing run the flak gunners had ample opportunity to perfect their aim, and as the formation approached the target the bursts became accurate and intense. This time the bombs went away and the navigator gave the return flight course. As the bombers withdrew it was possible to see that the island was in a shambles . . . destruction had been heaped on destruction. Great fires were burning and ships at the docks were in flames. An awsome sight and one to remember for a lifetime.'

Altogether, 167 bombers bombed Heroya and completely devastated the great industrial complex. The attack, so far from England, caught the enemy unaware, and many German dignitaries and Norwegian quislings attending a dedication ceremony were killed in the raid. No bombers were lost, although *Georgia Rebel*, in the 351st BG, was hit by flak and her crew landed safely in neutral Sweden.

Col Peaslee concludes: 'The bombing of Heroya has passed into history and is rarely recalled, except by those who made the trip and who still survive. To them it was the most successful and shrewdly planned and executed mission of the entire war.'

Meanwhile, 41 B-17s of the 4th Wing bombed Trondheim from 20,000 ft. Testimony to their accuracy was provided later by an RAF photo-reconnaissance Spitfire, which brought back photos of a sunken U-boat, a damaged destroyer and gutted workshops in the harbour area. The other 4th Wing groups crossed Bergen harbour at 16,000 ft, but the target was completely covered with clouds and 84 aircraft had to return to England and land with full bomb loads – something crews were never happy about. About 15 Junkers Ju 88s put in an appearance on the return leg, but caused no damage to the B-17 formations. Crews were upset about the failure to bomb Bergen; none more so than 'Pappy' Colby, who was flying with the 94th. 'It was 8 hours 45 minutes of flying for nothing,' he laments, 'but we did see some of the mountains of Norway and one peak was covered with snow. The country appeared rugged, as all the towns and small farms were located in fiords on the west coast. One of my memories of the mission was coming home down the North Sea all relaxed and listening to beautiful German opera music on our radio.'

The following day the Fortresses were again out in force, this time to targets in north-western Germany. One combat wing from the 1st Bomb Wing was despatched to Kiel; the remaining groups going to Hamburg to bomb the Blohm und Voss shipyards. As they neared the city crews could see a towering 15,000 ft column of smoke; a result of fires still burning after a raid by RAF Bomber Command the previous night. Crews in the first elements managed to bomb before thick cloud added to the smoke, and the shipyards were well hit. However, Hamburg's notorious flak and fighter defences accounted for 19

Fortresses, including seven in the unlucky 384th.

Meanwhile, 4th Bomb Wing Fortresses headed for Warnemünde on the north German coast. Clouds obscured the target, and they were forced to head for the submarine construction yards at Kiel. The 94th BG was attacked near the target by about 30 fighters, and Lt Keelan's B-17 was seen to ditch about 60 miles off the coast. Unfortunately, in getting into a life raft one of the gunners fell into the water, breaking the strap on his Mae West, and he could not swim! An RAF Halifax bomber spotted them and radioed Air Sea Rescue, who sent out a Lockheed Hudson to drop them a powered lifeboat. They sailed the boat some 120 miles, at which point they were picked up by a Danish fishing boat. The Danes agreed to take the crew to England and, instead of returning to Denmark, decided to join the Free Danish Navy operating from the British Isles.

There was no let-up in the American offensive, and 'Blitz Week' gained momentum. On 26 July more than 300 heavies were despatched to Hannover and Hamburg. Thick cloud over East Anglia hampered assembly and, despite the recent introduction of 'splasher' beacons for forming up, many groups became scattered and had to be recalled. Only two combat wings won through to their targets. Other elements bombed targets of opportunity along the German coast.

Among the 92 Fortresses which successfully attacked Hannover were 17 B-17s and two YB-40s from the 92nd BG. Shortly before it crossed the coast the formation came under frontal attack by Fw 190s. Lt Alan E. Hermance's B-17 was seen to hit the water about ten minutes from the island of Nordenay with one engine on fire and the tail badly damaged. Capt Blair Belongia's B-17 came under attack from seven Fw 190s, and two of his engines were put out of action. Belongia nursed the ailing bomber back across the sea and ditched about two miles off Sheringham, where the crew were rescued by a fishing boat after an hour in the water.

Other 92nd BG aircraft also suffered in the attack. They included *Ruthie II*, piloted by Lt Robert L. Campbell, who had brought the first *Ruthie* home from Nantes on 4 July, and his co-pilot, Flt Off John C. Morgan, a six-foot red-haired Texan who had flown with the RCAF for seven months before transferring to the 8th Air Force. The navigator, Keith J. Koske, later wrote: 'We were on our way into the enemy coast when we were attacked by a group of Fw 190s. On their first pass I felt sure they had got us for there was a terrific explosion overhead and the ship rocked badly. A second later the top turret gunner, S/Sgt Tyre C. Weaver, fell through the hatch and slumped to the floor at the rear of my nose compartment. When I got to him I saw his left arm had been blown off at the shoulder and he was a mass of blood. I first tried to inject some morphine, but the needle was bent and I could not get it in.

'As things turned out it was best I didn't give him any morphine. My first thought was to try and stop his loss of blood. I tried to apply a tourniquet, but it was impossible as the arm was off too close to the shoulder. I knew he had to have the right kind of medical treatment as soon as possible and we had almost four hours flying time ahead of us, so there was no alternative. I opened the escape hatch, adjusted his 'chute for him and placed the ripcord ring firmly in his right hand. He must have become excited and pulled the cord, opening the pilot 'chute in the updraught. I managed to gather it together and tuck it under his right arm, got him into a crouched position with legs through the hatch, made certain again that his good arm was holding the 'chute folds together, and toppled him out into space. I learned somewhat later from our ball turret gunner, James L. Ford, that the 'chute opened OK. We were at 24,500 ft and 25 miles due west of Hannover, and our only hope was that he was found and given medical attention immediately.

'The bombardier, Asa J. Irwin, had been busy with the nose guns, and when I got back up in the nose he was getting ready to toggle his bombs. The target area was one mass of smoke and we added our contribution. After we dropped our bombs we were kept busy with the nose guns. However, all our attacks were from the tail and we could do very little good. I had tried to use my interphone several times, but could get no answer. The last I remember hearing over it was shortly after the first attack, when someone was complaining about not getting oxygen. Except for what I thought to be some violent evasive action we seemed to be flying OK.

'It was two hours later, when we were 15 minutes out from the enemy coast, that I decided to go up and check with the pilot and have a look around. I found Lt Campbell slumped down in his seat, a mass of blood, the back of his head blown off. This had happened "two hours" before, on the first attack. A shell had entered from the right side, crossed in front of John Morgan and had hit Campbell in the head. Morgan was flying the 'plane with one hand, holding the half-dead pilot off with the other hand, and he had been doing it for over two hours!' [It was no mean feat, Campbell was a six-footer and weighed 185lb].

'Morgan told me we had to get Campbell out of his seat, as the 'plane couldn't be landed from the co-pilot's seat as the glass on that side was shattered so badly you could barely see out. We struggled for 30 minutes getting the fatally injured pilot out of his seat and down into the rear of the navigator's compartment, where the bombardier held him from slipping out the open hatch. Morgan was operating the controls with one hand and helping me handle the pilot with the other.'

The radio operator, waist, and tail gunners were unable to lend assistance because they were unconscious through lack of oxygen, the lines having been shattered several hours earlier. Morgan's action was nothing short of miraculous. Not only had he flown the aircraft to the target and out again with no radio, no interphone and no hydraulic fluid, but he had maintained formation the whole time. It was an incredible feat for a pilot flying one handed.

Morgan brought *Ruthie II* in to land at RAF Foulsham, a few miles from the Norfolk coast, and put down safely. Campbell died 1½ hours after they reached England. The other crew members survived, including Weaver, who had been put in a PoW camp after hospitalization. On 18 December 1943 listeners to the BBC's evening news learned that Flt Off (later 2nd/Lt) John C. Morgan (now with the 482nd Bomb Group) had received the Congressional Medal of Honor from Gen Ira C. Eaker in a special ceremony at 8th Air Force Headquarters, and heard him relive the events of 26 July.

On 27 July the 8th was stood down for a badly needed rest while the forecasters waited for the weather to improve over Europe. 'Blitz Week' was resumed on the morning of 28 July, when the 1st Wing made an ambitious attack on aircraft factories at Kassel while the 4th Wing had the dubious honour of flying the deepest penetration so far, to the fighter assembly plant at Oschersleben. The 94th BG with the Group CO, Col Fred Castle, flying in the lead ship, *Sour Puss*, led the strike force. Castle's pilot, Maj 'Pappy' Colby, recalls: 'On my map, Oschersleben was a little over 90 miles southwest of Berlin, but even with the new 'Tokyo tanks' it looked a hell of a long way. The plan called for the usual diversion thrust off the Friesian Islands with a 180° turn back towards England and then the real attack, crossing the coast near Emden and on to the target. Things began to go wrong early in the plan. The weather was supposed to be clear, but instead we were flying between layers of stratus clouds as we started the diversion. Then the navigation went wrong, because, instead of turning back some 60 or 70 miles west of the Friesian Islands, we went clear down on top of them and stirred up a hornet's nest of fighters based on Heligoland. They worked us over heavily, darting in and out of the clouds, and one group lost three ships from a fighter which hid in the clouds above the formation and then swooped down and dropped an aerial bomb which exploded in the formation. The cloud layers were so thick we had a very hard time making the turn back towards England, with the result that everybody got lost and, instead of leading a wing into the target, we only had 28 ships.

'Col Castle was much upset, as orders were not to go in with less than 20 aircraft. He was unhappy about my turning in towards the target, but I conned him into going, saying I could see three more of our 'planes in the distance. (I was not about to back after all the hell we had just been through.) We just started in over the coast without asking anybody and the other 27 'planes followed me. The fighters followed us for about 100 miles, but as we were now in tight formation they didn't attack.' [The 4th Wing had started out with 120 Fortresses, but all except the 94th and some in the 96th turned back.]

'So we sailed down towards the IP, which was covered with about 7/10ths cloud. The navigator picked the wrong town. I don't blame him in the least, as the stupid staff people had picked the central town in a row of three towns – all on the same railroad, and all about the same size. So we turned on the bomb run and suddenly found that the target, instead of being dead ahead, was off to our left some 30 miles. Nobody had any suggestions, so I told the bombardier to keep the target in sight and we would make a 180° left turn and bomb it on a westerly heading. We made a good bomb run and the photos showed later we did a good job hitting it in spite of the problems. Actually, the cloud cover was between 5/10ths and 7/10ths, but from 26,000 ft it's extremely hard to pick out landmarks. Despite the press story we had no fighters over the target, but heavy flak crossing the coast on the way home. We did evasive action and got home with no losses out of the 94th.

'Widewing [8th Air Force] gave Col Castle a very hard time about making two runs to hit the target (which was supposed to be very dangerous), and for about a week there were rumours that there might be disciplinary action taken; but then the photoship got back with pictures of the bomb damage and everything was rosy. They gave Col Castle the Silver Star for leading the mission. Bless his heart, he deserved it, if only for riding on a camp-stool behind a screwball like old "Pappy".' [Strike photos showed that the heavies had knocked out 50 per cent of the plant].

Fifteen Fortresses belonging to the 4th Wing were shot down on the Oschersleben raid, including one crippled B-17 which crashed into two others, bringing down all three. The 182 heavies which went to Kassel were limited in their bombing because of cloud which obscured the target. On the way home they were attacked by fighters which fired rocket projectiles, 8 ins in diameter, from beneath their wings. A long-range Thunderbolt fired a burst at a Fw 190, and his bullets set off a rocket under the right wing. The rocket soared off in a cloud of white smoke as the fighter disintegrated under the onslaught of the P-47's guns. Without the P-47 escort, losses in the bomber formations would have been heavy.

On 29 July the 8th set out for the fourth time in five days, the 1st Wing visiting the shipyards at Kiel and the 4th Wing going to the Heinkel assembly plant at Warnemünde, which had escaped the attention of the B-17s four days before. The strain was beginning to tell, and the 385th BG lost three B-17s in a mid-air collision during assembly at only 2,000 ft, two miles from the English coast. Only six parachutes were seen to leave the three aircraft. The bombing of the Heinkel plant was described as 'excellent' and Fw 190 production was severely curtailed.

On 30 July VIII Bomber Command brought down the curtain on 'Blitz Week' when 186 Fortresses from the 1st and 4th Wings went to the aircraft factories at Kassel – a round trip of some 600 miles. The weather was fine, and P-47 Thunderbolts equipped with long-range fuel tanks escorted the heavies almost to the target and back again. Without the 'Jugs' B-17 losses would have been alarming. The Fortress formations were hit by a ferocious onslaught of enemy fighters, as Howard E. Hernan, flying top turret gunner in *The Old Squaw* in the 303rd BG formation, recalls: 'We were hit by more enemy fighters than ever before. The estimate was well in excess of 300. At one time I counted 157 flying off to our right. A fighter came down through our formation, and then a whole gruppe of them got ahead of us and started making pass after pass. Most of them we fought off and turned them away at 700–800 yards. They would flip over on their backs and down they would go to get more latitude and then they would try again. A Bf 109 painted snow white dived on us. He had a beautiful Iron Cross painted on the wings and fuselage. I think he was coming so fast with a strong headwind behind him that he came right through the formation and was making a turn to the right. So help me God, he came between us and our wingman on the left, upside down, and went between our wings and never touched either one of us!'

The B-17 crews flew two-thirds of the six-hour round trip on oxygen, and Hernan's supply ran out over enemy territory. Arthur W. Miller, the co-pilot, had to feed him oxygen from walk-around bottles while he tried to shoot at incoming fighters. Hernan and Quick were each credited with one fighter apiece. On the way to the target the Fortresses had been assisted by a strong wind which had given them an indicated airspeed of 160 m.p.h. Now, on the homeward trip, the B-17s had to buck this wind. Howard Hernan picked out a landmark and looked down on it. Ten minutes later it was still there!

Number four engine quit, out of fuel, just as *The Old Squaw* finally reached the coast of England. Campbell glided down on to an airfield just before the number two began to splutter. Other aircraft were not so fortunate. Some ditched in the Channel and others crash-landed all along the coast as, one by one, they ran low on fuel. Altogether, 12 Fortresses were lost, including *Patches* in the 384th BG, which crashlanded at the fighter airfield at Boxted. Its parts were used later for other B-17s in the group.

On 31 July groups were told to stand down after a week of exhausting raids. Crews had flown themselves almost to a standstill and were glad of the rest, however brief. In a week of sustained combat operations VIII Bomber Command had lost about 100 aircraft and 90 combat crews. This reduced its combat strength to fewer than 200 heavies ready for combat. Meanwhile, in the blistering hot, arid North African desert the forgotten men of the Liberator groups were about to become world famous for a daring low-level mission across the Mediterranean.

Chapter Six

Ploesti

BETWEEN 11 AND 25 June the 389th BG, the third B-24 group to join the 2nd Bomb Division, flew into its base at Hethel, Norfolk, to train alongside the 44th and 93rd BGs for a secret low-level mission to the Rumanian oilfields at Ploesti. Col Jack W. Wood, the CO, was under pressure to get the group operational, and a temporary ground echelon was seconded to Hethel pending the arrival, on 6 July, of the regular ground personnel. Ploesti was the centre of an important strategic oilfield producing 60 per cent of all Germany's needs. By increasing the Liberator's fuel capacity to 3,100 gal they could just make it to the target from North Africa.

In June 1942 a detachment of 23 B-24Ds under the command of Col Harry H. Halverson, codenamed 'HALPRO', which was en route to join the 10th Air Force in China, had bombed Ploesti with limited results. No further raids were made on Ploesti, and then, on 6 March 1943, Field Marshal Erwin Rommel launched what proved to be his last offensive. It failed, and he was recalled to Berlin. The path was now clear for another strike on the Ploesti oilfields. In April 1943 bomber chiefs in London pressed Gen Lewis Brereton the CO of 9th Bomber Command, for another attack, but he was anxious to contain his bombing force for the Tunisian and Sicilian battles that lay ahead. On 6 May 1943 Operation 'Husky' – the invasion of Sicily – began, and the Liberators of the 98th BG, known as the 'Pyramiders', and the 376th BG, better known as the 'Liberandos', attacked Reggio di Calabria, the terminus of the San Giovanni-Messina ferry service to Sicily.

Early in June Brereton was informed that three 8th Air Force Liberator groups would join the 98th and 376th BGs for a second attack on Ploesti. After a five-day orientation course, the 44th Flying Eightballs, the 93rd Travelling Circus, and the 389th Sky Scorpions began flying low-level practice missions over East Anglia at less than 150 ft en route to their target range over the Wash. Rumour and speculation increased as ground crews sweated to remove the Norden bombsights and replace them with low-level sights. Heavier nose armament and additional fuel tanks in the bomb bays gave the men clues as to their new rôle.

At Hardwick, Col Addison Baker led his Liberators flying wingtip to wingtip at 150 ft over the hangar line on the base which served as a target. On some days the 93rd were joined by the 44th and the 389th in flights over the base in waves of three aircraft. The 44th, 93rd and 389th crews had been trained in the art of high-altitude precision bombing, and were quite unused to low-level flying. It led, on 25 June, to a mid-air collision involving two 389th Liberators. One B-24 made it back to Hethel, but the other crash-landed and one man was killed. The 389th were the youngest and most inexperienced of the three 201st (Provisional) Wing Groups. When they departed for North Africa at the end of June they had completed only two weeks' training in Norfolk.

By 25 June 41 Liberators were available at Shipdham for the Ploesti mission, which was codenamed 'Operation Statesman'. Five days later the three groups began their flight to North Africa via Portreath in Cornwall. Some 42 B-24s took off from Hardwick, and 30 more left the runways at Hethel. However, a few 389th aircraft remained behind in Norfolk for training and air-sea-rescue duties. For the 93rd the long overseas flight meant a return to the African desert they had foresaken in February 1943.

The 124 Liberators flew to Libya, where they came under the control of the 9th Air Force. The 93rd and 389th resided at bases near Benghazi, while the Eightballs were based at Benina Main, one of Mussolini's former airfields, 15 miles from Benghazi. Hundreds of wrecked Axis aircraft still littered the area for hundreds of miles around, and the words 'Believe, Obey, Fight' were inscribed on the walls of the hangars. Relationships between the 8th and 9th were never good. The 9th accused the 8th of being undisciplined and given to gross exaggeration of 'kills', while the 8th complained when it was

Fightin' Sam, *an original B-24D in the 566th Squadron, 389th BG, and crew commanded by Capt Tom Conroy in his early combat days with the Sky Scorpions. Conroy was killed in the Korean War. L–R back: Walt Taylor, waist gunner; Maj Conroy, 566th Squadron CO; Harley Mason, co-pilot; Al Ormsby, bombardier; Harold Roodman, navigator; Robert McNair, radio-operator. Kneeling: Doyle Kirkland, ball turret; Vic Scollin, waist-gunner; and two unknown gunners.* Fightin' Sam *was used as the squadron insignia.* (Russ D. Hayes.)

discovered that the 98th were witholding the best rations. By using up the less desirable items and keeping back the best foodstuffs, only the choicest rations would remain for the 98th when the 44th returned to England. Col Leon Johnson took the matter up with Col John 'Killer' Kane, the 98th's CO, but things did not improve during the Eightballs' stay at Benina Main.

One afternoon, crews at Benina Main were hastily summoned to report to the briefing room. Bill Cameron learned that his crew were to join his CO, Jim Posey's and another crew in a low-level sortie over Benghazi. Apparently, the natives were demonstrating in the town, putting pressure on the British for more local control. *Buzzin' Bear*, living up to its name, and the other two aircraft, buzzed the city in show of 'gunboat diplomacy'.

A few days later operations began in earnest, with missions in support of the Allied invasion of Sicily. The airfield at Lecce in Italy was bombed, and on 5 July the 93rd took off on the first of ten missions in support of the Italian campaign. Most of the missions were flown without escort, and soon losses began to assume the proportions sustained at the height of the raids on the U-Boat pens in France. On 17 July 80 Liberators raided Naples, where the flak was heavy and the fighters persistent. The gunners aboard *Buzzin' Bear* accounted for five enemy aircraft, including three Macchi MC 202s. Lt Joe Potter, a member of Lt Gentry's crew in the 44th BG, was killed by Italian farmers after he had baled out of the doomed aircraft.

On 19 July the Liberators made the first bombing attack on Rome. Although the Italian capital had been declared an open city, its railway yards had nevertheless remained the chief centre of supply for the Axis forces in Italy. Because of the city's cultural and religious significance the briefing for the raid was the most detailed and concise the combat crews had ever received. Lt Col Jim Posey concluded the 44th BG briefing with: 'And for God's sake if you don't see the target bring back your bombs'. He need not have worried. More than 100 B-24Ds bombed the Littoria yards, and the raid was declared an unprecedented success. Only one bomb 'got away' and slightly damaged a basilica. It was precision bombing at its best, but the conditions had been kind.

On 20 July the five Liberator groups were withdrawn from the campaign and 12 days' training for 'Tidal Wave' (the code name for Ploesti) began, with practice flights against a mock-up target in the desert. On 6 July Brereton had told his five group commanders that a low-level daylight attack would be made on Ploesti to achieve maximum surprise and ensure the heaviest possible damage in the first raid. Brereton had studied target folders for two weeks before making his decision. Most of the crews were apprehensive. This was no ordinary mission, and morale was not improved when Brereton told them that losses were expected to be as high as 50 per cent.

During the night of 31 July crews were briefed on the part they were to play in the momentous raid. It was barely daylight on the morning of Sunday 1 August 1943 when the Liberators took off. First away were 29 B-24Ds of the 376th BG 'Liberandos', led by the Group CO, Col

Keith Compton, and Brig Gen Uzal G. Ent (CO, 9th Bomber Command) in the command ship, *Teggie Ann.* (Brereton had intended to go in the command aircraft, but an order from Gen 'Hap' Arnold in Washington forbade it.) Behind them came 39 B-24Ds of the 93rd BG, led by Col Addison Baker and Maj John 'The Jerk' Jerstad in *Hell's Wench.* They were followed by 47 B-24Ds in the 98th formation, led by Col John 'Killer' Kane in *Hail Columbia*, and 37 B-24Ds of the 44th, led by Col Leon Johnson in *Suzy Q*. His intention to lead the Eightballs in *Suzy Q* had been jeopardized the night before, when a broken spark plug was diagnosed in number two engine. After an anxious night of maintenance and repair the sick patient was pronounced fit to fly.

Bringing up the rear of the formation were 26 B-24s of the 389th, led by Col Jack Wood in Maj Kenneth 'Fearless' Caldwell's Liberator. Some 389th crewmen flew with the 98th as fill-ins. Each of the Sky Scorpions' B-24Ds could carry only four 500 lb bombs because an additional 400 gal of fuel had been stored in the bomb bay. The 389th carried bombs with ten-second delay fuses, while the other groups carried 20-minute acid-core-fused bombs which would not explode until the bombs dropped by the 389th created a concussion wave in the target area. Any that did not explode in the concussion wave would eventually explode by means of the acid core fuse.

Brereton had decided on seven forces from the five groups. Col Compton would lead 30 B-24s to White I, the Romana American Refinery; Baker would take 21 B-24s to White II, Concordia Vega; Maj Ramsey D. Potts would lead the balance of the 93rd (15 aircraft) to White III, the Standard Petrol Block and Unirea-Spiranza; and Kane would lead 46 aircraft to White IV, the Unirea-Orion and Astra Romana. Johnson would lead 18 B-24s to White V, Columbia Aquila;

Captain Jack Dieterle and co-pilot Flt Off Thomas Baum flew their last mission, to Ploesti, on 1 August 1943, in The Little Gramper. *Dieterle became operations officer and Baum got his own crew. Capt Ben Walsh and his co-pilot, Sam Blessing, took over the* Gramper *and her crew after losing their B-24D over the Straits of Messina, near Sicily. Both were rescued by Sicilian fishing boats and returned to Benghazi. Tom Campbell, the crew's navigator, originally called the reptiles in the African desert 'Grampers', from which the ship got its name. Campbell was killed in an aeroplane crash in Sweden early in 1944. Here, Lt Col Tom Conroy congratulates Walsh after completing his last mission for him as squadron commander.* (Russ D. Hayes.)

while his deputy, Lt Col James Posey, would lead 18 aircraft to attack Blue I, Creditul Minier Brazi. Jack Wood's 389th were allotted Red I, Steaua Romana at Campina.

At 07:00 Lt Brian W. Flavelle's *Wongo Wongo!* in the 98th, lifted off from Berka Two. The other 174 Liberators followed them into the sky above the Mediterranean. One B-24 in he 389th, *Kickapoo*, which was flying with the 98th, had an engine failure on take-off and crashed on landing. Only two men, badly burned, scrambled out of the wreckage.

As the five-mile formation flew on to Corfu the inevitable malfunctions reduced the numbers, and seven of Kane's Pyramiders were forced to abort. Three more B-24s from other groups also returned early. Nearing Landfall at the German occupied island of Corfu, *Wongo Wongo!* began to go out of control. She veered up, fell over on her back, and plunged into the sea. Black smoke billowed up into the beautiful blue summer sky. *Brewery Wagon*, piloted by Lt John Palm, took its place at the head of the 376th.

After Corfu, crews veered right, to the east, and headed overland to Ploesti. At the Greek border commanders were confronted by the Pindus Range, rising to a height of, at most, 11,000 ft. The horizon was blotted out by cumulus clouds towering to 17,000 ft, and a decision had to be made whether to continue as briefed and risk collision, or climb above them. Compton elected to climb above the cloud tops to save fuel and time, and the 93rd followed him. 'Killer' Kane, whose Group was following the 376th, had the decision made for him. Many of the Pyramiders aircraft were not equipped with oxygen for this low-level mission, so the 98th circled and entered the cloud in threes and, after crossing the range, repeated the manoeuvre before setting course again. The 44th and the 389th adopted the same

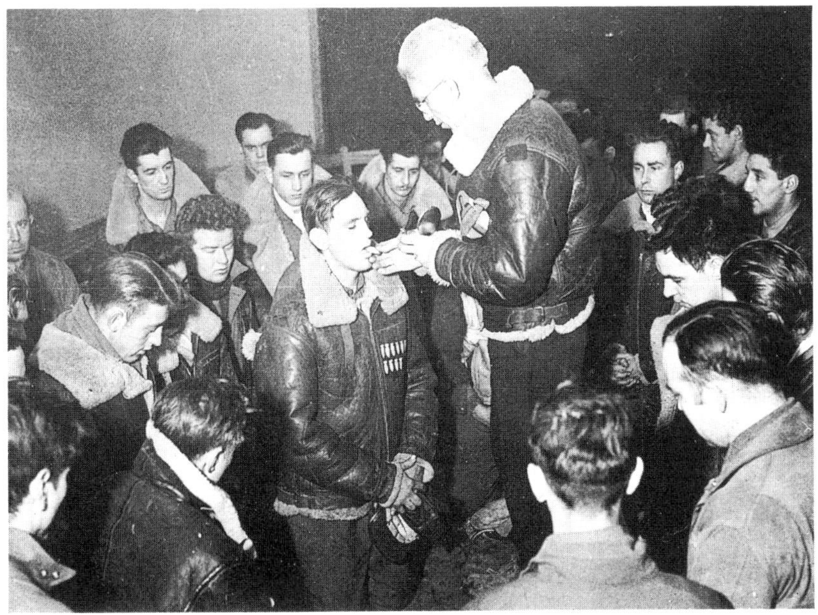

Father Gerald Beck, the Catholic chaplain at Hethel, distributes communion to the 389th combat crews after a mission briefing. Driving in his jeep at top speed, he went from B-24 to B-24, ensuring that no one was denied communion. In North Africa Father Beck was inside a B-24 administering the sacrament at take-off time and ended up being the observer for that mission! Russ D. Hayes believes that Father Beck was probably the most influential driving force behind the men of the 389th BG. (USAF.)

tactic and followed the 98th. This delay caused the 376th and 93rd BGs to become separated from the rest of 'Tidal Wave' by some 60 miles.

As they neared Ploesti Compton prepared to take the 376th over the refineries alone. He overtook *Brewery Wagon* and nosed *Teggie Ann* into the lead slot. Events now began to overtake the B-24s. Owing to a navigational error the Liberandos turned south too soon, at Targoviste, instead of at the correct IP at Floresti, and the 93rd followed. Only *Brewery Wagon*, which was on course, took the route as briefed, and was shot down soon after. The 376th's error led to the 93rd's subsequent tactical mistake in bombing the 98th's and 44th's targets, and caused approximately 20 ineffective 376th sorties.

When the mistake was realised, Compton and Ent decided to make the best of the situation and head for the Astro Romana complex. The Liberandos saw the 93rd already desperately fighting its way through to the target area, and split to attack targets of opportunity instead. As the Liberandos passed Ploesti and began climbing up the foothills east of the city they saw the Pyramiders coming towards them.

The plan was in ruins. Groups came in from the wrong directions and bombed any target which presented itself. The 93rd had followed Compton's force, and trailed over Ploesti. Some Rumanian fighters attacked the 93rd formation, and the tail gunner of *Joisey Bounce* became the first casualty of the Ploesti battle. Baker and Jerstad turned *Hell's Wench* 90° left and headed for the smokestacks of Ploesti. Ramsey Potts in *The Duchess* and the second formation of 93rd B-24s followed. The flak batteries enveloped the Flying Circus with their fire, and at only 20 ft the aircraft were sitting targets. During the five-minute bomb run the Group was torn to shreds. *Hell's Wench* was hit and caught fire. Baker jettisoned his bombs, but he and Jerstad decided to continue to the target. At Ploesti *Hell's Wench* was enveloped in flames and surged up to 300 ft before falling back and crashing to the ground. Both pilots were awarded posthumous Medals of Honor for their sacrifice.

Capt Walter Stewart, the deputy leader in *Utah Man*, took over the 93rd lead and, despite severe damage to the bomber, managed to land again in Libya, 14 hours later. K. D. McFarland, flying *Liberty Lad* on two engines, was the last home by another two hours. Nine other 93rd B-24s, including two which collided in cloud, did not return. Among the survivors were *Joisey Bounce*, which made it home with a shattered tail, *Thar She Blows*, *Ball of Fire Jr*, *Bomerang* and *The Duchess*.

Meanwhile, the 98th, led by 'Killer' Kane in *Hail Columbia*, and the 44th crossed Ploesti from the northwest. The Pyramiders suffered the highest casualties of all five groups, losing 21 of the 38 B-24s that started out from North Africa. At least nine were destroyed by the blasts from delayed action bombs dropped by the 376th.

The Eightballs arrived at Ploesti at 15:15, immediately plunging into a hail of flak and ripping tracers, smoke, fire and explosives. Several parts of the extensive plant were already ablaze, and to reach the specified target Johnson led his formation directly over this fiery and bursting cauldron of oil and through a veritable forest of

B-24Ds of the 93rd BG in close formation shortly after their return to Norfolk from North Africa. The nearest aircraft is Joisey Bounce, *41-24226, and 'C' is* Bomerang, *both veterans of the Ploesti mission of 1 August 1943.* (USAF.)

anti-aircraft guns. Modest barns and harmless-looking haystacks now revealed themselves as emplacements, and from everywhere, including the handcars on the sidings, flew a barrage of steel. Col Johnson headed for the Columbia Aquila plant, but through an error another group had already bombed the target assigned to the Eightballs.

Johnson decided to seek an alternative target. He changed course and headed straight and low through the smoke, flames, and floundering B-24s for a plant as yet untouched. Bombers went down on all sides and one, caught in the blast of an exploding bomb, pointed its nose upwards and soared about a hundred feet before falling helplessly on to its back. Johnson's *Suzy Q* came through the maelstrom, as did his two wingmen. Bill Cameron led the second wave in *Buzzin' Bear* and also got through safely. *Lil' Abner*, leader of the third wave, crashed 40 miles from the target. Altogether, nine of the 16 aircraft in the Eightballs' first formation were lost. Meanwhile, Col Posey's formation went after Blue target at Brazi, five miles south of Ploesti. Twenty-one B-24s went in and, incredibly, only two failed to emerge beyond the target. Posey's formation had knocked out the Creditul Minier Refinery.

The greatest success, however, went to the 389th, which brought up the rear of 'Tidal Wave' and struck for its target at Campina, although there were some anxious moments when the formation turned down the wrong valley. Led by Col Jack Wood and Maj Caldwell, the 389th pulled up and flew on for perhaps three or four minutes before turning to the right. They started down towards the refinery, which was marked by a great pall of smoke, and split into three sections to hit the target from three different directions.

The target was completely destroyed, but the success was marred by four Liberators being shot down. Another nine were forced to land in Turkey and Cyprus, and 17 returned to North Africa. The B-24s flew so low over the oilfields that enemy fighters hit the ground when they failed to pull out of dives after making their attacks on the bombers.

Bill Cameron poses in front of his new B-24D Liberator Buzzin' Bear. *(Cameron.)*

The bravery and determination of the men of the 389th was exemplified by the courage displayed by Lt Lloyd D. Hughes, who was posthumously awarded the Medal of Honor for refusing to turn back after shells had ruptured his fuel tanks. Although fuel was streaming over the fuselage, he piloted his B-24 low over the blazing target. Heat engulfed the bomber, and flames licked at its fuselage as the fuel ignited. Hughes struggled to complete the bomb run, but after 'bombs away' his starboard wing dipped and ploughed into the ground. Only two gunners survived.

Next morning the results of the mission were pieced together. Unfortunately, the plants the Liberators had sought to destroy were soon repaired, and were operating at pre-mission capacity within a month. Of the 177 B-24s which had set out, eight were interned in Turkey and 45 were brought down. Twenty-three had landed in Cyprus (including Kane's *Hail Columbia*), Sicily or Malta. Of the 88 that returned to North Africa, 55 had various degrees of battle damage. All five groups received Presidential Unit Citations, while Col Leon Johnson and Col 'Killer' Kane received Medals of Honor for their leadership. On 9 August Col Leland C. Fiegal, who was formerly with the 93rd during its training days in the USA, arrived from America to take command from Lt Col George S. Brown, who had been acting CO since the death of Lt Col Addison Baker.

Following a well-earned leave, the Liberator groups resumed raids on Axis targets in Austria and Italy. On 13 and 14 August the Liberators bombed the Messerschmitt factory at Wiener Neustadt in

389th BG strike photos taken from a 567th Bomb Squadron Liberator at 275 ft, showing their target at Campina in flames. (Earl Zimmerman.)

the first 9th Air Force raids on Austria. On 16 August the B-24s were allocated Foggia in southern Italy, despite reports that the Axis had been moving its defences and concentrating them there. On previous sorties into this territory the missions took on the nature of a 'milk run', and only the day before another bomb group had gone in without opposition. However, 16 August proved much different. Charles Joe Warth, a gunner in *Southern Comfort*, piloted by Lt H. W. Austin in

B-24D Lucky *in the 409th Bomb Squadron, 93rd BG, lived up to its name after surviving a direct flak hit on the Ploesti mission of 1 August 1943. The nose art was the crest of the 409th Squadron.* (USAF.)

the 506th Bomb Squadron of the 44th BG, recalls: 'We were told that the raid would be a "milk run". We were "fat, dumb and happy" to go there. But conditions change rapidly in a combat zone and the German High Command, getting word we were returning, laid a little trap for us.'

Joe Warth had missed the Ploesti raid because all 44th BG aircraft carried nine-man crews to permit more fuel to be carried. He was the only member of the crew to stand down that day. Foggia was to be the Austin crew's twelfth mission of the war. At around 04:30 on 16 August 25 Eightball aircraft began to take off from their desert airfield at Benina Main. The Liberators' propellers whipped up great sandstorms as the bombers taxied from their dispersal points. Two Liberators developed mechanical troubles shortly after take-off, and were forced to jettison their bombs in the Mediterranean and return to Benina. Twenty-three aircraft, including Austin's ship, *Southern Comfort*, headed for their target, the satellite airfield at Foggia North.

B-24D Jerk's Natural, *41-23711, flown on the first five missions by Lt John 'The Jerk' Jerstad (MoH for his action at Ploesti, 1 August 1943) of the 93rd BG, pictured at Hardwick shortly after its return from North Africa. (USAF.)*

This was reached at 10:33, and the Liberators released their 45-second tail delay and fragmentation bombs from 20,000 ft. The enemy flak was accurate, and several B-24Ds suffered minor damage.

Light scattered clouds over the target area afforded no protection at all, and upwards of 50 Bf 109s, Ju 88s and Me 110s tore into the Eightballs, using the unlimited visibility to good advantage. Joe Warth recalls: 'Our Liberator took an uncountable number of direct hits from the German fighters, which came at us from every direction. I know we shot down at least three of them when we heard the bale-out klaxon sound; three of our engines were shut off and on fire and the bomb bay was a blazing inferno. In the rear of the aircraft we were completely cut off from the rest of the crew. I made it to the camera hatch, turning round to see the door to the bomb bay vapourize in the flames. The four of us in the rear wasted no time in getting out, S/Sgts Lee and Purcell going out of their waist windows.

'*Southern Comfort* was a mass of flame as she spun down, crashing into an Italian hillside. There was a final blast of flame and noise as if she had but one desire left; to return to the earth as the ore from which she came.' Lt P. S. Singer, the navigator, and Lt S. Finder, the bombardier, lost their lives. Their bodies were later found by the Germans, who reported that their parachutes were bullet-ridden and had failed to work properly. The rest of the crew were captured by the Germans and sent to PoW camps, but Warth succeeded in escaping to England late in 1943.

Three Liberators in the 67th Squadron were also lost, including *Buzzin' Bear* and the seemingly indestructible *Suzy Q*. Capt Bill Cameron and 'Pappy' Moore again escaped disaster, Cameron having been promoted to squadron commander and Moore having completed his tour on an earlier mission to Naples. Following the bombing of Cancello on 21 August, the three 8th Air Force groups were ordered back to England to continue the air war against Germany. Their sojourn in the desert had been a harrowing experience, and life on their bases in Norfolk would never be the same again for the survivors.

Chapter Seven

The Schweinfurt raids

IN ENGLAND, DURING the Liberators' absence, the loss of about 100 Fortresses and men during 'Blitz Week' had been made good, and on 12 August the 390th BG from Framlingham helped swell the ranks of 330 bombers heading for targets in the Ruhr. Once again adverse weather was to dog the mission, and it caused many groups to seek targets of opportunity. Groups became strung out and the Luftwaffe seized the opportunity to strike at the widely dispersed formations. They hit groups time and again, inflicting heavy losses, particularly among the 92nd and 384th BGs, which lost four and five aircraft respectively.

Three days later VIII Bomber Command participated in the 'Starkey' deception plan, which was created to make the enemy believe that an invasion of the French coast was imminent. In theory it would relieve some of the pressure on Russia and halt troop movements to Italy. The Fortress formations roamed across France, Belgium and Holland, dropping their deadly loads of bombs on long-suffering German airfields. Friendly fighter support was generally

390th BG B-17F-60-DL 42-3426 releases its bombs. The group made its bombing debut on 12 August 1943, to the Ruhr Valley. (Via Ian McLachlan.)

described as 'excellent', and the Luftwaffe largely stayed on the ground. However, there was always the 'expected unexpected', and two aircraft in the 390th BG collided, tearing the tail off one. Both spun in.

Strikes against enemy airfields in France and the Low Countries continued on 16 August. Then, early that evening, operations staff stood by their teleprinters, awaiting orders for the morrow; the anniversary mission of the 8th Air Force. The Field Order for 17 August called for ambitious and daring strikes on the aircraft plant at Regensburg and the ball-bearing plant at Schweinfurt. Brig Gen Robert Williams, commander of the 1st Wing, would lead his force to Schweinfurt, while Col Curtis E. LeMay was to lead the 4th Wing to Regensburg. To minimise attacks by enemy fighters, LeMay's B-17s would fly on to North Africa after the target. The 1st Wing, meanwhile, would fly a parallel course to Schweinfurt to confuse the enemy defences further, returning to England after the raid.

Despite the planning, Eaker and his subordinates were under no illusions. They knew that the B-17 crews would have a running fight on their hands, but hoped that four P-47 fighter groups detailed to escort the Regensburg force would keep losses down. However, the long, straggling formation stretched for 15 miles, and presented the fighter pilots with an awesome responsibility. Up front was the 96th BG with Col LeMay at the helm. Behind came the 388th and 390th BGs, followed by the 94th and 385th making up the 2nd Combat Wing. Bringing up the rear of the formation were the 95th and 100th BGs, each carrying incendiaries to stoke the fires created by the leading groups.

To add to the problems, only one P-47 group rendezvoused with the bombers as scheduled. When the Luftwaffe attacked in strength the overburdened Thunderbolts could not possibly hope to protect all seven groups in the 4th Wing. Fortresses in the rear of the formation were left unprotected, and the 95th and 100th Bomb Groups bore the brunt of the ferocious attacks, which were mostly made from head-on. The unlucky Thorpe Abbotts' group lost two B-17s, and the 95th lost one. In the 1½ hr preceding the bomb run 17 Fortresses were shot down. The 385th BG lost three bombers, while others, badly shot up, barely made it over the treacherous snow-covered Alps.

The 2nd Combat Wing was forced to swing around in a 360° turn and make another bomb run after the target had been obscured by smoke from the leading wing's bombs. The bombing was extremely accurate, and this might well have been due to the presence of Col LeMay, an exponent of high-level bombing techniques, in the first wave. The 390th had placed 58 per cent of its bombs within 1,000 ft of the MPI and 94 per cent with 2,000 ft. The last two groups over the target, the 95th and 100th, added their incendiary clusters to the conflagration, which was now marked by a rectangular pillar of smoke towering to 10,000 ft.

Six main workshops were hit, five being severely damaged. A hangar was partially destroyed and storerooms and administrative buildings wrecked. Some 37 Bf 109s at dispersal were damaged, if not

B-17s cross Regensburg during the raid on 17 August 1943. (USAF.)

wrecked, and all production at the plant came to an abrupt halt. Although it was unknown at the time, the bombing had also destroyed the fuselage jigs for a secret German jet fighter, the Messerschmitt Me 262.

The surviving 128 B-17s, some flying on three engines and many trailing smoke, were attacked by a few fighters on the way to the Alps. LeMay circled his formation over Lake Garda to give the cripples a chance to rejoin the Wing, but two smoking B-17s, one belonging to

Aircraft debris hurtles past near a Fortress formation during the mission to Regensburg on 17 August 1943. (USAF.)

the 390th and the other, *High Life*, belonging to the 100th and flown by Lt Donald Oakes, glided down toward the safety of Switzerland, about 40 miles distant. Oakes landed wheels-up at Dubendorf, a military airfield near Zurich, and his aircraft became the first B-17 to land in Switzerland. Two B-17s in the 390th BG had been shot down in the target area, and a third, out of fuel, headed for Spain. It landed near Toulon in France, and the crew were made prisoners of war. An unidentified Fortress crashlanded in northern Italy and five more eventually ditched in the Mediterranean. Red lights were showing on all four fuel gauges in every aircraft, and it was a ragged collection of survivors which landed at intervals up to 50 miles along the North African coast. Nine of the 100th's 24 bombers failed to land in North Africa; the highest loss in the 4th Wing.

Although they did not yet know it, the 4th Wing had encountered so many fighters en route because the 1st Wing had been delayed by thick inland mists for 3½ hr after the 4th Wing had taken off. This had effectively prevented a two-pronged assault which might have split the opposing fighter force. The delay gave the Luftwaffe time to refuel and rearm after dealing with the Regensburg force and get airborne again. They attacked the Schweinfurt force with the same ferocity, shooting down 36 Fortresses. The coast of England was a welcome sight for the survivors. At bases throughout eastern England anxious watchers counted in the returning Fortresses. Eighteen had taken off from Grafton Underwood, but the watchers in the control tower counted no further than 13.

Two 96th BG B-17Fs over the Alps on 17 August 1943, en route to North Africa after bombing Regensburg. (Via Geoff Ward.)

Above *Colonel Curtis E. LeMay was displeased with the Army at Telergma after landing in North Africa following the Regensburg shuttle mission from England on 17 August 1943.* (Via Ian McLachlan.)

Above right *B-17F-35-VE* Shack Bunny, *42-5913, of the 385th BG, at the North African landing strip after the Regensburg shuttle mission from England on 17 August 1943.* (Via Ian McLachlan.)

The total loss of 60 bombers was more than twice as great as the previous highest, on 13 June, when 26 bombers were lost. Hardest hit in the 1st Wing were the 381st and 91st BGs, which lost 11 and ten B-17s respectively. The third highest loss of the day went to the 100th BG in the 4th Wing, which lost nine Fortresses.

The lack of facilities in North Africa ruled out any more shuttle missions in the immediate future, and VIII Bomber Command continued flying missions to France and the Low Countries. Then, on 6 September, Gen Eaker sent 338 B-17s to the aircraft components factories at Stuttgart. Some 69 Liberators, including the 392nd BG, recently arrived at Wendling, Norfolk, and equipped with the new B-24H and B-24J with power-operated nose gun turrets, flew a diversionary sweep over the North Sea.

The Stuttgart raid was a completely 'SNAFU' from the start. Cloud interfered with assembly over England and prevented accurate bombing at the target. The B-17 formations came under sporadic attack shortly after crossing the enemy coast – an indication that the bulk of the fighter force was massing further inland for a concentrated strike. Thick cloud was also building up inland, and the feeling among the B-17 crews was that the mission should be aborted. Brig Gen Robert B. Travis, who had assumed command of the 1st Wing from Brig Gen Williams, circled Stuttgart for approximately 30 minutes in a vain attempt to find the target. Claude Campbell, who was flying in the 303rd BG formation behind Travis, recalls: 'We flew around dodging flak, trying to find a hole in the overcast. Fighters were flying around as bewildered as we were. Eventually we dropped our bombs on God knows where [they hit a wheatfield] and began to fight our way home.'

Fighters shot down 11 B-17s of the 388th BG; the highest loss it had sustained on a raid since joining the 8th in June 1943. Many more Fortresses came off their targets with their bombloads intact, and some 233 bombers released their bombs on targets of opportunity en route to the enemy coast. Ten B-17s in the 100th BG attacked airfields in France for the loss of two Fortresses. One crashlanded and nine men were made PoWs, while *Raunchy*, piloted by Lt Sam Turner, was knocked out of formation and headed for Switzerland, where it was demolished while ditching on Lake Constance. Joe Moloney, the ball turret gunner, had been killed, hit by a 20 mm shell between the shoulder blades, but the remaining nine men in the crew survived despite some terrible injuries. By the time the B-17s were east of Paris red lights began to show on the fuel gauges, and many crews began to wonder if they would reach England. Three B-17s in the 92nd BG were forced to ditch in the Channel, out of fuel, and a fourth ditched two miles off the English coast.

Next day the 8th bombed enemy airfields in France and the Low Countries. It was joined for the first time by the 389th BG, newly equipped with the latest B-24H and J aircraft. On 13 September VIII Bomber Command was officially divided into three bombardment divisions. The nine groups in the 1st Bomb Wing formed the 1st Bomb Division, commanded by Gen Travis, and the six B-17 groups forming the 4th Bomb Wing were renamed the 3rd Bomb Division, under Col Curtis E. LeMay. All four 202nd Combat Bomb Wing (Provisional) Liberator groups became the 2nd Bomb Division, under the command of Gen James Hodges, with its headquarters at Ketteringham Hall. Col Leon Johnson moved from the 44th to command the 14th Combat Wing, and Lt Col James L. Posey was promoted to command the Eightballs.

On 15 September a few heavy bombers flew a night mission with the RAF against the Montlucon Dunlop tyre factory. During the day almost 140 bombers attacked the Renault works and a ball-bearing plant at Paris, while a comparable force attacked airfields at Chartres and Romilly-Sur-Seine. Crews could have been forgiven for thinking they were now engaged on nocturnal missions because their return was made in darkness, as S/Sgt John W. Butler, a gunner in *Tarfu* in the 93rd BG, who was on only his third mission, recalls: 'We hit our target, which was the airfield at St. Andre, pretty damn good. We really were on the beam. On the way back it was pretty dark and some fool started firing at a Flak burst. Then someone mistook a B-24 for a bandit and set his number two engine on fire. They all started to fire at the poor devil. Four 'chutes got out. I really sweated it out as tracers were going all over Hell. It was also the first night landing in the ETO. We landed back at Hardwick at 21.25 hours. There was an air raid on when we arrived back over England and the sky was really lit up with searchlights.'

Next day the long-range B-17s of the 3rd Bomb Division flew a 1,600-mile, 11-hour round trip to Bordeaux to bomb an aircraft plant, and their return was also made in darkness. Before this mission crews had, however, practised taking off in squadrons and assembling as a group at night. Just off the southwest coast of England the B-17s encountered heavy rain squalls, and these, plus the impending darkness, dispersed the formation. The storm front knocked radio altimeters about 1,000 ft out of calibration, and many pilots got into difficulties. Three B-17s ditched in the North Sea and two others crashed, killing all ten crew in one Fortress and one crewmember in the other. The 1st Bomb Division encountered heavy fighter opposition on its mission to the port installations at Nantes, while most of the 21 B-17s in a diversionary force which headed for Cognac airfield failed to bomb because of thick cloud over the target. In all, the 8th lost 13 bombers on the day's raids.

The 44th, 93rd and 389th BGs were ordered to North Africa again for a short time in mid-September, when the Salerno landings appeared to be in jeopardy. Meanwhile, on the morning of 24 September crews were alerted for a mission to Stüttgart again, but adverse weather forced its cancellation. 'Pappy' Colby recalls: 'At 11:30 they decided to have a wing formation practice mission, following a Pathfinder aircraft and bombing a simulated target in the North Sea'. Bomb loads were hastily changed and machine guns re-installed. The B-17s completed assembly without incident, but over the North Sea they were bounced by about 15 German fighters. 'Of course we had no fighter cover,' says Colby. 'They shot down one ship in the group behind me. As it glided down one 'chute came out and then it blew up. Seven Bf 109s came on through and one started an attack on us, as I was the last airplane. Luckily, our tail gunner had gotten his twin fifties installed and he fired a long burst and the fighter turned away.'

In the 100th formation, *Damdifino II* came in for some particularly heavy attacks by fighters using the sun to excellent advantage. They raked the fuselage, and a 20 mm shell started a fire in the oil tank behind the number three engine. Lt J. Gossage, the pilot, held the aircraft steady while all the crew baled out. Theodore J. Don, the bombardier, baled out at 1,000 ft and hit the sea almost at the instant his 'chute deployed. He was later rescued by a flotilla of MTBs en route to the Dutch coast, but the co-pilot and the navigator were dead when they were picked up. The two waist gunners and the ball turret gunner were never found. The bomber hit the sea nose down and quickly began to sink. Gossage was trapped, but managed to pull himself free and float safely to the surface.

The H2S radar trials carried out on 23 September proved so impressive that Gen Eaker instructed that similarly equipped Fortresses should accompany the force of 305 bombers to Emden on 27 September. This small port was handling about 500,000 tons of shipping a month as a result of damage inflicted on Hamburg. Emden was also chosen because of its proximity to water, which would show up reasonably well on the cathode ray tubes. In all, 244 bombers hit the target, and the Fortresses which bombed with the aid of H2S-equipped B-17s did remarkably well. One of the three combat wings in the 3rd Division managed to bomb visually after exploiting a gap in the clouds, but subsequent photographic reconnaissance proved that only the H2S-assisted formations had achieved a fair concentration of bombs on Emden. Other bomb patterns ranged as far as five miles away from the city.

The H2S sets seemed to provide the answer to the 8th's problems, and Eaker was anxious to use them again as soon as possible. A period of bad weather gave the technicians time to iron out some of the teething troubles before the bombers were despatched to Emden again

B-17F Bomb-Boogie, *42-5763, in the 401st Bomb Squadron, 91st BG, which was shot down on 6 September 1943 on the Stüttgart mission when it was flown by 1st Lt Elwood D. Arp.* (USAF.)

on Monday 2 October with two H2S-equipped aircraft from the 482nd BG. Brig Gen Robert W. Travis led the mission in *Little America*. This time the H2S sets worked perfectly, although inexperience resulted in one pathfinder aircraft releasing its bombs too early and many B-17s dropped their loads short of the target. Winds also carried away smoke markers and spoilt the aim of the following formations.

Further radar bombing was delayed because the 482nd BG had insufficient aircraft and crews to participate in a major mission, and there were several days on which conditions were suitable for visual attacks in western Germany. On 4 October 361 bombers were despatched but, without PFF, cloud ruled out accurate bombing at all primary targets. Twelve B-17s were shot down, and losses would have been higher had it not been for the strong P-47 escort and a diversion mission flown over the North Sea by 30 B-24Hs of the 392nd BG, together with six Liberators from the 44th and 93rd. (These two Groups, and the 389th, newly returned from North Africa, were still licking their wounds, the 44th having lost 16 B-24s shot down or written off in crash landings three days before on a mission to Wiener Neustadt.) They certainly flushed the fighters, for over the North Sea they were jumped by 30 Bf 109s and Fw 190s.

Capt Myron H. Keilman, Operations Officer of the 579th Bomb Squadron, was flying deputy group lead. 'The rate of closure was so fast,' he recounts, 'that I hardly had a chance to spot them before I saw their guns blinking fire. They dove below our formation and circled for another pass. Then there was a second wave of five or six of them, and another – and another. I lost track of how many. I am sure that they were surprised at having our new nose turrets returning their fire, but it didn't seem to deter them. Each B-24H had four turrets of twin .50 calibre guns plus a flexible '50 at each waist window.

'Sitting there, I was dismayed for something useful to do. After the third attack or so I couldn't sit there any longer, so I slapped the airplane commander on the arm and hastily took over flying the airplane. That lasted only a few minutes because he couldn't stand watching those fighters either. This exchange continued for the duration of the battle. Besides the 13 mm and 20 mm guns of the '109s and Fw 190s there were occasional large single flashes of fire from their 210 mm rockets. Each packed the wallop of a large anti-aircraft artillery shell and could readily blow up a B-24. We were lucky, though. Because they were time-fused, the time and distance of launching the rockets was very critical for them to explode among the airplanes of our formation. With closing speeds of 700 m.p.h. or more this wasn't easy. The use of head-on attacks was relatively ineffective, but it was real scary.'

The low squadron, containing the 44th and 93rd flights, were well worked over by the fighters because they did not have the new nose turrets. A German fighter rammed into one of the lead aeroplanes in the High squadron, which had 579th Squadron CO Maj Donald Apport aboard, and this, in turn, crashed into another B-24. All three went down. Myron Keilman was assigned 579th Squadron Commander that evening. (His brother Paul, who was a bombardier in the 44th BG, had been killed in a mid-air collision with a fighter over the North Sea eight months before, on 23 January.) Altogether three B-24s were lost, but the American gunners claimed 19 fighters destroyed.

On 8 October the Fortresses were assigned the port at Bremen. To split the enemy fighter force, the 1st Division approached the target from Holland while the 3rd Division crossed the North Sea and approached the target from the north-west. Meanwhile, the 2nd Bomb Division flew a long, curving route over the North Sea to Vegasack. Unfortunately, after the P-47 escort had withdrawn, low on fuel, the B-17s encountered enemy fighters in strength. The unfortunate 381st BG, flying as low group in the 1st Division formation, lost seven of its 18 B-17s, including the lead ship.

To crews in the 3rd Division, though, it seemed that everything was going according to plan, but the German flak defences had already

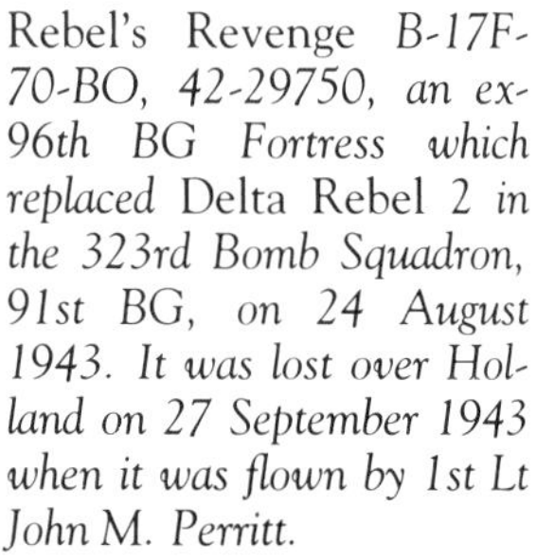
Rebel's Revenge *B-17F-70-BO, 42-29750, an ex-96th BG Fortress which replaced* Delta Rebel 2 *in the 323rd Bomb Squadron, 91st BG, on 24 August 1943. It was lost over Holland on 27 September 1943 when it was flown by 1st Lt John M. Perritt.*

calculated the height and speed of the previous wing, and had no need to alter those calculations as the 100th sailed over the target at much the same height and speed. The lead aircraft, *Just a Snappin'*, flown by Capt Everett E. Blakely and Maj John B. Kidd, the command pilot, was hit repeatedly and lost 3,000 ft before Blakely and Kidd regained control. The 100th lost seven B-17s, including the one flown by Maj 'Bucky' Cleven, CO of the 350th Bomb Squadron, and Bill MacDonald's *Salvo Sal.* Fighters attacked, killing waist gunner Douglas Agee, and *Salvo Sal* turned over, spun slightly and burst into flames. All six enlisted men and John James, the co-pilot, were captured by German patrols shortly after landing. Carl Spicer, the navigator, evaded capture and reached England via France and Spain. MacDonald and Frank McGlinchey, the bombardier, also evaded capture and travelled along the evasion lines to Spain, only to be caught at a crossing point on the Pyrenees. They were sent to Stalag Luft I at Barth. The four surviving B-17s owed their survival to the 390th BG leader, Maj Robert O. Good, who encouraged them to move in tightly behind his 20 B-17s after the target. The 8th lost 26 bombers, including 14 from the 3rd Division.

On 9 October 378 heavies were despatched on the day's operation, which involved three targets. The 1st and 41st Combat Wings despatched 115 aircraft to the Arado aircraft component plant at Anklam near Peenemünde as a diversion for 263 bombers attacking the Polish port of Gydnia and the Focke-Wulf plant at Marienburg. For Howard E. Hernan and two other members of Claude Campbell's crew in the 303rd BG at Molesworth, the Anklam raid marked their 25th and final mission of the war. Maj Calhoun, the 359th Squadron CO, replaced Claude Campbell in the *Eightball*, and Gen Travis, the 1st Bomb Division commander, took the co-pilot's seat. Hernan recalls: 'On our approach to the target there was little flak, although there was a lot around Peenemünde. There did not appear to be many fighters either, so I had an opportunity of watching the bombs drop from 12,500 ft. We completely saturated the target and headed back over Denmark and the North Sea.' (The Anklam force lost 14 B-17s, all from the 1st Combat Wing).

The Gydnia force had continued on its 1,500-mile round trip to the docks area. Leslie G. Thibodeau, flying his third mission with the 388th BG, says: 'Our group made two runs on the target area before we dropped our bombs because we were confronted by a great smokescreen thrown up by German destroyers in an effort to protect the ships and installations. However, the 550 ft-long liner *Stüttgart* was on fire and the docks, railways and workshops were hit.'

The third force of B-17s, which bombed Marienburg, achieved the greatest success of the day. The normally unfortunate 385th BG led the raid and lost only two aircraft, one through engine trouble. Major Colby led the 94th BG, which followed closely behind. 'The target was completely demolished,' he writes. 'As we turned for home one gun fired three bursts at least a mile away, proving that we had complete surprise. They just didn't believe we could bomb so far from England.' Anti-aircraft defences had been thought unnecessary so far

Smoke trails from B-17F, Roger The Lodger II 42-30377, of the 412th Bomb Squadron, 95th BG, shortly before it went down in flames on the Marienburg mission on 9 October 1943. Fighters scored hits in the No.2 engine and put a rocket in the No.3 engine. Seven of Lt Ehert's crew baled out but two of the parachutes were on fire. The five survivors perished in the freezing waters of the North Sea. Robert Wing, the bombardier, had a premonition the night before that he would not return. (USAF.)

from England, and their absence meant that the force could bomb from between 11,000 and 13,000 ft. At such heights accuracy was almost guaranteed, and 60 per cent of the bombs dropped by the 96 Fortresses exploded within 1,000 ft of the MPI and 83 per cent fell within 2,000 ft. Before the raid the Marienburg plant had been turning out almost 50 per cent of the Luftwaffe's Fw 190 production. The results were devastating and Gen Eaker called it 'A classic example of precision bombing'. Hernan adds: 'We finally arrived back at Molesworth to be welcomed by the same throng, possibly more, that had seen us off. I was overwhelmed, and of course my good pilot, Claude Campbell, was there to greet us.'

The raid which followed, to Münster on Sunday 10 October, heralded a surprising switch in bombing policy. For the first time in the war the 8th Air Force was to bomb a residential area to deprive the Germans of its rail workers, who were practically all billeted in the town. At Framlingham, home of the 95th BG, which would lead the 3rd Bomb Division to Münster, crews were told: 'Your MPI will be Münster Cathedral, and you are going to bomb the workers' homes . . .' A maximum effort was ordered, 264 B-17s from the 1st and 3rd Divisions being despatched. Crews were told that approximately 245 single-engined and 290 twin-engined fighters could be expected to oppose the mission. Despite a planned direct route, the 1st and 3rd Division forces would be given a strong Thunderbolt escort, and Liberators of the 2nd Bomb Division would fly a diversionary sweep over the North Sea.

At 13:48 Col John K. Gerhart, CO of the 95th BG, took off from Horham to lead the 13th Wing and the 3rd Bomb Division over the North Sea towards Münster. Following closely behind came the 390th and the 100th, led by Maj Egan and John Brady in *Mlle Zig-Zag*. By the time the Third Division crossed the Dutch coast at 14:16 no fewer than 27 aircraft had aborted with mechanical problems. The 100th Bomb Group for instance, had lost seven of its original 21 aircraft, including one which had failed to take off from Thorpe Abbotts.

Unfortunately, fog over England prevented the next relay of Thunderbolt escorts from taking off, and the B-17s had to continue alone. Then the diversionary force of B-24s was forced to abort, and as the formation turned for home the German controllers redirected their fighters towards the 3rd Division instead. The Luftwaffe picked up the leading 13th Wing and, concentrating on the low group, proceeded to tear the 100th BG apart. *Mlle Zig-Zag* was hit by a rocket and went down. 'Bucky' Egan baled out and was ultimately made a PoW. The 100th reeled under the incessant attacks, and 11 aircraft were shot down before the target was reached. Only Capt Keith Harris in the 390th BG who was flying in *Stork Club* in the 100th BG formation, Lt Robert Rosenthal, and Lt John Justice's *Pasadena Nena* reached the target. (Justice was shot down on the homeward leg.) *Royal Flush*, which was flown by Robert Rosenthal because *Rosie's Riveters*, his usual aircraft, was still under repair following *Rosie's* debut on the disastrous mission to Bremen, lost two engines over Münster and a rocket shell tore through the right wing, leaving a large hole. Despite this, Rosenthal completed the bomb run and instigated a series of violent manoeuvres to throw the aim of the flak guns.

The 18 B-17s in the 390th BG also felt the full impact of the Luftwaffe attacks. In about 25 minutes the 390th lost eight of its bombers as the rockets exploded among them. Next, the Luftwaffe turned on the 95th BG. Five of the 19 B-17s were shot down. The survivors continued to the target, desperately fighting off the intense Luftwaffe attacks. Beyond the target *Tech Supply*, flown by Lt John G. Winant Jr, son of the US Ambassador to Great Britain, was hit by a rocket and exploded. It was Winant's 13th mission. (Winant was

B-17F Spot Remover *in the 390th BG, piloted by Capt Keith Harris, taxies past the control tower at Framlingham on 12 August 1943. On the mission to Münster, on 10 October, Harris flew a spare aircraft because* Spot Remover *was undergoing repairs for damage sustained on the raid on Bremen.* (Via Mike Bailey.)

among those who were made PoWs).

Shortly after *Tech Supply* went down, *The Eightball* in the 390th formation was hit in the starboard wing by a rocket. 'The rocket sheared a path through the top half of the right wing (about 15 feet from the end),' recalls Richard H. Perry, the co-pilot. 'The wing tip flapped up and down in the windstream and caused us to lose the lift that we should have gotten from the wing.' The combined efforts of Perry and Bill Cabral, the pilot, were not enough to keep the bomber from falling out of formation, so Ferris was called to the controls. He stood between Perry and Cabral and managed, despite his injuries, to put a hand on each of the control wheels and help the pilots keep *The Eightball* straight and level in formation.

It was a great relief to one and all when the white vapour trails of the Thunderbolt escort were seen directly ahead. There were few B-17s for the 'little friends' to protect. The 390th was now down to a pitiful ten bombers, and even the survivors were not sure they would reach England. Those that did were badly damaged, with wounded crews and pilots, and put down as best they could. Bill Cabral and Richard Perry landed at Thorpe Abbotts after bad weather prevented a landing at Framlingham. Despite the fog, all ten aircraft in the 390th made it to Suffolk. It had been a black day for the 13th Wing, which had lost 25 of the 29 B-17s lost by the 3rd Division. The 390th had lost eight and the 95th five. Worst of all, the 100th BG had lost 12 bombers. This brought its total losses to 19 in three days.

In all, 88 bombers had been lost on three successive days, and the losses came at a time when intelligence sources revealed that Luftwaffe fighter strength was increasing. Some put the figure at around 1,100 operational fighters. In reality, the Luftwaffe could call upon 1,646 single- and twin-engined fighters for the defence of the Reich; 400 more than before the Pointblank directive. The Allies' figures confirmed their worst fears. The decision was therefore taken to attack the ball-bearing plant at Schweinfurt for the second time in three months, in the hope that VIII Bomber Command could deliver a single, decisive blow to the German aircraft industry and stem the flow of fighters to Luftwaffe units.

On the afternoon of 13 October Brig Gen Orvil Anderson, Commanding General of VIII Bomber Command, and his senior staff officers, gathered at High Wycombe for the daily Operations Conference. They were told that good weather was expected for the morrow. At once a warning order was sent out to all three bomb division headquarters with details of a mission, No. 115, to Schweinfurt. The orders were then transmitted over teletape machines to the various combat wing headquarters.

Anderson hoped to launch 420 Fortresses and Liberators in a three-pronged attack on the city. The 100th Bomb group was still licking its wounds after the severe maulings of 8 October, when it lost seven crews, and 10 October, when it lost another 12 crews. Despite these extremely serious losses, the 'Bloody Hundredth' was still expected to contribute to the tonnage of bombs to be dropped on Schweinfurt.

The plan called for the 1st and 3rd Bomb Divisions to cross Holland 30 miles apart, while the third task force, composed of 60 Liberators, would fly to the south on a parallel course. The 923-mile trip would last just over seven hours, and this meant that the B-17s of the 1st Division which were not equipped with 'Tokyo tanks' would have to be fitted with an additional fuel tank in the bomb bay, with a consequent reduction in bombload. Each division would be escorted by a P-47 group, while a third fighter group would provide withdrawal support from 60 miles inland to halfway across the Channel. Two squadrons of RAF Spitfire Mk.9s were to provide cover for the stragglers five minutes after the main force had left the withdrawal area, and other RAF squadrons would be on standby for action if required. Despite these precautions, 370 miles of the route would be flown without fighter support. The 96th BG, which would be flying in the van of the 45th Combat Wing, would lead the 3rd Division, while the 92nd BG, at the head of the 40th Combat Wing, would lead the 1st Division.

The plans, then, were laid, but the unpredictable weather intervened before take-off and hampered the B-24s' assembly, finally ruling out their participation. It seemed that the Fortresses' participation was also ruled out, but an American-crewed Mosquito, 35,000 ft over the Continent, radioed back that all of central Germany was in the clear. The 40th Combat Wing took off and led the 1st Division over the coast of England, 20,000 ft above Orford Ness. Further south, the 45th Combat Wing led the 3rd Division over the Naze. Behind the 45th Wing came the 4th Combat Wing, followed by the 13th Combat Wing. Fifteen of the 164 aircraft in the 1st Division and 18 aircraft of the 160 in the 3rd Division either turned back with mechanical problems or became lost in the cloudy conditions. The long and complicated assembly also diminished the Fortresses' vital fuel reserves, especially in those aircraft carrying bombs externally to compensate for the internal tonnage lost to bomb bay fuel tanks. Many of these crews were forced to dump their wing mounted bombs

B-17F-115-BO 42-30727, piloted by Lt William C. Bisson in the 367th 'Clay Pigeons' Bomb Squadron, 306th BG, was lost on the Schweinfurt raid on 14 October 1943 when flak knocked out two engines and fighters riddled the rear fuselage, killing S/Sgt Thompson E. Wilson, the tail gunner. Only 2nd Lt Charles R. Stafford, the co-pilot, who exited through the side cockpit window, and four crewmen in the aft section escaped death. (Richards.)

in the Channel or abort the mission.

The 3rd Division encountered some fighter opposition and lost two Fortresses before the Thunderbolt escort withdrew, but, by the time it entered the target area, the 1st Division had lost 36 bombers shot down and 20 had turned back. Although the 1st still had 224 Fortresses, most of the groups had been torn to shreds and some were barely skeleton formations. The 306th had lost ten of its 21 Fortresses, and by the time the 305th BG could see the city of Schweinfurt, 12 miles distant, it had lost its entire low squadron of five aircraft and parts of the high and lead squadrons. Only three of the original 18 aircraft remained, and they were joined by a Fortress from another group. There were not enough aircraft for effective bombing, so Maj Normand, the group leader, decided to join the depleted 92nd and 306th formations for the bomb run. Of the 37 Fortresses in the 40th Combat Wing which had crossed the Channel, only 16 remained. Worse was to follow.

At 14:39 the 91st began dropping its bombs on the streets, houses and factories of Schweinfurt. The 91st was to claim the best overall bombing results for the 1st Division. However, the 351st BG, from the same wing, the 1st, was the most accurate, Capt H. D. Wallace, the squadron bombardier in part of the group formation, placing all his bombs within 1,000 ft of the MPI. The three surviving bombers in the 305th bombed the centre of the city. Immediately after 'bombs away' the group's 13th victim was claimed by fighters, leaving only Maj Normand and another B-17 from the 18 that had set out from Chelveston. The two survivors turned away from the target and followed the lead group home.

The 40th Combat Wing dropped its bombs and headed in the direction of the 1st Combat Wing, which was now making for the French border. The third and final wing, the 41st, added its bombs to the conflagration and turned off the target to allow the 3rd Bomb Division, flying six minutes behind, to take its turn. First over the target was the 96th BG at the head of the 45th Combat Wing. Its target was obscured by smoke from the preceding bomb runs, but crews had not flown this far to be thwarted, and released their bombs anyway. The second group in the wing was the 388th, with 16 aircraft. The lead bombardier was unable to identify either the Kugelfischer ball-bearing works or the marshalling yards located to the south, so he set his sight on the bridge over the River Main and released his bombs slightly to the right of the ball-bearing plant. The bombs cascaded down into the southern half of Schweinfurt and the western end of the marshalling yards. The 13th Combat Wing was the last wing in the 3rd Division to cross Schweinfurt. Crews eagerly released their bombs and headed for home.

The city of Schweinfurt had soaked up over 483 short tons of high explosives and incendiaries. The 3rd Division had dropped the most bombs on target, and the 390th was the most successful. Although the lead ship had experienced difficulty, all 15 aircraft placed 50 per cent of their bombs within 1,000 ft of the MPI. The B-17s turned off the target and flew an almost complete 180° circle around Schweinfurt. A

B-17s of the 306th BG weave their way through heavy flak over Schweinfurt on 14 October 1943. Altogether, the group lost ten Fortresses, the second highest loss in the 1st Division. (Richards.)

group of Fw 190s headed for the 1st Division formation and singled out the trailing 41st Combat Wing. The leading 379th BG lost four B-17s in the first pass.

Both divisions headed for their respective rally points and began forming into combat wings again for the return over Germany and France. Approaching the French coast, the two surviving aircraft in the 305th BG sighted the 92nd and 306th BGs for the first time during the mission. Luckily, the two B-17s had met little fighter opposition on the way home, for they had used almost all their ammunition before reaching the target. The Fortresses' return to England was hampered by the same soupy weather that had dogged their departure. At 16:40 the 1st Division bombers crossed the Channel coast and were followed, just five minutes later, by those of the 3rd Division.

Altogether, the 1st Division had lost 45 Fortresses on the raid, the 305th had lost 16, and the 306th ten. The 92nd BG had lost six, and a seventh was written off in a crash landing at Aldermaston. The 379th and 384th BGs had each lost six B-17s in combat, and three crews from the latter group had to abandon their aircraft over England, making nine in all. The 303rd BG lost two aircraft, including one which crash-landed after the crew had baled out near Riseley. The 91st, 351st and 381st BGs each lost one B-17.

The 3rd Division had lost 15 aircraft, the 96th had lost seven, and the 94th six. The 95th and 390th had each lost one B-17. The 100th, 385th and 388th BGs suffered no losses, although few aircraft, if any, escaped scot-free. Of the bombers which returned to England, 142 in both divisions were blackened and charred by fighter attacks and holed by flak. Sixty Fortresses and 600 men were missing. Five battle-damaged B-17s had crashed in England, and 12 more were destroyed in crashlandings or so badly damaged that they had to be written off. Of the returning bombers, 121 required repairs, and five fatal casualties and 43 wounded crewmen were removed from the aircraft. Only 88 of the 1,222 bombs dropped actually fell on the plants. Production at the Kugelfischer plant, the largest of the five plants, was interrupted for only six weeks, and the German war machine never lacked for ball-bearings throughout the remainder of the war. As in many other German industries, dispersal of factories ensured survival for the German ball-bearing industry, and careful husbanding of resources meant that some forms of machinery needed fewer ball bearings or none at all.

Chapter Eight

The best of days, the worst of days

THE DAY AFTER the second Schweinfurt mission, all heavy bomb groups were stood down to lick their wounds while replacements were sent in. One of the recent replacements at Bury St. Edmunds was Cliff Hatcher, the co-pilot in Lt Johnny Pyles' crew. 'When I arrived,' he recalls, 'the group had lost 30 aircraft up until 27 September, and ten more aircraft were lost while I underwent training. For a few days we learned formation flying and generally learned the ropes.'

The losses, and a spell of bad weather, restricted the 8th to just two more missions in October. Then on 3 November, the 8th was assigned Wilhelmshaven. Altogether, 555 bombers and H2X ships from the 482nd BG were despatched to the port. H2X or 'Mickey Mouse' (later shortened to 'Mickey') was a recently developed American version of the British H2S bombing aid. Some groups carried incendiaries, and, in the words of Capt Claude Campbell, who was flying his 24th mission in the 303rd BG, in *The Eightball*, they 'intended to burn up the city'.

For Cliff Hatcher and Johnny Pyles it was their first mission. Hatcher recalls: 'We took off in *Lil' Butch* and flew in "Purpule Heart Corner". A new crew always flew in the tail-end of the formation, and

Frank Walls poses in his co-pilot's window of B-17F Shack Bunny *in the 551st Bomb Squadron, 385th BG. This aircraft, and Lt Lyle V. Fryer's crew, was lost over France on 20 October 1943 on the mission to Duren, Germany. All of the crew were captured and made PoWs.* (William Nicholls.)

"Purple Heart Corner" was on the left wing of the second element leader of the low squadron. We were the lowest 'plane in the formation. The opposite was "tail-end charlie", which was in the top position off the right wing of the second element leader in the high squadron.

'A Bf 109 hit us and knocked out our numebr two engine. There were lots of contrails and we hid in them, flying behind our group. It proved successful and we got home, although later our ground crew chief at Bury St. Edmunds told us he found a .50 calibre bullet in the inverter beneath my seat! Obviously one of our boys in the 94th thought we were a German fighter! The group lost only one aircraft. Lt Brunson in the 322nd Squadron was set on fire by a combination of flak and fighters. One to six 'chutes were reported.'

The Lockheed P-38 escort all the way to the target kept losses to a minimum, and crews were quick to praise their 'little friends'. 'I saw about 25 enemy fighters,' says Claude Campbell, 'but our boys kept them at bay. They came in real close and gave good protection to the stragglers. My hats off to them, and I hope we could get more of them over to England. The target was covered by clouds, and bombing results could not be determined. There were no casualties in our group, and I thought: "Bring on the next one (my 25th and final mission".'

The 8th was again out in force on 5 November when 374 Fortresses were despatched to the iron foundry works and marshalling yards at Gelsenkirchen, led by five Oboe-equipped pathfinders. For two weeks afterwards the weather grew worse and resulted in many aborted missions. It was not until 11 November that the 8th was in the air again, this time to Münster, the scene of such devastation a month previously.

Maj 'Pappy' Colby led the 94th BG and Lt Pyles' crew flew their third mission this day, in *Lil' Operator*. This B-17 had the face of Esky, the little man who appeared on the cover of *Esquire* magazine, on its nose. Pyles' crew were assigned the 'tail end Charlie' slot in the high squadron, which was reckoned to be the most dangerous position after 'Purple Heart Corner'. Everything went well until shortly before bomb release. *Lil' Operator* was rocked by an explosion just forward of the engines on the port side. Oil began pouring out of number two engine and streaked back across the cowling and wing. Pyles told Hatcher to keep an eye on the oil pressure and feather the number two propeller if necessary. The pressure quickly dropped to zero, and Hatcher punched the feathering button. *Lil' Operator* continued its bomb run and Lt Adolph J. Delzoppo, the bombardier, released his bomb load over the target.

The loss of an engine had considerably reduced their speed, and they were now alone. 'Bandits at 2 o'clock,' crackled over the interphone, and Hatcher peered into the strong sun. Suddenly a Bf 109 appeared out of nowhere and dived so close that for a moment the crew feared they were going to be rammed. The German pilot opened fire and several explosions occurred in the cockpit of the B-17, filling it with smoke. *Lil' Operator* fell off to the right and dived for the ground at alarming speed. Hatcher and Pyles opened their side windows to let out the smoke, and for the first time both men realized that they were going down fast! Straining on their control columns, Hatcher and Pyles managed to right their bomber. Hatcher was sure that the number three engine was wind-milling, but three and four engine instruments had been shot out in the fighter attack.

Pyles levelled off at 15,000 ft and applied full left rudder to keep the bomber on course. The throttles for engines three and four were dead, and Pyles decided to shut down number three. Then Ervin Smith, the ball-turret gunner, called up on the interphone that the undercarriage was in the 'down' position. Ross Andrews, the engineer, discovered a large hole in the right forward bulkhead of the bomb bay which had been caused by two 20 mm shells exploding in that area. It had cut off all electrical supply to the righr hand side of the aircraft, and only the armoured pilots' seats had saved Hatcher and Pyles from flying shrapnel. Amazingly, the top turret gunner had escaped injury when fragments had whistled around his legs.

Pyles lost height and headed for some clouds. An aircraft with one-and-a-half engines out and a lowered undercarriage was an open invitation to any enemy figher pilots. Soon, five fighters had ganged up on the crippled bomber. Harold Norris, the tail gunner, saw them first, approaching from the rear. *Lil' Operator* dodged in and out of cloud, and soon the bomber was down to just 500 ft, flying over towns and villages at rooftop height. Milburn Franklin resisted the temptation to strafe the streets, and instead the gunners took on the enemy fighters that continued to harass them until they were clear of the coast. Two enemy fighers were claimed destroyed.

At the coast Pyles eased up to 1,000 ft and the crew began throwing out all excess equipment. As a result the airspeed picked up a little and *Lil' Operator* flew on over the Channel without getting her feet wet, thanks to the gentle manipulation of the number one throttle. Number four engine had been providing good power, but failed to respond to the throttle, indicating that the supercharger had been inoperative at altitude.

Pyles put the *Operator* down at Bury St. Edmunds but number four engine resisted all Hatcher's attempts to 'kill' it until the last minute. Both pilots hit their brakes hard, and the aircraft stopped just short of the end of the tarmac. Smoke and dust shot into the air, and the crew sat there for a few seconds until the very real threat of fire prompted them to evacuate the aircraft.

Then came the distant scream of vehicles and the 'blood wagons' arrived with Col Castle at the helm. Castle made sure that no wounded were on board, and then demanded to know why Pyles had stopped on the runway, because other aircraft were about to land with wounded on board. Pyles explained the situation and pointed out that they could not taxi away on one engine. Col Castle walked across to the *Operator*, rubbed his chin, and returned to the crew. 'You boys have had a trying day,' he said, 'but you had better head for debriefing and then perhaps you can get some well deserved rest.'

For the first two weeks of November 1943 England was blanketed by thick, woolly fog, and airfields were lashed with intermittent showers and high winds. The weathermen predicted that the bad weather would lift on the morning of 16 November. However, crews were told to make ready for a special mission to Norway, where visual bombing could be used to advantage. Col Myron H. Keilman, CO of the 579th Bomb Squadron, 392nd BG, at Wendling, recalls: 'Enthusiasm generated by this intriguing mission was paramount. That night (15th November) the Division Field Order specified that the target was the secret German heavy water plant situated near the little town of Rjukan. It was a small target located in the mountains, about 75 miles from Oslo, and was difficult to identify. Bomb loads had to be reduced because the distance involved a round trip of about 1,200 miles. Only ten 500 pounders were carried in each aircraft, which were to bomb from an altitude of only 12,000 ft.

Meanwhile, the 1st Division was assigned the molybdenum mines at Knaben, and the Third was to attack a generating plant at Vermark in the Rjukan Valley. Intelligence sources indicated that both targets were connected with the German heavy water experiments, which would help give the Nazis the atomic bomb, but crews were not told this at the time.

At all 1st Bomb Division bases Fortresses were rolled from their muddy dispersal sites and lined up for the green light at the end of the runways. At Molesworth, the occasion was of special significance for the 303rd BG's group *Knockout Dropper*, which was flying its 50th mission. If it completed the raid it would set a new 8th Air Force record for a B-17.

Knockout Dropper was something of a 'good luck' ship, but the same could not be said of *Shady Lady II*, a B-17 which had flown with the 351st BG from Polebrook on the group's first mission, to Schweinfurt on 14 May 1943. Repairs to damage sustained on a recent mission had only just been completed, and the original crew refused to fly it any more. It was decided, therefore, that it be assigned to a new crew, led

An early B-17G 42-31134 in the 569th Bomb Squadron, 390th BG, en route to Rjukan, Norway, on 16 November 1943. (USAF.)

by Lt Joseph Wroblewski. As he recalls, *Shady Lady II* was the first aircraft assigned to the 351st to have a chin turret. This reduced the airspeed by 10 m.p.h. and made it a very clumsy and difficult aircraft to fly in formation.

'Knaben was my crew's first mission of the war,' Wroblewski recalls. 'I didn't expect to go with them on this one. Normally, an inexperienced pilot performed duties as a co-pilot with another crew on his first mission. The 'plane was heavily loaded with 2,500 gal of gas' and 12 500-pounders, but she made take-off easily. After forming we headed for Knaben, almost 700 miles distant. Groups of formations were scattered around in every direction, leaving vapour trails. All I could see of Norway were the mountains covered with snow. This mission was flown at 15,000 ft and it was very cold. All but the co-pilot and myself wore heated suits.'

Twenty B-24s had taken off from Wendling, and had joined with the rest of the 2nd Bomb Division over the North Sea. Landfall was made at Lanngesünd Fiord, where Luftwaffe fighters could be expected from Denmark. The formation flew past the city of Skien and north-west to the target. The 392nd lead crew overcame navigational problems caused by scattered and broken cloud which blotted out the landscape, and the Group made the IP on schedule. The bombing run was made using Automatic Flight Control Equipment. Bombardier 'Doc' Welland and the formation dropped bombs simultaneously on the nuclear energy development plant. The 389th however, encountered opposition, albeit weak, about 100 miles from the target. Three Ju 88s flew alongside the formation at 3 o'clock and each made three passes, but the Sky Scorpions suffered no serious damage and continued to the target. Only 40 mm cannon-fire greeted them as the group left the target at about 15,000 ft.

Meanwhile, the 3rd Division struck at Rjukan, about 75 miles due west of Oslo. As the formation approached the target area there was no opposition, confirming the belief that the Germans would not be expecting a raid so far north. The 94th BG arrived ten minutes early and had to make a 360° turn. Crews had been told to make certain that Norwegian workers were not on their shift when the bombs were released. As the Fortresses crossed the target for the second time thick cloud obscured the plant from view, and the formation was forced to make another 360° turn in the hope that they would clear.

Ruben Fier,the bombardier in Edward J. Sullivan's Fortress in the 94th formation, recalls: 'While doing our 360° turns off the coast, a B-17 from the 390th began doing slow gyrations in the sky without the benefit of anyone shooting at us. It felt like we were sitting in the balcony of a theatre watching an actor perform before us. The B-17 finally sliced into the water in an inverted position. We did not see any parachutes, nor could we understand what caused the unfortunate incident. Small ships were seen to head out towards the crash site, but we were unable to see survivors or what happened when the boats arrived on the scene.

'Our 'plane, momentarily attached to the 100th BG, began our run into the target behind other 'planes in formation before us, but due to the cloud they were unable to drop their bombs. When the 100th approached the target the clouds drifted away and we dropped the first bombs on the target, which were what appeared to be large concrete buildings nestled in the mountains, with flat roofs. As we later described to the *Stars and Stripes* reporter on our return to Bury, I could see the bombs mushroom into the flat roofs and, after a short period of time, flames of many colours escaped through the roofs. By the time we turned off the target and began flying out to sea, parallel to the course we flew in, the target area was engulfed in black smoke rising to the sky. The following groups were seen to be dropping their bombs into the smoke, and licks of flame were seen coming up from the target area. Little did we realize at the time that the heavy water was essential to the Germans in their early stages of nuclear research.'

The raid by approximately 155 bombers destroyed the power station in addition to other parts of the plant, causing a complete stoppage of the entire manufacturing process. The Germans later decided to ship their remaining heavy-water stockpile to Germany. However, all 546 tons of the heavy water were sent to the bottom of Lake Timm when the ferry boat being used to transport it was blown up by SOE agents over the deepest part of the lake.

The round trip to Norway was slightly shorter than the 1,800-mile circuit to Trondheim on 25 July 1943, and the 1,600-mile round trip to Heroya. Joe Wroblewski returned to Polebrook at 15:00 with 750 gal of fuel remaining. 'We were lucky to draw an easy mission first time out,' he says, 'although the going was rough coming into the English coast, with rain, snow and low ceilings. We gained some idea of what to expect for the future.'

Lt John P. Manning brought *Knockout Dropper* back to Molesworth to make it the first B-17 to complete 50 missions in the ETO. Crews told waiting newsmen that the only anti-aircraft fire they had encountered had come from a single flakship in one of the fiords. Crews in the 3rd Division rejoiced over their accurate bombing of Rjukan, saying that the explosion had lifted their aircraft suddenly,

95th BG Fortresses drop bombs on Wilhelmshaven in November 1943. The nearest aircraft is B-17F-30-DL 42-3153, Devil's Daughter. *(USAF.)*

'. . . as if a giant hand was pulling them upwards. As it was we hit it right on the nose.'

On 18 November the Liberators received a 'frag' order for a mission to bomb the Ju 88 assembly plant at Oslo-Kjeller and industrial targets in Oslo, while 127 B-17s were despatched to Gelsenkirchen. However, the Oboe sets aboard the leading Fortresses gave trouble and directed the formation too far north of the target. After an unsuccessful battle with the elements the B-17s were forced to return to England. The Liberators went all the way to Norway, and crews could quite easily distinguish the city of Oslo when the B-24s turned at the IP. At 12,000 ft the 392nd lined up for the bomb run. The skilled navigator-bombardier team of Swangren and Good systematically checked off the course heading, landmarks, true airspeed, wind drift and minutes to 'bombs away'. Myron Keilman, flying deputy lead, saw the target ' . . . standing out in the late morning sun,' and thought that ' . . . it would be a shame to miss it'.

'Bombardier Joe Whittaker was following through with every essential detail of a bombing run,' says Keilman. 'Should anything have happened to the lead airplane and it had suddenly aborted the bomb run, Joe had his bombsight cross-hairs on the aiming point of the assembly plant. If he had been given the command "take over", he could have successfully delivered the bombs.' Lt McGregor, in the lead aircraft, held his B-24 precisely on altitude and airspeed, and he and the 20 bombers following released the 210 500-pounders on the target simultaneously.

On the return leg the same scattered to broken clouds lay across the Skagerrak beneath the formation. Suddenly the gunners spotted German fighters skimming across the cloud tops opposite the B-24s' line of flight. A dozen-plus Ju 88s climbed to make fast diving passes as they circled in behind the bombers. Liberator 'outriders' moved into a tight formation providing the mutual protection of concentrated firepower. Diving in pairs, the German twin-engined fighters lobbed rockets and 20 mm explosive sheels into the 392nd. Tail and top turrets responded with bursts of machine gun fire, and the ball turret gunners opened up below as the fighters broke off the attack.

Sergeant T. E. Johnson, flying with Lt Everhart, shot up one fighter so badly that it burst into flames and was last seen in an uncontrollable dive. Two Liberators were hit and began to lose power. They could not keep up with the rest of the formation, and as they fell behind the Ju 88s concentrated their fire on them. The B-24 pilots dived for cover and sheltered in the clouds. For a time they played hide and seek as the fighters circled, and eventually the bombers were lost from view.

Wave after wave of enemy fighters pressed home their attacks, but Sgt Forrest Clark, the tail gunner aboard Lt R. C. Griffith's aircraft in the 44th, succeeded in shooting down one Ju 88. 'Sitting in the tail position,' he recalls, 'I could look back and see a line of seven to ten fighters lining up to attack our rear. "They're waiting in line to get at us," I called over the intercom, pressing the mike to my throat. Suddenly they attacked from all sides. Two shells went through the turret directly over my head, missing me by inches. I followed one after the other as the Luftwaffe pilots zoomed in at our tail and then dove beneath us to come up in front and swing and line-up for another pass. One after another they came. Closer and closer. I tracked them with my twin .50-calibre guns, but could not get a good lead on any until they passed under us and then shot up again for the waist gunners to get shots at them.

'Finally, I fixed one in my sights as he levelled out and came in faster and faster. "So close," I said to myself. "He's going to hit us: he's going to ram us." I gripped the triggers of both guns, levelled them out and pressed down. I kept holding the triggers down, hoping they would not jam the belts. I could see my tracers going out in long lines right into his wing roots. Bright flashes of fire and traces kept boring into his wings until he came so close I could see the outline of the German pilot's head in the cockpit. Just as he slipped under us I saw a thin trail of smoke coming from the engine.' Clark was almost completely out of ammunition, and a 20 mm shell hit Sgt Bill Kuban, the ball gunner, who was bringing him more rounds, in the head, knocking him unconscious and bleeding to the floor. Clark heard the bale-out bell, but at first he had difficulty in getting out of his shattered turret. Two men, Sgts John Gibboney and L. J. McAndrews, were getting ready to jump through the open camera hatch. Clark prayed, because he knew he would not survive long in the ice-cold sea if he jumped: 'I actually went down on my knees and prayed. Much to my surprise, just about that time the fighter attacks suddenly stopped and the Germans left us to what they must have thought was our death.'

Lt Houle's B-24, which was severely damaged, tottered gallantly to within 50 miles of the English coast with safety in sight. But by now his fuel indicators were reading zero and he was forced to ditch. The aircraft seemed to break in two, and four minute figures were seen to slip into the icy waters of the North Sea. Griffith, himself flying on three faltering engines, circled over the scene while his radio-operator called ASR. With his own fuel supply running low, Griffith dipped his wing in salute to his fallen comrades and turned towards his base. ASR were unable to trace any of the crew or the aircraft. Griffith's Liberator spluttered on, just above the sea. Clark adds: 'More than once the call went out from the pilot to prepare to ditch, but we had a wounded gunner who would surely die if we ditched in the icy water. We limped on, and more than once it seemed all engines quit and the 'plane stuttered as if in its death throes. But the 'plane would not die.'

Griffith made it back to Shipdham, where the landing gear failed to work. The flight engineer Earl Parrish tried desperately to crank it down by hand, but this failed too. Griffith ordered everyone to bale out. Forrest Clark was certain he had landed in Holland, but a Norfolk farmer holding a pitchfork soon reassured him. Clark fell to the ground and gripped it with both hands in a gesture of relief and thanskgiving. Griffith managed to land the badly damaged B-24 on one wheel and Kuban's life was saved. Two hours later repair crews checking the wreckage found two unexploded German shells in the one good engine that had brought the crew home.

Six B-24s were lost on the Oslo raid, including three Liberators, one

Lieutenant R. C. Griffiths' B-24, 41-29161, in the 67th Bomb Squadron, 44th BG, which crash-landed at Shipdham after the mission to Norway on 16 November 1943. (Ursel P. Harvel.)

each from the 93rd, 392nd and 44th, which were forced to land in Sweden. *War Baby* in the 93rd landed at Orebro, as did one from the 392nd. The 44th BG aircraft circled the airfield at Trollhatton, firing signal flares to inform the Swedes that it was about to land. US policy at that time called for the burning of any aircraft that landed in neutral territory, and the 44th crew set fire to their Liberator shortly after landing.

The bad weather continued over the next few days, but did not prevent RAF Bomber Command bombing Berlin on the night of 22 November. This led to rumours of an American follow-up raid being mounted on the capital the next day, but it was cancelled because of bad weather.

On Friday 26 November 633 bombers, the largest formation ever assembled by the 8th, were directed against targets as far apart as Bremen and Paris. Two new B-17 groups, the 401st and 447th, had joined the 8th during November, and the 401st made its combat debut this day. Col Harold W. Bowman's outfit helped swell the 1st Division stream to 505 bombers briefed for the port area of Bremen, while 128 B-17s of the 3rd Division for Paris. Unfortunately the skies were unexpectedly cloudy, and the 3rd Division was forced to return with its bomb loads intact.

A 94th BG B-17, piloted by Lt Johnny Pyles, was rammed by a Bf-109 near the target, at Ivry. The German pilot was thought to be already dead as he approached the formation, and the fighter flew straight at Pyles' ship and hit it between the number two engine and the fuselage. Cliff Hatcher, Adolph Delzoppo and Erwin Smith were not flying with Pyles that day. They had been replaced by three other crewmembers for combat indoctrination. The only survivor was the tail gunner, Harold E. Norris. The tail broke free during the impact explosion, and Norris managed to bale out before it fluttered like a leaf to the ground. He evaded capture and was passed along the French Underground to Spain, where he recovered from frostbite and was returned to England.

The 1st Division, enroute to Bremen, encountered persistent fighter

Fortresses of the 96th BG release their bombs on the Focke-Wulf factory at Bremen on 26 November 1943. The nearest aircraft is B-17F-45-VE Winnie C, *42-6099, in the 337th Bomb Squadron, which was felled by 'friendly' bombs over Orianenberg on 22 March 1944. Second Lieutenant Nathan Young and his crew failed to return.* (USAF.)

attacks by up to 100 German fighters. Claude Campbell, flying the 25th and final mission of his tour with the 303rd BG Group that day, recalls: 'Focke-Wulfs jumped us before we reached the enemy coast, but I did evasive action and the boys shot 'em off. All kinds of enemy fighters were in the air, including old Stuka dive-bombers; a perfect illustration of Hitler's shortage of first-line fighters. We ran into a typically heavy barrage of flak over Bremen. The target was covered with clouds, and bombing results could not be determined. P-47s picked us up and escorted us from the target so the enemy stayed away.' The 8th lost 29 Fortresses and five fighters.

On 30 November 'Pappy' Colby flew his 25th and final mission when the Fortresses were despatched to Solingen. Pappy made it despite a leaking oxygen system. 'As long as I live,' he says, 'I will never forget the first glimpse of the English coast which told me I was coming home for good. I remember saying to myself, "Pappy, with God's help you made it".'

The next day, 1 December, Col Budd J. Peaslee led a PFF attack on industrial targets at Solingen. S/Sgt John W. Butler in *Tennessee Rambler*, in the 93rd BG, wrote: 'We had to fly 15 minutes into France before we picked up our P-47 escorts. I was very glad to see those babies. We were attacked by Jerry, and he really pressed his attacks. We were under attack for 45 minutes, and I really sweated it out. There was also plenty of flak. We couldn't see the target, so we had to go around to the secondary. There was plenty of flak there, too, and *Iron Ass*, on our wing, had his wing shot off. Red Carey, our right waist gunner, shot a Ju 88 down. Four yellow-nosed Bf 109s came diving down so close I could see the 'chute harness on Jerry. Carey fired at them, but no luck. I fired over 90 rounds at a Me 110, a Bf 109 and a Ju 88, but I really didn't get a good shot at them. I saw one bandit attack *Southwind* and it was in trouble. Three 'chutes came out, then five more bandits came down and they shot off the left wing. It went into a spin and burst into flames. It was T. U. Collins, my pilot's, 25th and final mission, so he was very happy.' More than 20 bombers were lost on the raid.

B-17G-5-BO Fletcher's Castoria *42-31220 in the 100th BG, named for Lt William Fletcher, crashed on take-off from Thorpe Abbotts on 4 December 1943.* (Via Robert E. Foose.)

On 5 December about 550 bombers set out for airfields in France, but thick cloud prevented any bombing. Some crewmen, like S/Sgt. John Butler, the tail gunner in *O Carole N Chick* in the 93rd BG feared that the mission would not count towards their tour. Butler recalls: 'I had just called the navigator over the interphone that it would be nice if we could run into some flak so we could get credit for a mission, when all of a sudden I had all the flak I wanted. A ship in the 389th received a direct hit and blew into a million pieces. Two 'chutes got out. The whole wing came off in one piece and dropped by itself, turning lazy circles. It was all on fire and reminded me of a cartwheel from the Fourth of July.'

On 11 December the weather cleared sufficiently for 523 bombers to hit Emden, but rocket-firing Me 110s and Me 210s accounted for the loss of 17 heavies, including the lead ship piloted by Capt Hiram Skogmo in the 390th BG. Two days later 640 of 710 B-17s and B-24s

L–R: Alvar Woodall, top turret gunner; Harold L. Morris ball turret gunner; and John R. Ward, all from Lt Forrest V. Poore's crew in the 385th BG. Woodall and Morris were, killed flying in Mary Ellen III, *one of three 385th BG B-17s lost on the mission to Emden on 11 December 1943.* (William Nicholls.)

Blondie II, *B-17F-90-BO 42-30182 of the 95th BG, was shot down on the Emden mission on 11 December 1943. (Mike Bailey.)*

despatched bombed targets in Germany. The 2nd Bomb Division, which included 12 Liberators of the 445th BG Group from Tibenham on their first mission, attacked the U-boat yards at Kiel, while the Fortresses hit Bremen and Hamburg. On 16 December 535 bombers, including Liberators of the 446th BG based at Bungay (Flixton), making their 2nd Bomb Division debut, made a follow-up raid on Bremen. On 20 December metal foil strips called 'Window', or 'Chaff', were dropped over the city during the third raid in a week, to confuse enemy radar. More than 470 bombers hit the port area, but 27 heavies were shot down by fighters.

The 8th was stood down on 21 December, but the following day 439 B-127s and B-24s attacked marshalling yards at Osnabruck and Münster. The 2nd Bomb Division, its numbers increased by the addition of the 448th BG, was assigned Osnabruck. Sgt Francis X. Sheehan, an armourer-gunner in *Harmful Lil' Armful*, flown by Lt Alvin D. Skaggs, recalls: 'Osnabruck turned out to be heavily defended. Although flak was minimal, the fighters were there in abundance, as we found out. My first encounter with combat

A B-24H in the 445th BG loses part of a wing after a direct hit, and begins its death spiral. The 445th made its debut on 13 December 1943. (Mary Beth Barnard via Mike Bailey.)

B-24 Liberators of the 446th BG in formation. The Bungay group made its debut on 16 December 1943. (USAF.)

commenced with black puffs of flak dotting the sky around us. It was something we never did get accustomed to. The effectiveness of this was shown when part of a ship began trailing smoke and parachutes. As we approached the target the aircraft to our immediate right dropped its entire bomb load on the left wing of a wingman that had drifted down and under him. Stunned, I watched the damaged aircraft fade left and over on its back. I prayed for 'chutes to appear, but none did. I was brought back to reality by the call over the intercom – "Fighters!" Twin-engined enemy aircraft were lobbing rockets into a formation of bombers to my right. At first they seemed oblivious to our presence. I fired at one of the fighers, which began trailing smoke and fire and went down through the clouds. I was later given credit for this.'

John Butler, flying left waist gunner in *Judith Lynn* in the 93rd BG formation, also had his hands full. 'Me 110s fired rockets into the formation behind us. One hit one of our 'planes and put a large hole in the vertical stabilizer. Another B-24 had about 10 ft of his wing shot off by fighters. She went into a spin and pulled out of it, then went

B-17G-1-BO Pee Tey Kun, *42-31033, of the 613th Bomb Squadron, 401st BG, after crash-landing at Deenthorpe on 16 December 1943. This aircraft and 1st Lt Stephen J. Nasen's crew failed to return on 11 January 1944. (Via Mike Bailey.)*

Crews take a breather below the tail of 390th BG B-17G-30-BO 42-31892 before their next mission. (Via Holmes.)

into a steep dive. There were no 'chutes. Another B-24 hit by fighters went into an inside loop and started down in a dive. She exploded and broke into three pieces. There were no 'chutes.' Althogether, 13 Liberators were lost, including two each from the 446th, 448th and 445th BGs.

On Christmas Eve the bombers were despatched to V1 flying bomb sites in France, which went under the code-name 'No-ball'. To Joe Wroblewski it seemed that 'every 'plane in Britain was up' on 24 December. The Fortress formations were further strengthened by the 447th BG from Rattlesden, which made its debut this day as the 26th heavy bomb group to join the 8th. Some 670 bombers bombed 23 V1

Bombs away from a 390th BG B-17G high over Germany. (Via Ian McLachlan.)

sites without loss. VIII Bomber Command was stood down from Christmas Day until 30 December, when 658 heavies, escorted by P-38s and P-15s, bombed oil plants at Ludwigshafen near the German-Swiss border. Cliff Hatcher, who flew with the 94th BG, recalls: 'We were attacked by Me 110s, Me 210s and Fw 190s, which caused a lot of damage. The German fighters lined up wingtip to wingtip off to our right, out of range of our .50 calibres. About 18 of them were lined up like a row of battleships, and when they fired simultaneously it was like a naval broadside. They fired air-to-air rockets, and one went right over our right wing by about 5 ft. I felt sure it would hit the top turret, but it missed us.'

Sgt Sheehan in *Harmful Lil' Armful*, in the 448th BG recalls: 'Lt Tom Foster's crew was flying our right wing in a very tight formation when suddenly a Bf 109 appeared in a head-on attack with tracers streaming at our left side over and under our ship. Shells began to rake the front and top of Foster's 'plane. The Plexiglas on the top turret shattered and S/Sgt James Brant slumped over, fatally injured. At the same time bullets tore through the pilots' compartment, killing Foster. Francis Rogers, the co-pilot, took over and moved out of formation. The whole centre section above the bomb bay was aflame. We could still see crewmen in the waist position as the ship began to fade away from the formation. Several men managed to bale out only seconds before a terrific explosion caused their 'plane to completely disintegrate.' Altogether, 23 bombers and 12 American fighters were lost on the raid, and 23 German fighters were claimed destroyed.

On New Year's Eve VIII Bomber Command completed its second year in England with all-out raids on airfields in France. Robert 'Peck' Wilcox, a bombardier in the 351st BG at Polebrook, recalls: 'The Bordeaux area was covered with thick cloud cover, and we headed for Cognac. There were some scattered clouds but no flak and no fighters. Up ahead I saw our target. Already the lead bombardier was sighting in on it, and on we flew. I wondered why we weren't doing any evasive action. We were closing fast and all of a sudden all hell broke loose. The lead 'plane was the victim of a direct hit. (Col William Hatcher, the CO, was later reported to be a PoW.) Our 'plane was hit; the air was turbulent. A big hole had been blasted in the nose. I dropped our bombs, but no-one had a chance to look down. 'Planes seemed to be going down all over. The formation was shot to pieces, I would say. We had an engine on fire and Bender, our pilot, asked Collins about the damage and the fire. We made a circle all by ourselves and we were all alone. I mean all alone. What was left of the formation had headed for England.' Altogether, the 351st lost nine B-17s.

Bender's crew baled out. Andy Anderson walked out through Spain in one month, and Harold Freeman followed him out in three months. 'Peck' Wilcox remained at large in France until September 1944, when he linked up with the 7th Army during the liberation. The rest of the crew were made PoWs. After landing, the one regret 'Peck' Wilcox had was: 'It was a long way from home and I wasn't going to be in Peterborough for any New Year's Eve party.'

Baling out of an aircraft over occupied France was usually a hit and

385th BG crew deep in thought at a mission debriefing at Great Ashfield. (Via Ian McLachlan.)

miss affair. Sometimes, like the majority of Bender's crew, crew members were rescued from the clutches of the Germans by the Resistance. Others were not so fortunate. However, at least one downed crew recall their sojourn with the French as a memorable time in their young lives. A crew who baled out near Paris were 'grabbed' by the Free French. Instead of being hidden in a farmhouse, six of the crew were taken into the French capital and hidden in a house of prostitution. One of the crew, who was 20 years old, recalled that he weighed 160 lb when he baled out and, several months later, when they were moved, he weighed 140 lb. Apparently he could not be confined without sampling the merchandise!

Chapter Nine

The battles of 'Big Week'

FOG AND RAIN grounded the bombers until 4 January, when over 500 bombers attacked the shipyards at Kiel. The next day bad weather interfered with the mission, and only 216 bombers of the 1st Bomb Division returned to the port. The 91st BG lifted off from Bassingbourn to become the first group in the 8th to complete 100 missions, although it had paid dearly for the privilege, losing more aircraft and crews on mission than any other group.

Meanwhile, Fortresses of the 3rd Division flew to airfields in France. The 94th BG was assigned Bordeaux airfield. Cliff Hatcher in *Belle of Maryland* whose 10th mission this would be, recalls: 'For some reason the powers-that-be decided that the best route to Bordeaux was to fly straight in as if we were going to Germany, then turn due south and fly the whole length and breadth of France and out to sea, hitting the target as we went.'

Ralph K. Patton, the co-pilot in Glenn B. Johnson's crew, adds: 'We had been briefed, and it wasn't very reassuring, that we could expect heavy flak. There was also an operational training group of young fighter pilots about 60 miles south of Bordeaux, and they had at least 60 fighters. Our fighter escort wouldn't be able to stay with us over the target because of fuel limitations. We could expect the "schoolboys" to be there in force.' The crew's usual ship, the *Horrible*

B-17F-120-BO 42-30767 of the 367th 'Clay Pigeons' Bomb Squadron, 306th BG, crashed on take-off at Thurleigh on 5 January 1944, killing the pilot, Capt Ian R. Elliott, who was flying almost his last mission, and seven of the crew. (Richards.)

Hanks, was out of commission with a cracked air intake, and their replacement ship, '212, had been badly shot up and had only just managed to make it back to England on a previous mission.

Hatcher continues: 'We came under constant enemy attack from the time we hit France until we headed out to sea. Three Fw 190s queued up as we approached Bordeaux, and the leader turned in towards our formation for a head-on attack. The two wingmen must have been trainees, because they peeled off and headed for home. The leader was shot down, but another three queued up, this time in front of us. They must have been veterans because they barreled in, straight at us. Trimble, the bombardier, shot at the three as they bore in and was credited with one "kill" and with damaging the other. All three were burning. Our left waist gunner and our tail gunner each claimed a Bf 109.'

Patton noted: 'Just after we had dumped our bomb load a shock hit the 'plane. Johnson and I struggled to right it. Black anti-aircraft puffs were all around us. As we moved out of range the call came in over the intercom – "Bandits, 12 o'clock high!" Then they came in at 3 o'clock. Suddenly, five Fw 190s in single file came in from 1 o'clock level. On the second pass we knocked one of them down. On the third pass they fired four canon shots in the tail before turning and heading back. Suddenly the tail assembly began shuddering, and we had to reduce our speed to 150 m.p.h.

'Slowly the formation pulled ahead of us. When we reached the Breton coast the rest of the formation was almost eight to ten miles ahead of us. Suddenly, as anti-aircraft fire began to burst close to us and as we swerved to elude it, our gunners spotted two Fw 190s hiding in the glare of the sun. Our tail gunner called out: "Here he comes!" As he released his microphone switch I could hear his guns open fire. Those were the last words I heard him speak.' The Fortress was raked by 20 mm cannon fire and the tail gunner and Jim Stewart, the ball-turret gunner, were killed. Johnson felt the control pressure go limp as the nose shot up violently, and gave the order to bale out. Sgt William A. Munson, the waist gunner, was killed on the way home. Patton, Jack McGough the bombardier, and Glen Johnson all landed safely and were eventually returned to England via the 'Bonaparte' evasion lines. Ralph Hall, the engineer, returned in August after crossing the Pyrenees into Spain and coming home via Gibraltar.

Still under attack, the remaining B-17s in the 94th BG headed for the temporary safety of the sea until the time came to recross the Normandy Peninsula. Cliff Hatcher continues: 'When we were over the Bay of Biscay I motioned Kacsuda, the pilot, to take over, but I couldn't take my hand off the throttles. My hands were literally frozen to the throttles (we had been under constant attack for maybe three hours).

'Over Normandy we ran low on ammo'. Trimble had exhausted his in the chin turret, and joined Ball, the navigator, in the nose. He began firing the flexible .50-calibre cheek gun. Ball fired the flexible .50 on the port side. Suddenly, their guns jerked to a stop. They looked at their guns in disbelief, only to discover that they had both been firing from the same ammo' belt!' *Belle of Maryland* made it back to Bury St. Edmunds, but four other B-17s of the 94th did not.

The 5 January missions were the last under the auspices of VIII Bomber Command. The 15th Air Force had now been established in Italy, and it was decided to embrace both the 8th and 15th in a new headquarters called US Strategic Air Forces, Europe, at Bushey Hall, Teddington, Middlesex which had previously been Headquarters, 8th Air Force. 'Tooey' Spaatz returned to England to command the new organization. Lt Gen Ira C. Eaker was posted to the Mediterranean theatre and replaced at 8th Air Force (whose HQ moved to High Wycombe) by Gen Jimmy Doolittle, the famed Tokyo leader and former air racing pilot.

The first mission under the auspices of the USSAFE was flown on 7 January, when 420 B-17s and B-24s caused considerable damage to chemical and substitute war material plants at Ludwigshafen and the engineering and transport industries in the twin city of Mannheim. Major James M. Stewart, the famous Hollywood actor, who in 1940 had won an Academy Award for his role in *The Philadelphia Story* and now CO of the 703rd Bomb Squadron, led 48 B-24s of the 445th to the I. G. Farben Industrie plant at Ludwigshafen. As the bombs doors opened a shell burst directly under his wing, but Stewart managed to regain control and complete the bomb run. Beyond the target he joined the wayward 389th BG, which had strayed off course, and although the 389th lost eight aircraft, his action probably prevented total annihilation.

One of the 389th Liberators, flown by Capt Wilhite, was lost when it was attacked by a rocket-firing Fw 190 near Paris. A rocket exploded

Maj James Stewart, who became 453rd BG Operations Officer on 30 March 1944, with crew members of Male Call *at Old Buckenham.* Male Call *was originally assigned to Charles A. Ward's crew in the 734th Squadron. It flew 95 missions and was the only original group aircraft which was still flying at the end of the war.* (Frank Thomas.)

Capt Wilhite's crew in the 389th BG had returned to combat duty after being released from internment in Portugal in the summer of 1943, after engine trouble prevented them from continuing to North Africa in July 1943 for the Ploesti mission. Back row, L–R: Sam Flatter, James McConnel, Lt Harry, Capt Wilhite, Rudy Salties, Harold Saunders. Front Row, L–R: Charles 'Denny' Dewett, Max Snyder, Roger Caplinger, Bob Sweatt. All the men in this photo except Sweatt were killed (Harry did not fly the 7 January 1944 mission). (Russ D. Hayes.)

in the cockpit, and other hits signalled the end of the bomber. S/Sgt Robert H. Sweatt, the only survivor, recalls: 'The Fw 190 knocked our right wing off at about 21,000 ft, and by the time I got my 'chute on the 'plane was spinning and burning. I was halfway out of the waist window when the B-24 exploded, and I was blown out. Wendell Dailey, my co-pilot managed to get out, but the Germans killed him when he landed on the ground. [The rest of the crew were never found.] I fell about a mile before I could get the 'chute open. My jugular vein was punctured, and I had to pinch my neck to stop the flow of blood. Later, when I landed, I filled the hole with mud.' When the French found him Sweatt was unconscious and seriously ill from wounds and fever. The French hid him in a secret medical facility for several weeks until he recovered. While he was in hospital his watch, which had been attached to his steel helmet when he baled out, was found, still running, and returned to him. Sweatt was later transferred to Paris, sent along the French 'Bonaparte' underground line, and ultimately reached England on 23 March 1944.

A host of enemy fighters had attacked the returning bombers near the Biscay coast. John Butler, tail gunner in *Texas Rambler*, piloted by Lt L. D. Lange in the 93rd BG, wrote, 'They shot down seven B-24s in our group, including both 'planes flying on our wing. The "Abbeville Kids" really are very hot pilots and they don't scare very easily. I noticed four Bf 109s at about 1,200 yards at 7 o'clock. I had my guns on them to see what they would do. They were just milling around. Then one peeled off and came into attack. I held my fire until he was about 500 yards. Then I opened up. I fired about 70 rounds. He started to burn and peeled off toward 8 o'clock. Then he threw his belly up. I let loose about 30 rounds. The pilot baled out and the 'plane started down and then exploded. My right waist gunner shot

B-17G-1-VE 42-39822 of the 333rd Bomb Squadron, 94th BG, piloted by 2nd Lt Donald D. Sharp, was shot down at 13:10 on 11 January 1944 over Rheine, Germany, on the mission to Brunswick. (Hans-Heiri Stapfer.)

down a Fw 190 and the pilot baled out as the 'plane exploded.' Altogether, the 8th lost 12 bombers and seven fighters on the 7 January raids.

On 11 January a maximum effort involving more than 570 B-17s and B-24s was attempted against aircraft factories at Waggum, Halberstadt and Oschersleben in the Brunswick area, a city notorious for its flak and fighter defences. However, the fighter escort soon became lost in the cloud layers over England and many were forced to abort the mission. Two hours into the mission the 2nd and 3rd Divisions were ordered to abandon the operation but the 1st Division, which was about 100 miles from Brunswick, was allowed to continue, with disastrous results. Some 34 of the 174 B-17s despatched to Oschersleben were shot down, while two wings assigned the plant at nearby Halberstadt came through practically unscathed. The 303rd lost ten bombers and the 351st seven. The 94th lost seven bombers and an eighth, *Belle of Maryland*, piloted by Cliff Hatcher, was so badly damaged that it never flew again. Sixty bombers were lost on the three raids. The 94th received its second Presidential Unit Citation, and in August 1944 all of the 1st Division groups which took part in the raid were similiarly awarded.

Vast banks of strato-cumulus clouds covering most of Germany prevented the visual bombing of targets, so throughout the remainder of January and early February attacks on targets in France became the order of the day. One exception occurred on 30 January, when a record 778 heavies were despatched to the aircraft factories at Brunswick. Some 701 aircraft bombed using PFF techniques, while 51 dropped their bombs on targets of opportunity. Twenty aircraft were lost on the mission.

Of the 29 missions flown during January and February 1944, 13 were

B-17G-20-BO Minnie The Mermaid, *42-31614, joined the 533rd Bomb Squadron, 381st BG, on 22 January 1944.* (Via Mike Bailey.)

to V1 rocket sites. These strikes were no longer regarded as 'milk runs' because the Germans, having realized their vulnerability to air attack, had moved in additional flak batteries, and the bombing altitude was raised to 15,000 ft and higher. On 5 February the bomber formations were swelled by the addition of B-17s of the 452nd BG, commanded by Lt Col Herbert O. Wangeman, and B-24s of the 453rd BG, commanded by Col Joe Miller. Both groups were based near Norwich, at Deopham Green and Old Buckenham respectively. Three days later, 237 bombers attacked Frankfurt-on-Main while 127 bombers attacked V1 sites at Watten and Siracourt and another 78 bombed targets of opportunity.

On 12 February 85 B-24s returned to the St. Pol/Siracourt area and

B-24H 41-25654 of the 453rd BG amid contrails over Germany in early 1944. The 453rd made its debut on 5 February 1944. (USAF.)

The crew of Reddy Teddy *of the 93rd BG, with whom Butler flew his 25th and final mission, as right waist gunner, to the V1 sites at St Pol/Siracourt on 12 February 1944. Standing, L–R: 1st Lt Glenn E. Tedford, pilot; 1st Lt Kenneth E. Keen, co-pilot; 1st Lt William N. Roberts, bombardier; 1st Lt Norman C. Hansen, navigator. Kneeling, L–R: T/Sgt McAffee, engineer; S/Sgt Wolfe, left waist gunner; T/Sgt Keenan, radio operator; S/Sgt Neim, ball gunner; S/Sgt Williams, right waist; S/Sgt Dunkel, tail gunner. (John Butler.)*

bombed the V1 sites again. John Butler, who was flying his 25th and final mission of his tour, – was right waist gunner in *Reddy Teddy*, piloted by Lt G. E. Tedford in the 93rd BG. He wrote: 'We took off at 07:30 to bomb Siracourt from 18,000 ft. Flak was pretty good, but none was close to us. It was minus 22. When I left the French coast behind I was very happy. I never wanted to see the French coast again except on a postcard or on a newsreel. It was a good mission to finish up on. I was a pretty happy guy when I landed.'

General Doolittle had been biding his time, waiting for a period of relatively fine weather in which to mount a series of raids on the German aircraft industry. The meteorologists informed him that the week of 20–25 February, which was to go down in history as 'Big Week', would be ideal for such an offensive. Myron Keilman recalls: 'The weather had been so bad that the 392nd had flown only 16 missions since 1 January. But by 20 February we had been both alerted and briefed, and had taxied for take-off nearly every morning since Gen Doolittle had taken command. We waited for hours in the dense fog before the red flare fired from the control tower signalled "mission cancelled". Then back to airplanes' dispersal pads; back to the dank Nissen huts and back to the damp, ice-cold cots for needed sleep and tomorrow's alert. Damn the foggy weather, damn the war and damn Gen Doolittle too.'

Like so many mornings in England, the sky in the early hours of 20 February was clear, but a few stray clouds drifting in from the North Sea gave warning of an instrument assembly above 10/10ths cloud by take-off time. A force of over 1,000 heavies was assembled as the anticipated cloud scudded across eastern England, bringing snow squalls which threatened to disrupt the mission. The 1st and 2nd Bomb Divisions were briefed to hit the Bf 109 plants at Leipzig, which had been bombed only a few hours earlier by RAF Bomber Command. The 3rd Division, meanwhile, would fly an equally long and arduous

Friendship between the US 8th Air Force and the people of Britain in World War Two was never greater than when Americans came calling with gifts and sweets for young British children near the bases. (Via Pat Everson.)

route, to Poznan in Poland.

Lt Lowell Watts, pilot of *Blitzin' Betsy* in the 388th BG, who was flying his 19th mission that day, viewed the map in the briefing room at Knettishall with a senses of foreboding. 'The map was covered as always, but there was an extension on the right hand side of it. Our regular map, which reached from England to east of Berlin, was too small for this raid! The cover was pulled away and there it was! The red tape ran out from England over the North Sea to Denmark, across it, out over the Baltic Sea, then back in over eastern Germany and into Poland. Poznan was our target. It lay almost 1,000 miles away.

'Just before taxi time we started the engines. There was no point using any gas we could save. We took off, climbed through the clouds and assembled. The rendevous time was cut in half and we started out over the North Sea, tightening up the formation more as we went along and climbing to 11,000 ft before levelling off. We used the lowest possible power setting and the lowest r.p.m. possible, and flew as smoothly as we could in an effort to make our gas last.

'Near Denmark the clouds began breaking up, and by the time we crossed the Danish coast it was as clear as a bell beneath us. Something else met us besides good weather: Jerry fighters. Off on our left a group was under heavy fighter attack. Two bombers went down. Later, we saw ten 'chutes drop from another crippled 'plane but, pilotless as it was, this ship, slowly losing altitude, continued on eastwards, and not until we were across the Danish peninsula did we lose sight of it.

'The Fw 190s attacking us kept sweeping in until we were well out over the Baltic and the quaint red-roofed villages of Denmark had blended into the horizon beneath us. We changed course to the south-east and climbed to 17,000 ft. Clouds were piling up beneath us again, and the German coast was covered by them. On and on we flew. We were almost to Poland now and Ju 88s, Me 110s and Me 210s had replaced the Focke-Wulfs, making steady, unrelenting diving attacks on our formation. Nowhere could we see a break in the undercast. There was a ruling that no target in occupied country would be bombed except by contact bombing. Targets in Poland came under this category, so after flying those hundreds of miles, many of them under fighter attack, we had to turn back, still carrying our bombs, tired, hungry, with the fighters still on us and a feeling of frustration in the knowledge that Poznan's factories would still be turning out Focke-Wulfs on the morrow.

'We checked our gas tanks. They were less than half full, and we were still lugging our bombs. The loss of only one engine would be enough to make us run out of gas. As it was, it would be nip and tuck. We should just make it, but maybe we wouldn't. We were still at 17,000 ft, using a lot more gas than we would had we dropped our bombs and gone back down to 11,000. Sixteen of our 21 'planes were still in formation. Our other two groups were a little better off. We had lost the left wing and the "diamond" ships in our element, the second element of the low squadron. The VHF crackled to life. "Wolfgang Yellow, Wolfgang Yellow, this is Wolfgang White calling. Open bomb bay doors. We're approaching our target." Now over Germany, we were going to bomb a secondary target by PFF through clouds.

'Our bomb doors swung open as we fell in behind the 96th Bomb Group, which had the PFF ship. Suddenly, flak appeared: big, ugly, mushrooming billows of black, blossoming out around the angry red flash of the shell's explosions. The flak became thicker and more accurate as we neared the point of bomb release. Our ship bounced as the sound of ripping metal brought a lump to our throats. A big jagged hole had made its appearance between our number one and two engines. The number two gas gauge still showed no indication of a leak. There were two rips in the number two cowling, but the oil pressure was up and the engine was running smoothly. Up ahead two long streams of white arched down beneath the lead ship in the 96th formation. Those were the marker bombs of the PFF ship. In a few seconds we were nearing those markers. As we passed them we dumped our bombs, happy to feel the 'plane leap upwards, free of its load. The flak pounded us for about a minute longer, then it began to disappear. At last we were heading home, free of our bombs and able to cut down on our power settings. Only a few Ju 88s were around. Now and then they would lob a rocket at us, careful to stay out of range of our .50s. One formation of 88s lined up behind us and started pumping rockets at us. The projectiles sailed into the high squadron, bursting like flak. Fire broke out on the right wing of one 'plane. It flew for a minute longer, then rolled up on one wing and started down. Suddenly, there was a flash, a huge billowy puff of smoke and jagged pieces of broken, twisted metal fluttered aimlessly earthwards.

'The hours dragged on. We'd been up almost eight hours now, and we were crossing Denmark with the North Sea still separating us from

England. Leaving the coast, we let down to 10,000 ft and loosened the formation as the fighters fell away. A glance at the gas gauge was anything but heartening. It would be a close one getting back today. We checked everything we might need if we should have to ditch.

'The sun was riding low in the west as we neared England. Every few minutes one of our 'planes would drop out of formation to save gas. A few we heard calling pitifully to Air Sea Rescue, and soon below us one of the lone 'planes would glide with a splash into the sea, its gas exhausted. "Pilot from navigator, we're over England. You can see a spot of coastline off to our right through that little hole in the clouds." "Good deal. Guess we'll make it if this let down doesn't take too long."

'We watched the radio compass swing around, telling us we were passing over our field. Our squadron leader zoomed gently up and down. His left wing ship peeled off and was followed by the squadron lead ship, his right wing ship, and then our 'plane. The ships were letting down on a heading of 90°. disappearing one by one into the fluffy folds of white below us. Soon we were skimming the clouds, then we were in the soup, dark, lonely and uninviting. I was watching only the instruments now, heading 90°, flaps one third down, wheels down, airspeed 150, vertical speed 500 ft per minute. Down, down, down we went, the gloom darkening each second. At 1,000 ft we were still on instruments. We were all dead tired, but during the let-down we forgot it for the moment while eager eyes tried to pierce the murk for signs of the ground or other 'planes which might hit us. At 750 ft we broke out. It was raining but visibility was fair. We turned almost 180° until the radio compass read '0' and we flew until landmarks became familiar. Finally, we saw flares up ahead and soon the runway became visible. A 'plane was on his approach. Another, too close to him, pulled up and went around again. We started our approach and let down with the fuel warning lights on and the gas gauges reading almost empty. We couldn't stay up much longer. Kennedy turned the turbos full on in case we should need the power if we had to go around again. Old *Blitzin' Betsy* settled down, floated a second and touched the runway. We rolled to the end of the runway, another mission completed. Then we realized how tired we were.'

The same tiredness was prevalent on the 1st Division's mission to Leipzig and the 2nd Bomb Division's strike on Brunswick and Magdeburg, which proved costly. As the 1st Division formation crossed into Germany it encountered single- and twin-engined fighters of almost every type. The German pilots adopted American single-engined-fighter tactics in an effort to gain favourable attacking positions, as Joe Wroblewski, in the 351st BG formation, recalls. 'About 20 Bf 109s hit us just before the target and came in four at a time, head-on. They flew right through our formation and slow-rolled beautifully while shooting. In the excitement some gunner from our own formation shot through one of our engines, cutting a gas balance line and mixture control cable. Besides having a few screwed-up indicators on the panel and a worried mind, everything was okay.'

In a last attempt to deter the 1st Division the Germans employed cable bombing methods. It did not work. The leading 401st BG, led by Col Harold W. Bowman, the CO, leading the 94th Wing, flew on to the briefed point west of Brunswick and diverged to bomb the target. Despite a heavy flak barrage during the bomb run, which heavily damaged Col Bowman's aircraft, the formation bombed with excellent results. Direct hits were achieved on the principal assembly shop at the Erla Maschinenwerk Messerschmitt production factory, and its other large assembly building was observed to be on fire as the bombers left the target area.

Three medals of Honor were won this day. Lt William R. Lawley, a pilot in the 305th BG, brought his badly disabled B-17 back with a dead co-pilot and eight wounded crew, despite being badly hit in the face. In the 351st BG Sgt Archie Mathies, a ball-turret gunner, and Walter Truemper, a navigator, were posthumously awarded the Medal of Honor for gallantly flying their severely damaged bomber, *Mizpah*, back to England after the co-pilot had been killed and the pilot rendered unconscious. Despite a valiant attempt to land the aircraft, both men were killed on their third attempt to crash-land the crippled bomber at Polebrook.

There was no let-up in the campaign against the German aircraft industry, and on 21 February the heavies were out again. The bomber stream was swelled by 36 B-17s of the 457th BG, commanded by Col Luper and based at Glatton, Huntingdonshire, which was making its debut. The principal targets were the aircraft factories at Brunswick, but thick cloud obscured the objectives and 764 bombers bombed using PFF techniques. Many groups attacked targets of opportunity, and airfields and aircraft depots were heavily bombed.

The following day the elements caused collisions during assembly. Eventually, conditions became so bad that the 2nd Division received a recall while flying a scattered formation over the Low Countries.

B-17G-10-DL 42-37796 of the 350th Bomb Squadron, 100th BG, a 'squadron spare' piloted by Lt William Fletcher, who normally piloted Fletcher's Castoria, crash-landed in Holland at Halfiveg after bombing airfields at Alhorn and Vorden on 21 February 1944. All ten men were made PoWs. (USAF.)

Some groups dropped their bombs on targets of opportunity, while two B-24s in the 445th BG, which did not receive the recall, bombed their assigned target at Gotha. Two 92nd BG B-17s collided in cloud during a diversionary raid on Aalborg, Denmark. The 3rd Division was forced to abandon its mission, but the 1st Division, led by Col 'Mo' Preston, CO of the 379th BG, continued to the Junkers works at Oschersleben and Bernberg. The bombing was 'successful', but 39 Fortresses were lost on the day's missions, including seven in the 306th BG.

On 23 February crews received a much needed respite when weather conditions were the prime reason for keeping the heavies on the ground. Maintenance crews worked around the clock, attempting to get every bomber possible ready for combat. They were needed the next day, 24 February, when Doolittle despatched 867 bombers to targets throughout the Reich. Hearts sank at 1st Bomb Division group briefings when the curtains were pulled back to reveal that the target was the ball bearing plant at Schweinfurt. Some 231 B-17s bombed the target for the loss of 11 Fortresses, while 236 B-17s of the 3rd Division attacked their secondary target at Rostock after overcast had ruled out the primary objectives at Poznan, Tutow and Krzesiny.

Meanwhile, 238 B-24s attacked the aircraft factories at Gotha, 420 miles due east of the white cliffs of Dover. Eight groups crossed the target and a ninth, the 458th from Horsham St. Faith near Norwich, flew a diversionary sweep over the North Sea. Some 28 B-24s in the 445th joined with the 389th and 453rd to form the leading 2nd Wing. The 14th Wing's 44th and 392nd BGs flew behind them, while the 20th Wing brought up the rear.

Flak was heavy over Lingen, Holland, and the Liberators encountered persistent attacks by the Luftwaffe. Even the arrival of three P-47 Thunderbolt groups just after 12:00 was unable to prevent five 445th Liberators being shot down in the space of six minutes. Over 150 enemy fighters ferociously attacked the formation all the way to the target, despite close attention from escorting fighters. The Division beat off incessant attacks as it flew on over the Dummer Lake, where it veered south-eastwards to Osnabruck and the bombed-out airfields near Hannover. Three more 445th B-24s were shot down before the formation turned south near Gottingen at 12:35. Nine minutes later the ninth 445th Liberator, belonging to the 703rd Squadron, was shot down.

Lockheed P-38 Lightnings and North American P-51 Mustangs took over from the hard pressed P-47s near Hannover and orbited the formation as it proceeded to Gotha. Undaunted, German fighters attacked and raked the B-24s with cannon and rocket fire. Using the Liberators' dense vapour trails to excellent advantage, they often struck at any lagging bomber from below and behind. The Luftwaffe even attempted to disrupt the large and unwieldy combat wings. At 13:09 the Division changed course to the south-east, with a feint towards Meinegen. Some confusion arose at the IP when the navigator in the 389th lead ship suffered oxygen failure and the aircraft veered off course. The bombardier slumped over his bombsight and accidentally tripped the bombs. Altogther, 25 Liberators bombed the

388th BG insignia pictured on 15 July 1972 on a wall in the long since demolished briefing hut at Knettishall, Suffolk. (Steve Gotts.)

8th Air Force in colour

B-17G *Skyway Chariot 43-37521 of the 351st Bomb Squadron, 100th BG, under repair at Thorpe Abbotts. On 18 March 1945 this was one of four 351st B-17s shot down in an attack by four Me 262s on the final Berlin mission of the war when 1,329 heavies were despatched in the largest ever raid on the German capital. Six men in Lt Rollie King's crew bailed out before the ship exploded killing all four gunners in the rear.* (100th BG Memorial Museum.)

B-17s of the 100th Bomb Group at dispersal at Thorpe Abbotts. (100th BG Memorial Museum.)

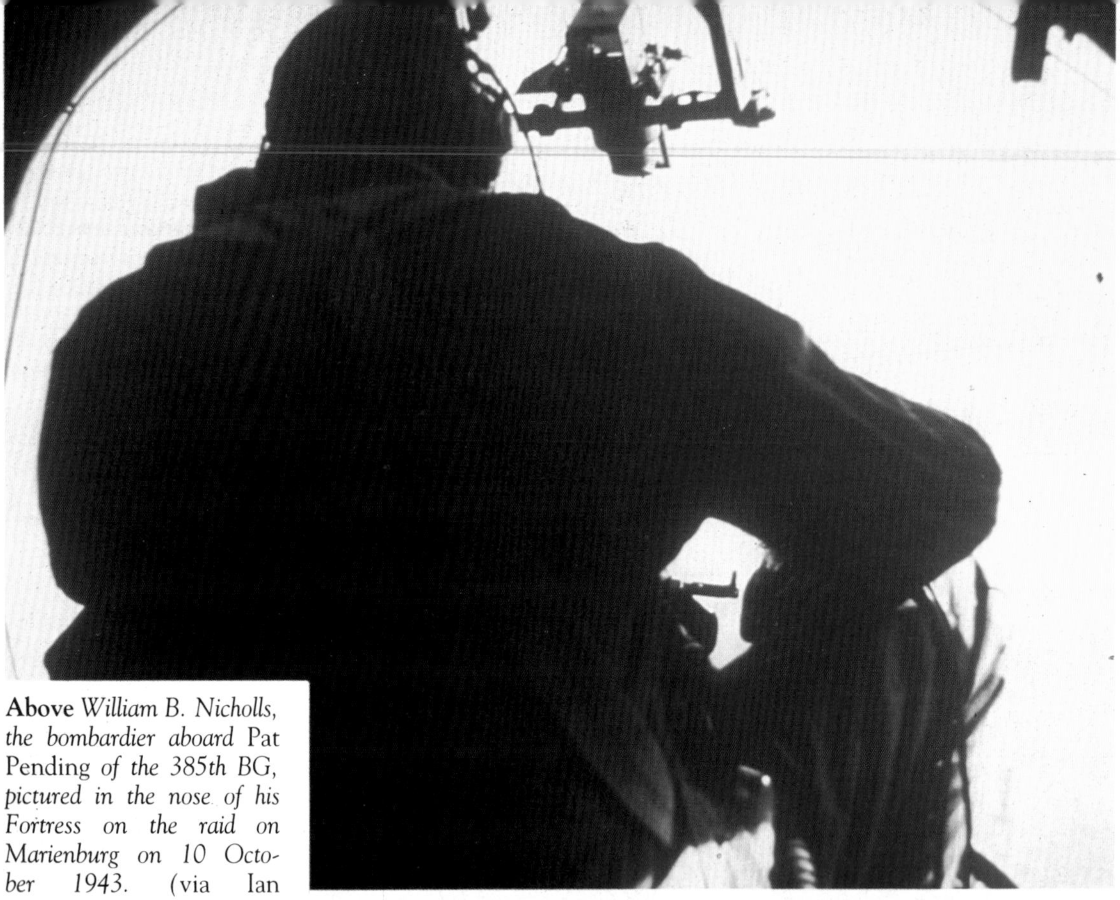

Above *William B. Nicholls, the bombardier aboard* Pat Pending *of the 385th BG, pictured in the nose of his Fortress on the raid on Marienburg on 10 October 1943. (via* Ian McLachlan.*)*

Above right *B-17G 43-37792 in the 413th BS, 96th BG, taxies out at Snetterton Heath. This aircraft, flown by Lt Henry Chrismon, was lost on the mission to Osnabruck on 21 November 1944. (via* Robert Foose.*)*

Far right *B-17G* Little Joe *42-102586 of the 339th BS, 96th BG, waits its turn for take off from Snetterton Heath. (via* Robert Foose.*)*

Right *Remains of Lt Arthur J. Reynolds' 482nd BG (PFF) B-17F 42-5793 which crashed at Brome, Suffolk on 10 November 1943 en route to lead the 100th BG, killing 13 crew and four British road menders. (*100th BG Memorial Museum.*)*

Above *England was 'one giant aircraft carrier' as this picture of hundreds of Fortresses during the build-up for the Normandy invasion shows.* (USAF.)

Above right *Liberators of the 458th BG over Norfolk.* (USAF.)

Far right *B-24J 42-100295 of the 68th BS, 44th BG flown by Lt Robert Rose and Jack B. Williams which crashed at Thorpe Abbotts on 2 March 1944 after an engine fire. It was repaired and flew again, only to be abandoned over England on 16 January 1945 returning from Dresden with Lt Lindsay's crew.*

Right *B-17G* Mason and Dixon *42-31412 was painted by Sgt Frank Stevens of the 100th BG for Capt 'Buck' Mason, and navigator Bill Dishion.* (via Robert Foose.)

Above *B-24 Liberators of the 493rd BG, nicknamed 'Helton's Hellcats' after its CO, Col Elbert Helton, taxi out at Debach, Suffolk.* (Robert Foose.)

Above right *Lead and Low squadrons of the 487th BG cross the Brittany Peninsula after bombing Royan, 15 April 1945.* (Robert Foose.)

Far right *P-51D Mustangs of the 352nd Fighter Group, based at Bodney, escort 458th BG Liberators en route to their target across the North Sea.* (USAF.)

Right *B-24H* Big Dealer *of the 493rd BG at Debach in 1944.* (via Robert Foose.)

Hardwick flying control 1944. (via Mike Bailey.)

Officers of the 100th Bomb Group socialising with English girls near Thorpe Abbotts. (100th BG Memorial Museum.)

Col Jack Wood (centre), Capt Kenneth 'Fearless' Caldwell (left) and other officers plan a 389th BG mission from the North African desert in August 1943. (USAF.)

secondary target at Eisenach. Before the small 445th formation reached the target its 10th and 11th victims fell to the German guns. By now the 445th consisted of only 14 Liberators, three having aborted before entering Germany. Another 445th B-24 was shot down just after leaving Eisenach.

The 13 remaining 445th B-24s, realizing that they had veered off course, continued alone. They arrived over the target at 13:25 and executed an eight-minute bomb run. The 180 500 pounders dropped from 12,000 ft inflicted considerable damage on the Gotha plant. Other groups, totalling some 171 B-24s, dropped another 468 tons of assorted bombs from varying altitudes and directions. A 13th B-24 belonging to the 445th fell victim to the German defences minutes after 'bombs away'.

Myron Keilman, who was flying deputy lead to Lt Col Lorin J. Johnson, recalls: 'The weather was very clear as we turned to the target. Red flares from the lead ship signalled "bomb bay doors open". The bombardier removed the heated covers from the bombsight [they had heated blankets before we did!]. He checked his gyroscope's stabilization and all bombing switches "on". Our high and low squadron fell in trail and all seemed great. Then pilotage navigator Kenny, in the nose turret, observed the lead wing formations veering away from the target heading. A fast and anxious cross-check with lead crew navigator Swangren and a recheck of compass heading and reference points assured command pilot Lorin Johnson that the target was dead ahead. Within minutes Good, the lead bombardier, called over the intercom: "I've got the target!" Lead pilot McGregor checked his flight instruments for precise 18,000 ft altitude and carefully levelled the aircraft on autopilot. He then called back: "On airspeed, on altitude. You've got the aircraft." Making a final level of his bombsight, Good took over control of steering the aircraft with the bombsight.

'At 18,000 ft it was 40° below zero, but the bombardier never felt the cold as his fingers delicately operated the azimuth and range controls. He cross-checked all the bomb and camera switches to the "on" position, especially the radio bomb-release signal switch which simultaneously releases all the bombs of the other aircraft in the formation. Maintaining perfect formation, the 392nd fought its way through the German flak defences and bombed the Gotha works with pinpoint accuracy. After Lt Good had dropped the bombload the camera recorded the impact of the bombs. Lt McGregor took over and swung the formation to the outbound heading and the rallying point. Despite the now accurate flak, the second and third squadron bombardiers, Lts Ziccarrilli and Jackson, steered their squadrons to the precise bomb delivery points too. Of the 32 B-24s which took off that morning, 29 of them delivered their 12 500-pounders precisely on target as briefed.'

The 392nd was extremely accurate, dropping 98 per cent of its bombs within 2,000 ft of the aiming point. The average percentage of bombs dropped by the 2nd Bomb Division which fell within 2,000 ft on visual missions under good to fair visibility in February 1944 was

Crew members in Mac's Sack *bid farewell to Jim McGregor's lead crew in* Big Fat Mama *in the 579th Bomb Squadron, 392nd BG, as they prepare to leave snowbound Wendling for the USA on 26 January 1945. McGregor's crew flew lead from September 1943 to January 1945, including the notable strike on Gotha on 24 February 1944, when they led the 14th Wing.* (Keilman.)

only 49 per cent. (In comparison, the 1st Division achieved 76 per cent and the 3rd 77 per cent.) The 44th had also achieved a highly accurate bomb run. Intelligence described Gotha as ' . . . the most valuable single target in the enemy twin-engine fighter complex,' and later estimated that six to seven weeks' production of Me 110s was lost. However, the 392nd paid dearly for its accuracy. Strung out in trail, and with some B-24s slowed down by flak damage, the three

B-24J Liberators in the 706th Bomb Squadron, 446th BG, en route to the Me 110 assembly plant at Gotha on 24 February 1944. The nearest aircraft is 42-100360. (USAF.)

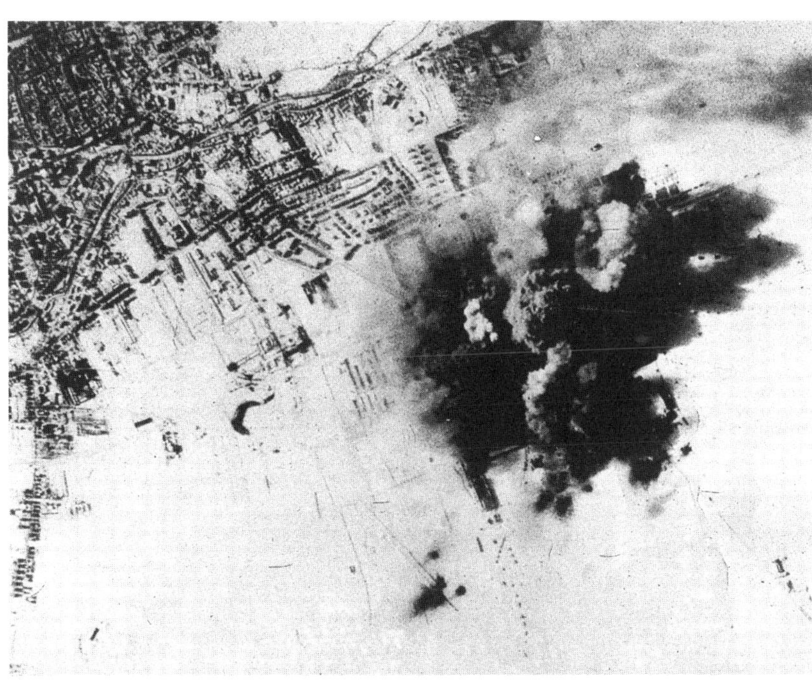

Gotha strike photo taken by the lead crew in the 392nd BG. Some 98 per cent of the 392nd's bombs fell within 2,000 ft of the aiming point. (Keilman.)

squadrons became vulnerable to vicious fighter attacks. For an hour after bombing the 392nd was subjected to head-on passes and tail attacks from singles and gaggles of Luftwaffe fighters. When the group returned to Wendling at 15:30, seven hours after take-off, seven B-24s were missing and another 13 landed with varying degrees of damage. Sixteen enemy fighters were confirmed destroyed by 392nd gunners.

Six 389th Liberators were also shot down in quick succession during

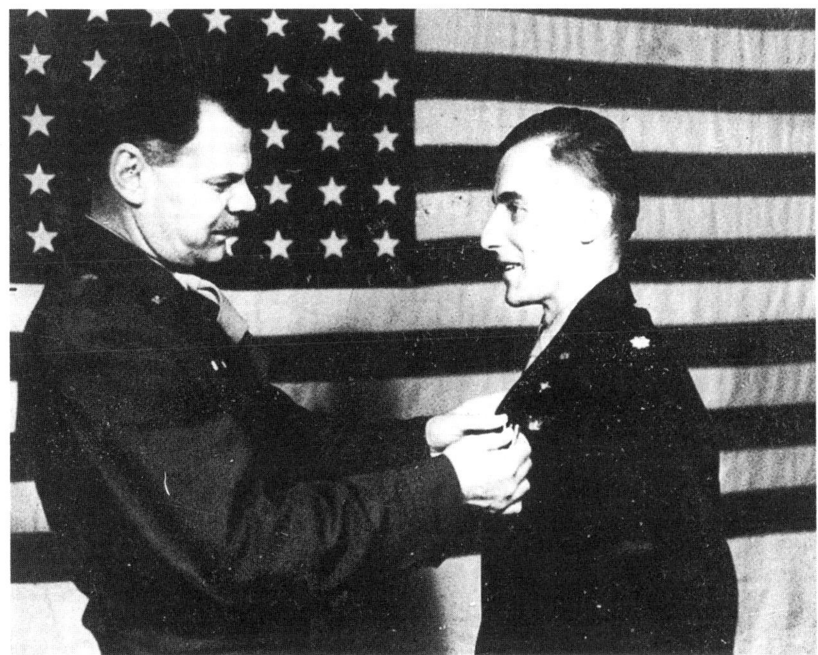

Col Myron Keilman (right), CO, 579th Bomb Squadron, 392nd BG, received the Distinguished Flying Cross from Col Leon Johnson, CO, 14th Combat Wing. (Keilman.)

the raid, while the survivors received further punishment on the homeward journey. The 13 surviving 445th Liberators, nine suffering from varying degrees of battle damage, limped into Tibenham at about 15:45. Altogether, they had lost 122 men on the bloody mission, including Maj Evans, the 702nd CO, and most of the operations staff. Capt Waldher, Operations Officer of the 700th Squadron, was also lost. The group's gunners were credited with the destruction of 21 enemy fighters, plus two probables and two damaged. Both the 445th and 392nd BGs were later awarded Presidential Unit Citations for their part in the raid.

The next day, 25 February, marked the culmination of 'Big Week', when the USSTAF readied some 1,154 bombers and 1,000 fighters for the deepest raid into Germany thus far. The 1st Bomb Division was assigned the Messerschmitt experimental and assembly plants at Augsburg and the VFK ball-bearing plant at Stüttgart, while the 2nd Bomb Division attacked Furth, near Nurnburg. Crews in the 3rd Division, extremely tired after the exertions of the long and tiring 12-hour mission to the Baltic, were mortified to learn that their target was the Bf 109 plant at Regensburg-Prufening – the first time the B-17 crews had need to return to the city since the fateful raid on 17 August 1943, when they had suffered devastating losses. The Germans had given top priority to the reconstruction of the Regensburg plant, and within six months had restored production to something like its previous output. Although most of the old buildings had been destroyed, several main buildings had been rebuilt, including a long assembly shop on a site where three had once stood. This time the Italy-based 15th Air Force would bomb the target before the England-based force arrived over the city.

Very considerable damage was caused to the Bf 109 plants, first by 149 B-17s and B-24s of the 15th Air Force, and then by the 3rd Bomb Division. They arrived over Regensburg an hour after the 15th Air

A formation of B-17Gs of the 368th 'Eager Beavers' Bomb Squadron, 306th BG. The nearest aircraft is B-17G-20-BO 42-31454. (USAF.)

Force bombers, to see smoke pouring upward and rising to about 20,000 ft. Unlike their Italy-based colleagues, the 3rd Bomb Division met only token fighter opposition. The joint bombing was highly effective, and output was severely reduced for four months following the raids. Also, the 1st Bomb Division heavily damaged the Messerschmitt plants at Augsburg and the ball-bearing plants at Stüttgart. The raids cost the 8th Air Force 31 bombers.

Thereafter, cloud banks over the continent brought a premature end to 'Big Week'. Higher command assessed the results and implications of their actions over the past five days. Despite the loss during 'Big Week' of 226 8th Air Force bombers, Spaatz and Doolittle believed that the USSTAF had dealt the German aircraft industry a really severe blow. However, although the 8th had flown some 3,300 bomber sorties and had dropped 6,000 tons of bombs, the destruction was not as great as at first thought. Luftwaffe *gruppes* were certainly deprived of many replacement aircraft, and fighter production was halved the following month, but it had cost the USSTAF 400 bombers and 4,000 casualties. Furthermore, although the small high-explosive bombs destroyed factories, the machine tools, lathes and jigs were left virtually untouched beneath the wreckage. It was only a matter of time before this equipment was recovered from the wrecked plants and put into use again. Nonetheless, Doolittle and his staff officers now felt sufficiently confident to strike at Berlin, the biggest prize in the Third Reich.

Chapter Ten

Bomb bays over 'Big-B'

A RAID BY the 8th Air Force on Berlin had been scheduled for 23 November the previous year, but had been postponed because of bad weather. RAF Bomber Command had been bombing the capital nightly for some time, but Berliners had never before been subjected to the round-the-clock bombing which had devastated so many other German cities. Finally, on the morning of 3 March, briefing officers pulled back the curtains to reveal red tapes reaching like groping fingers all the way to Berlin, in the heart of Nazi Germany. Whistles and groans greeted the news. 'What a birthday treat,' thought Cliff Hatcher, as he sat through the briefing at Bury St. Edmunds. Only the day before he had celebrated his 21st birthday.

The weather, which was bad when the B-17s took off, grew worse, and eventually the mission was 'scrubbed', but not before a tragic collision occurred. Hatcher recalls: 'We were midway in the streams of the vicinity of Kiel, and we kept trying to climb above the fog and cloud. Unfortunately, we did not get the recall signal until after the groups in front of us, and they turned before we did. Suddenly, I looked up and saw what looked like hundreds of B-17s, heading straight for us. Lt Alwardt's ship collided with an approaching B-17, and I flew right through the middle of a black cloud. I could feel the heat from the explosion. I thought we had had it, but incredibly we survived and began heading back. We were maddened by the wasteful and needless collision.'

The 94th BG dispersed in chaos after the recall, and aircraft flew home in twos and threes, dropping their bombs en route. Hatcher dropped his bombs over Heligoland, and only just made it back across the North Sea when his B-17 iced up at 30,000 ft during an attempt to get over the top of a bad storm front. He flew back hugging the sea, and only the de-icers on the propellers prevented the aircraft from going headlong into the water.

'Next day, 4 March, I walked into the briefing room at Rougham as scared as hell,' recalls Hatcher. '"Big-B" was splashed all over the target map, and I thought: "I won't make it".' However, the weather intervened again and crews were recalled. One wing, composed of two squadrons from the 95th BG and one from the 100th BG, did not receive the call signal and continued to the capital alone. Fortunately the Mustang escorts were still with the wayward bombers and provided support in the target area. They prevented a débâcle because, 14 minutes from the capital, they were attacked by German fighters. The 95th lost four aircraft and the 100th lost one, piloted by Stanley M. Seaton. Crews claimed to have dropped the first American bombs on Berlin: they were right. The 95th was awarded its third Presidential Unit Citation and the 100th was similarly awarded later.

On 6 March the 8th despatched 730 heavies escorted by almost 800 fighters to Berlin. The 1st Division was assigned the ball-bearing plant at Erkner, a suburb of Berlin, and the 3rd Division was assigned the Robert Bosch Electrical Equipment factory. Lt Lowell H. Watts, a pilot in the 388th BG, pulled on his clothes in the inky blackness of early morning at Knettishall. 'Perhaps I should have had a premonition of disaster,' he ponders. 'If not then, maybe the briefing should have left me anxious and worried. We were all set for our final combat mission, the mission which would relieve the strain of combat and give us at least a month at home with our friends and families. How we looked forward to going home again. That trip was almost within our grasp. Just a few more combat hours, that was all. But those hours were to be spent deep on Germany over a city the 8th had twice before tried to bomb without success. Berlin, "Big-B", defended in full force by the Luftwaffe and hundreds of flak guns manned by some of the best gunners on the European continent.

'On the previous recalled missions to "Big-B" a dog-leg route had been planned. There would be no bluff on this mission. We were to fly straight in and straight out. In addition to this grim prospect, we were to lead the low squadron of the low group of the second section of our combat wing. In short, our squadron would be the lowest and furthest back and, therefore, the most vulnerable spot in the wing to aerial attack. As I walked out to the briefing room Maj Goodman, our squadron commander, gave me a pat on the back and said his good wishes. He was assured that *Blitzin' Betsy* would be back on the line that evening and, if not, it would have cost plenty to bring her down.

'I walked under a faded white half moon through the pre-dawn darkness to our equipment room. The stars seemed cold and unfriendly. I had gradually grown calloused to many of the dangers of combat. Sure, the fighters and flak brought out the sweat and a tinge of nervous energy, but the thought of actually being shot down seemed like something that just wouldn't happen. Still, there was one thing certain, no chances would be taken on this last mission. I was deadly serious in checking over every detail of our 'plane and equipment. Still, I could show plenty of confidence when I told Harry Allert, our crew chief, to expect a first-class buzz job over his tent when we got back.

'The sun crawled up and peeked over the eastern horizon, casting a pink tinge on the fluffy, scattered clouds that seemed to forecast a clear day. Had we known, could we have seen a few hours into the future, we would have taken that pinkish tinge as a portent of the blood that was to be shed above those clouds. But then, it just looked like another day with better than average weather.'

Throughout the east of England Fortresses and Liberators began taxiing from their hardstands to take up position on the runways. The 1st Division groups would be in the van on the formation, with the 3rd filling in behind them, and the Liberators of the 2nd Division would bring up the rear. At Knettishall 12 B-17s of the 'B' Group took off, followed by 21 Fortresses of the 'A' Group.

Lowell Watts continues: 'Our take-off was perfect. We slid into our formation position without trouble, the rest of the squadron pulling up on us a few minutes later. Everything was working perfectly: engines, guns, interphone. Every man on the crew was feeling well and in good physical condition. We were all set for this final and greatest combat test. I wondered then if all this was a harbinger of a smooth mission or the calm before the storm. The question was to be answered very definitely within a very short time.

'While we were assembling the wing and division formations over Cambridge, the lead ship of our section of the wing aborted. Our group took over the wing lead. I felt better then; at least we weren't in the low group now. We crossed the English coastline and the gunners tested their .50 calibres. The Channel passed beneath us, then the Dutch coast dropped under the wings and fell away behind us. We sailed over the Zeider Zee and were almost over the German border when the storm broke.'

Over the Dummer Lake the 1st Division was attacked by fighters which concentrated on the leading groups, and the 91st, 92nd and 381st were given a thorough going over. The 457th BG was met by head-on attacks, and one Bf 109 which did not pull out in time crashed into Lt Roy Graves' B-17. The combined wreckage fell on Lt Whelen's Fortress, and all three fell to earth.

Next it was the turn of the 3rd Division groups to feel the weight of the enemy attacks. The leading 385th BG, at the head of the 4th Combat Wing, came in for persistent fighter attacks. Brig Gen Russell Wilson was flying in an H2X-equipped Fortress, and his crew included Medal of Honor recipient 1/Lt John C. Morgan. Just as the formation approached the Berlin area the flak guns opened up and bracketed the group. Gen Wilson's aircraft was badly hit, but continued on the bomb run with one engine on fire. Maj Fred A. Rabbo, the pilot, gave the order to bale out when the bomber began losing altitude, but before the 12 crew members could take to their parachutes the aircraft exploded, killing eight of them. Incredibly, Morgan survived, being somersaulted out of the aircraft with his parachute pack under his arm. He managed to put it on after several attempts, and was saved from possible injury when a tree broke his fall. Morgan was captured and sent to Stalag Luft III.

The unprotected 13th Combat Wing, comprising the 95th, 100th and 390th BGs, caught the full venom of the enemy fighter attacks. It was another black day for the 100th in particular, as Robert J. Shoens, pilot of *Our Gal' Sal'* in the 351st lead Squadron, which flew lead, recalls: 'I was part of "Fireball Yellow", and the group was going in with 20 'planes; one short. It was a spectacular day, so clear it seemed we could almost see Berlin from over England. Somewhere over

Crew of B-17G Blitzin' Betsy 42–37886, 388th BG. Back Row L–R: 1/Lt Lowell H. Watts, pilot; 2/Lt R. Kennedy, co-pilot; 2/Lt Emmett J. Murphy, bombardier; 2/Lt E. J. Kelley, navigator. Crouching L–R: T/Sgt J. B. Ramsey, top turret; S/Sgt R. E. Hess (KIA 6 April), right waist; T/Sgt I. Finkle, radio; S/Sgt R. H. Sweeney (KIA) ball gunner; S/Sgt H. Brassfield (KIA), tail gunner; S/Sgt Don W. Taylor (KIA), left waist (Watts).

eastern France we suddenly realised that we hadn't seen our fighter escort for several minutes. We had been without escort for about 20 minutes, which meant that a relay had not caught up with us. (The German fighters had engaged them somewhere behind us, knowing it would leave us without fighter escort.)

'The reason wasn't long in coming. Ahead of us, probably ten miles, there appeared to be a swarm of bees; actually German fighters. Guesses ran as much as 200. They were coming right at us, and in a few seconds they were going through us. On that pass they shot down the entire high squadron (350th) of ten 'planes. When an airplane went down you had to shut out the fact that it took men with it. On this raid it became most difficult because so many were lost. One loss in particular was an example of this. The crew from our own barracks were flying off the right wing of our airplane. Suddenly, during one of the fighter passes, their entire wing was on fire. In the next instant there was nothing there. The fighters made two more passes and, when it was over, *Our Gal' Sal'* was all alone. The last airplane from the group that I had seen flying was Capt Swartout in the 351st Squadron lead flying in *Nelson King*, piloted by Lt Frank Lauro. He was struggling along with about six feet missing from his vertical stabiliser, and was the only other airplane from the squadron who came back with us.

'We saw another group ahead of us, so we caught up with it. The airplanes had an "A" in a square on the tail, so they were from the 94th. We flew on to Berlin with them and dropped our bombs. The flak was heavy, but over Berlin the sky was black. The target was on the southeast side of Berlin. For reasons we couldn't figure out, the group we were with chose to turn to the left and go over Berlin. Since we were not part of the group we decided to turn to the right and get out of the flak. When we did that a Germany battery of four guns started tracking. They fired about 40 rounds before we got out of range. None of them came close because of the evasive action we had taken. Higher up and ahead of us we saw another group, so we climbed and caught up with it. It was also from our wing, having a "Square J" on its tails [390th]. We flew the rest of the way home with them without further incident. It was still a beautiful day, and with a chance to relax we began to wonder what had happened to our group. It couldn't be that we were the only surivivors of "Fireball Yellow".

In 30 minutes the enemy pilots had shot down 23 Fortresses in the 13th Wing, or had damaged them so badly that they were forced to ditch or crashland on the continent. Worst hit had been the 100th BG, which lost 15 B-17s.

Lowell Watts witnessed the decimation of the 13th Combat Wing, flying three miles ahead. 'Their formation had tightened up since I last looked at it. Little dots that were German fighters were diving into those formations, circling and attacking again. Out of one high squadron a B-17 climbed slowly away from its formation, the entire wing a mass of flame. I looked again a second later. There was flash, then nothing but little specks drifting, tumbling down. Seconds later another bomber tipped up on a wing, rolled over and dove straight for the ground. Little white puffs of parachutes began to float beneath us, then fell behind as we flew on toward our target. Our interphone came suddenly to life. "Enemy fighters, 3 o'clock level!" "Enemy fighters, 1 o'clock high!" They were on us. One could feel the tension, the electrifying impulse that swept through each individual crew member when the Fw 190s sailed through our formation. We were now fighting for our lives, for the 'plane and the crew, for the formation and for the group upon which much of our safety hung. Should that formation be badly chewed up now, we'd catch a great deal of hell during the next six hours.

'Roy Island, flying on my left wing, peeled off and headed west. His place was taken by another ship flown by a swell kid with three missions behind him. This fourth one was all he'd get. Another of our 'planes feathered an engine and began dropping behind, the target for several of the fighters. Two silvery streaks flashed past us. They were P-47s; our fighter escort had caught up with us. As the '47s came in the Jerries dropped away, making only sporadic passes. Once again we could breathe a little easier.

'The rest of the way in we had good fighter cover. Violent dogfights flared up ahead of us, forcing several of our fighters to drop their tanks and head for home. With their cover spread more thinly the Focke-Wulfs picked up the pace of the attack. They hit us hard twice before we reached the IP, taking several of our bombers out. Near the IP I looked off to the left where Berlin lay, just north of a heavy, low cloud bank. One bomb wing, the 13th, was making its run, just entering the flak. A dark, puffy veil that hung like a pall of death covered the capital city. It was the heaviest flak I had ever seen. It almost seemed to swallow up the bomber formations as they entered it, but somehow the 'planes kept coming out of the other side. True enough, there were losses. One ship blew up from a direct hit and three others dropped away from their formations, but still they went on to drop their bombs. It didn't seem like anything could fly through that, but there they were, Flying Forts sailing proudly away from the scene of their devastation. It wasn't too comforting to realise that we were the next group over the Hellish scene.

'Our group leader opened his bomb bay doors and we followed suit. However, the turn into the target was not made. Instead we were making a wide, sweeping circle to the left around the city. Our leading groups were already out of sight, heading for home. But still we swung on around Berlin. Precious seconds mounted into minutes, and still we flew without a bomb run. Tempers mounted and the radio crackled with curses and challenges to the men aboard our lead 'plane. "Get that damn thing headed towards the target. What in Hell do you think this is? The scenery may be pretty, but we're not one damned bit interested in it. If you ain't got the guts to fly through that, let somebody else lead the formation." And so went the radio challenges to a crew who, through incompetence or some error, had lost us precious time and muffed a lead responsibility that posed no peculiar problems other than courage and a clear head. Finally, northeast of our target, our lead ship turned toward the centre of Berlin. Our bomb doors came open and we settled down for the bomb run. This was it with a capital "I".

'For maybe a minute or two we flew on, flattening out and tightening up the formation. Then the flak hit us. They didn't start out with wild shots and work in closer. The first salvo they sent up was right on us. We could hear the metal of our plane rend and tear as each volley exploded. The hits weren't direct. They were just far enough away so that they didn't take off a wing, the tail, or blow the 'plane up – they would just tear a ship half apart without completely knocking it out. Big, ragged holes appeared in the wings and fuselage. Kennedy, the co-pilot, was watching nothing but instruments, waiting for that tell-tale story on some instrument that would indicate a damaged or ruined engine, but they kept up their steady roar, even as the ship rocked from the nearness of the hundreds of flak bursts.

'In quick succession the crew reported from nose to tail. Everybody was okay, with four of the crew on walkaround bottles. Flak was coming up as bad as ever but increasing in intensity. Above and to the right of us a string of bombs trailed out of our lead ship. Simultaneously, our ship jumped upwards, relieved of its explosive load as the call "Bombs Away!" came over the interphone. [The bombs hit a residential district between the marshalling yards and the Oranienburg Canal, just east of the Heinkel plant at Annahof.] Our left wing ship, one engine feathered, dropped behind the formation, leaving only four of us in our low squadron. A few minutes later, it seemed like a long time, the flak stopped. We had come through it all and all four engines were still purring away. After getting through that, nothing should be able to knock us down.

'A call came on the VHF radio from our low group. They still had their bombs. As if things hadn't already been enough of a nightmare, we still had another bomb run to make! Wittenburg lay off to the northwest, a big, easily spotted factory visible on its outskirts. We headed over it with our other group and took another blast of flak while they dropped their bombs. A big column of smoke began pouring out of the factory as the bombs hit.' [They fell on to a textile works on the banks of the Elbe.]

'By this time we were 31 minutes late. It proved to be an eternity for a good many men. Our fighter escort had long since headed for home and our other bombers were nowhere to be seen. There we sat, two lone and shot-up groups in the heart of Germany with no friendly fighters in the sky.

'I checked the ships in the formation. We had 15. We should have had 21. Only three ships still flew in our low squadron where there should have been seven. A check of our low group showed only 15 'planes there; a total of 30 in all.

'As we settled down into the routine of the trip home I began to feel a glow of happiness. We had come through hell without an injury on the crew. Shot up as we were, the 'plane was still flying smoothly. We had been over Berlin and had contributed to the carnage that was to be almost complete by May 1945. Now we were headed home. There was an immeasurable relief in knowing that a target had been crossed for the last time, at least in our present combat tour. No longer would we worry about the alerts that meant fitful sleep before another mission. On into the west we flew, while the minutes turned to hours and the miles clocked beneath us in endless and fatiguing procession. The sun swung low into our faces, streaming through the windshield in a bright but eerie light. Off to our right we could see the much bombed cities of Bremen and Hamburg. In a few minutes Holland would be beneath us.

'The interphone came to life. "Fighters at 10 o'clock high! Hey, they're '47s." Oh, what a beautiful and welcome sight they made as they swooped over us, dipped their wings and wheeled away. With our first sight of them a terrific sense of relief swept away the horrible feeling of loneliness and danger that had ridden the skies with us all the way from Berlin. We were now protected and in twenty minutes would be over the English Channel. I began to think about the buzz job I was going to give Harry, and also to wonder how I 'd word the cable back home to Betty when we landed. For a second a wave of extreme and indescribable happiness swept over me. Completion of our combat tour in the 'Big League' of aerial warfare seemed at hand.

'For us, the mission was a lot nearer finished than we realised. The P-47s, after their first pass over us, turned tail for England. We didn't know then that they had been sent out looking for us. Not until they were just about to return for lack of gas did they spot us. But the sight of them had been reassuring. With only 15 to 20 minutes' flying time to the Channel, we felt we could fight our way through anything and we hadn't seen a Focke-Wulf for almost an hour.

'I had just settled wearily back into my seat, relaxing from the first tenseness of seeing the fighters and subsequent relief of knowing they were friendly, when I noticed the high squadron leader was relaxing too much. He was flying back out of position with his squadron by what looked to be 400 or 500 ft. Things settled down for that last weary haul across Holland and the Channel.

'The interphone snapped to life. "Focke-Wulfs at 3 o'clock level!" Yes, there they were. What seemed in a hurried count to be about 40 fighters flying alone, just out of range beside us. They pulled ahead of us, turned across our flightpath and attacked from ahead and slightly below us. Turrets throughout the formation swung forward and began spitting out their .50 calibre challenge to the attackers. Some of the Focke-Wulfs pulled up above us and hit us from behind, while most of them dove in from the front, coming in from 11 o'clock to 1 o'clock low to level, in waves so close that only every second or third 'plane could be sighted on by the gunners. Still they came, rolling, firing and diving away, then attacking again. As the first of these vicious attacks began to ease off, flame shot from Gridley's 'plane, flying our wing. 'Chutes began dropping from it one after the other. "Those poor guys," somebody said. "They've got in 21 missions too."'

'The stimulation of mortal combat took hold as we settled down to see this last battle through to its bitter, bloody end. I had old *Blitzin' Betsy* pulled into the tightest possible formation and was cursing the high squadron leader, who was still trying to get into a decent position.

'The fighters began their second attack. I saw only what was visible from the corner of my eyes. I was flying formation, as steady and as tight as humanly possible. The Focke-Wulfs swept through our formation, especially between our lead and high squadrons. Somebody would pay for the gap left up there by lax flying. They couldn't get between us and the lead squadron, so they began concentrating attacks on our ship, now the lowest one in the formation. Enemy fire swept the nose and front of the cockpit. Dust began flying and the smell of powder from the exploding 20 millimetres was strong and pungent in my nostrils. The second wave passed and the fighters queued up for still another attack. Two more of our 'planes had been badly damaged and were dropping in flames from the formation.

'Brassfield called from the tail position: "I got one, I got one!" Then, with almost the same breath, "I've been hit". No sooner was the interphone cleared from that message when one more ominous crackled into the headsets: "We're on fire!" Looking forward I had seen a Focke-Wulf come at us from dead level at 12 o'clock. Our top and chin turret fire shook our B-17. At the same instant his wings lit up with the fire of his guns. Twenty-millimetres crashed through the nose and exploded beneath my feet in the oxygen tanks. At the same time they broke some of the gasoline cross-feed lines. Flames which started here, fed by the pure oxygen and the gasoline, almost exploded through the front of the ship. The companionway to the nose, the cockpit and the bomb bays were a solid mass of flame. While this happened, gunfire from Ramsey's and Kelley's forward turrets began tearing the attacking 'plane apart. Flames could be seen, and as the fighter fell apart, throwing pieces of metal in his path, he swept a few feet over our cockpit, obviously finished and out of control.

'I took a last look at Clark's 'plane on my right wing and our only remaining ship in the squadron. Then the flames blotted out all vision. I called the crew to bale out and started to set up the automatic pilot to fly the ship after we cleared the formation. I looked over to Kennedy's seat for help. He had gone. Ramsey had left the top turret, now nothing but a furnace. I had been too busy to even see them leave the cockpit.'

Emmett J. Murphy, Lowell Watts' navigator, also flying his 25th and final mission, takes up the story. 'The fighters attacked us six abreast and fired their 20 mm cannon as soon as they were within range. One Fw 190 actually passed within 50 ft of our 'plane after firing and continued on throught the formation. Some of us believed we hit him because we saw smoke from his engine, but we could not be certain as it all happened extremely fast. During the frontal attack we were hit by 20 mm shells in both inboard engines, with one shell coming through the Plexiglas nose, just missing Edward Kelley's, the bombardier, head and mine and exploding in the oxygen tanks below the pilots' cabin. Everything began to burn, so Kelley went out through the front hatch and I followed, getting my eyebrows singed as I went out. In addition to being hit hard from the front, we were also attacked from the rear as Taylor, one of the waist gunners, called out over the intercom that he had been hit in the eye. After Kelley and I got out Kennedy followed. He had to beat out the fire on his chest pack before putting it on.'

Lowell Watts was not yet ready to give up the struggle. He shoved the nose down to clear the formation and reached for the autopilot with his left hand. Just as he touched the switches he noticed for the first time that the two inboard engines were flaming out and there was no hope of stopping them. Suddenly *Blitzin' Betsy* jarred, shuddered, and went out of control. Watts continues: 'I didn't know what had happened (it was not until I talked with Monty Givens that I learned we had come up under our lead 'plane, piloted by Capt Paul Brown. Apparently, we rolled over upside down after hitting the other 'plane. It was this collision, I am sure, that smashed our windshield and knocked most of the top of the cockpit off. Because of the fire I did not see what happened, and thought we were gradually dropping below the formation. The tail damage, which was reported to have shredded the tail fin, probably damaged our elevators and sent the 'plane out of trim, causing it to crash.)'

Blitzin' Betsy's propellers had cut off the leading edge of Brown's port wing and had torn a hole in the number three engine's fuel tank on the starboard wing, which erupted in flames. Part of the crew baled out, but as the aircraft went into a flat spin Brown and Lt Lechowski, his co-pilot, were forced on to the roof of the cockpit. The aircraft exploded, Capt Job, the lead pilot, was killed and both pilots were sucked out. Lechowski was not wearing his parachute. Dupray, the navigator, and Gill, the bombardier, were believed to have been blown out of the nose. Paul Brown and Roy Joyce, who was also blown out of the aircraft, survived and were made PoWs.

Lowell Watts remained at the controls of *Blitzin' Betsy*, unaware of what had happened. All he knew was that he had rolled upside down: 'My safety belt had been unbuckled after the P-47 escort found us. I fell away from the seat but held myself in with the grasp I had on the control wheel. After a few weird sensations I was pinned to the seat, unable to move or even raise my left hand to pull off the throttles or try to cut the gas to the inboard engines. My left foot had fallen off the rudder bars while we were on our back. I couldn't even slide it across the floor to get it back on the pedal. Flames now swept past my face, between my legs and past my arms as though sucked by a giant vacuum.

'Unable to see, I could only tell that we were spinning and diving at a terrific rate of speed. With all the strength I had, I pulled back on the wheel. Horrible seconds passed and the controls failed to respond. I knew that Sweeney could never have gotten out of that damned ball turret. I fought the controls with no response. The fire was too heavy to even bother trying to jump from the nose hatch or the bomb bay. My 'chute would have burned off in nothing flat. I pulled my side window open, gasping for air. Then the 'Gs' began easing off. I thought of trying to jump out of the side window, but at best that was a tight fit and a rough way to bale out. I was still worried about Sweeney. He couldn't possibly have gotten out yet. Then I noticed that there was no windshield, no top turret and no roof to the cockpit! At least I could bale out by jumping through the roof.

'The ship felt like it was levelling off, but still the fire kept me from telling just what our real position was. I thought I'd fight it out a few seconds longer to give the men in the back a better chance; then jump. I fully expected to see the earth crashing through the front of the 'plane. Which would it be: that, or death from the flames that were searing past? I couldn't help but feel sorry for Betty and her baby boy. I remembered with a flash of pain that Don Taylor had called from the waist less than ten minutes before we hit to tell us his boy was a year old that same day. Death in itself didn't seem so frightening as I had imagined it might be. That wild, eerie ride down the corridors of the sky in a flaming bomber was to haunt my memories for the rest of my life, but it wasn't just the terror of death that would sear these memories across my brain; it was the unending confusion and pain of a hopeless fight, and the worry of nine other men who were my responsibility. Contrary to the usual stories, my past life failed to flash through my mind. I was too busy fighting to keep that life.

'As those thoughts combined with the struggle to maintain control of the 'plane, I felt myself suddenly catapulted through space, spinning so fast I couldn't pull my arms and legs into my body for several seconds. Something jerked heavily past my face. It was my flak suit. Then my oxygen mask flew off, followed by my goggles and helmet.'

Emmett J. Murphy, who had fallen to about 7,000 ft before pulling his ripcord, witnessed the last moments of *Blitzin' Betsy*. 'When I last saw our 'plane, while hanging in my harness, it was on its back in a steep dive, burning like a blow torch. Its four engines were screaming and running away. Then it exploded, blowing Watts, Ramsey and Ivan Finkle, the radio operator, clear of the aircraft, where they pulled their ripcords.'

Watts continues: 'Automatically, I reached for my chest. Yes, there was the ripcord, right where it should have been. Until then I hadn't once thought about my 'chute. I jerked the ripcord and waited. Nothing happened. I jerked it harder. There was a soft swish, then a hard, sharp jerk and I was suspended in space, hanging in the most complete silence I had ever known. I anxiously looked up at the billowy white nylon of my 'chute, fully expecting it to be on fire. I knew a great relief when I saw it intact. Above me the formation roared on into the west, the battle still raging. I looked for our 'plane. An engine went by, still burning. A few pieces of metal wrinkled on down, and farther away I caught sight of the bright yellow dinghy radio falling through space. What a screwy time to notice that radio but, ever since, the sight of it has stayed in my mind more clearly than anything else. I could see nothing else of our 'plane. Up above me were three 'chutes. There should have been nine. Just three. Damn! Sweeney never had a fighting chance.

'Off to the west our formation faded from sight. As the sound faded, a surge of anger and helplessness swept through me. I had flown a solid eight hours of formation. I took no chances. Our gunners had taken their toll. We had taken at least two, probably three, and possibly four German fighters down with us. We had done everything possible, yet here I hung on the shroud lines of a parachute. There were three more 'chutes, and what of the others?

'A Focke-Wulf swept towards me in a slow, deliberate circle. Then he came straight at me. I thought: "Damn, do these bastards shoot guys in their 'chutes?" The fighter flew on until he was almost on top of me. I tried to swing the 'chute, feeling very helpless. Then I noticed he was still turning, going on by me. A few seconds later he crashed. Not until then did I realize that a dead pilot had just flown past me. I looked down and saw three other 'planes burning on the ground.

'With a start I suddenly realized that I wasn't just hanging in space. I was drifting, and backwards at that. My burns, which I had begun to notice, were forgotten as I swung up, hanging to the shroud lines. The ground came up faster, faster. I jerked on the shrouds. In a very definite but unceremonious manner I had set foot upon the European continent. As I tumbled on to the wet, snow-covered earth, the wreckage of *Blitzin' Betsy* fell in scattered litter around me. With it fell the hopes, the faith and the efforts of everything I had trained, worked for and built during the past year and a half. The miles back to Colorado seemed farther than human comprehension as I looked helplessly into the western sunset.'

Sweeney, Brassfield, Hess and Taylor were found dead in or near the wreckage. The rest of the crew were rounded up and eventually sent to PoW camps in the Third Reich. Altogether, the 388th lost eight crews.

The 452nd BG formation of six B-17s, flying as the High Squadron, also suffered loss. Hank Gladys, the bombardier aboard *Flakstop*, flown by Lt Charles F. Wagner, recalls: 'Flying back from the target, we were about halfway through Germany when our fighter escort had to leave us as we were behind schedule because of our second pass over the target. Immediately, the Germans came up after us. Later, I learned that there were 33 of them after us. *Flakstop* was hit after the 388th collision occurred [Watts and Brown], during a ferocious fighter attack. The first attack came from the rear, killing our tail gunner, Sgt

G. L. James. Then the attack shifted to the front, where they knocked out our left engine and damaged our wing on the right side.'

Allan R. Willis, the co-pilot, says: 'The German fighters came like the proverbial swarm of bees. Six Bf 109s and Fw 190s took the 452nd as their quarry, and the fun really began. Virtually all passes were made from 10 to 12 o'clock high. Our intercom was "kaput", and I could make no attempt at fire control. A second pass raked the fuselage from nose to tail. The third did the crucial damage. It must have hit the starboard side oil, electrical and fuel lines because both starboard engines, numbers three and four, began to splutter. The tach's immediately indicated nearly total loss of r.p.m.s. I hit the feathering switches, but nothing happened. The props simply windmilled. The wide variation in r.p.m.s started *Flakstop* vibrating, and we fell out of formation. Both Charlie Wagner and myself fought the vibrating control columns to try and maintain straight and level flight. There was no panic yet. We could see the Zeider Zee on the horizon. We didn't want to bale out over Germany because of the stories we had heard about the German treatment of downed fliers.

'I saw one of our gas caps fly off. The only explanation I could think of was that the intense vibration had loosened them. The airstream over the starboard wing must have set up a siphoning action, and the gasoline and the hot oil might have come together. What I did know was that the entire starboard wing was, in a flash, a sheet of orange flame! In that single moment *Flakstop* gave up her rôle as a mighty Flying Fortress and became a flying coffin. It didn't take an aeronautical engineer to inform us that it was much safer outside than in. As I hit the bale-out bell (thank God that was working!) I glanced at the altimeter; 1,400 ft over Holland!'

Clyde J. Martin, the navigator, was first out of the front escape hatch. Allan R. Willis followed. Hank Gladys continues: 'During all this Lt Wagner was trying to set the automatic pilot, as he didn't know what the situation was in the other part of the 'plane. Right after I'd baled out, *Flakstop* went into a spin and crashed within my sight. Of the four remaining crew members in the back, three were killed and Sgt Lloyd Freeman, our ball turret gunner, was seriously wounded. He landed near Sgt Porter, who was advised by the Dutch Underground workers to leave him, as the Germans were very near and searching for us. I never learned the fate of Sgt Freeman. The Dutch Underground said that one of our 'chutists was strafed and killed while floating down by one of the attacking Fw 190s. Two other crew members' 'chutes failed to open after they baled out.' Six months later Willis and Gladys were liberated by the American Army.

The first American air raid on Berlin had certainly flushed the Luftwaffe just as Doolittle had hoped it would. The B-17 and B-24 gunners and the fighter pilots claimed more than 170 German fighters destroyed, but the Americans had lost 69 bombers, the highest number lost by the 8th in a single day, plus a further 102 seriously damaged. The 1st Division lost eighteen B-17s, while the 2nd lost 16 B-24s, including *Hello Natural* in the 448th, which was forced to seek refuge at Bulltofta airfield in Sweden. It was the first of 19 Liberators

A reporter interviews Ray L. Sears (later Lt Col, CO of the 735th Bomb Squadron, MIA 29 April 1944) and co-pilot Jim Kotapish from the Reluctant Dragon *in the 453rd BG on their return from Berlin on 8 March 1944. 'On this clear day there were aircraft as far ahead and as far back as the eye could see. A mass of 1,200-plus bombers and fighters that somehow made the sweating out of the bomb run a little more endurable.' The 453rd lost four B-24s on the 6 March Berlin raid and one on 8 March. (Jim Kotapish.)*

in the group which would be forced to land in Sweden during the war; the highest total of all the B-24 groups.

The 3rd Bomb Division lost 35 B-17s, with the 'Bloody Hundreth' again suffering unmercifully at the hands of the Luftwaffe, as Robert Shoens, pilot of *Our Gal' Sal'* recalls: 'When we got home we found that we were one of only five B-17s to return to Thorpe Abbotts. We had lost 15 airplanes. To say the least, we were upset, as was everyone on the base. Lt Col Ollen 'Ollie' Turner, the 351st Squadron Commander, met us as we parked the airplane. He was in tears. Most of the losses had been from his squadron. It was hard to take, but this was what we had been trained for.'

Air Chief Marshal of the RAF Arthur Harris sent a message to his opposite number, Carl Spaatz, at High Wycombe: 'Heartiest congratulations on first US bombing of Berlin. It is more than a year since they were attacked in daylight, but now they have no safety there by day or night. All Germany learns the same lesson.'

The 8th was stood down on 7 March, but the following day 600 bombers returned for the third raid on 'Big-B' in a week. The 3rd Division led the 8th to the VKF ball-bearing plant at Erkner, in the suburbs east of Berlin, while the 1st Division flew in the middle and the 2nd again brought up the rear. More than 460 bombers bombed Erkner with 'good results' (while 75 others bombed targets of opportunity), but once again the price was high. The leading 3rd Bomb Division encountered fierce opposition and lost 36 Fortresses, including 16 in the 45th Combat Wing. The worst-hit group in the 3rd Division during the series of Berlin missions had been the 100th BG.

1/Lt William F. Cely, in the 385th BG, is carried away from his B-17 on the shoulders of his crewmen after their return from the 8 March raid on Berlin. Cely had added the Silver Star to his DFC and Air Medal for bringing his battered 94th BG B-17 Frenesi *back from Brunswick on 11 January 1944, after five members of his crew and a cameraman had baled out over enemy territory.* (Via Ian McLachlan.)

In the first American operation to Berlin, on 4 March, the 'Bloody Hundredth' had won through to the target with the 95th while all the others had turned back. Raids on the capital that week cost the group 17 aircraft. (A year later, the 100th BG was awarded a second Presidential Unit Citation for its Berlin actions on 4, 6 and 8 March.)

On 9 March 1944 about 300 B-17s bombed Berlin again, but ten/tenths cloud prevented visual bombing, while 158 B-24s bombed other targets in the Brunswick, Hannover and Nienburg areas. The Luftwaffe was conspicuous by its absence, but nine heavies fell victim

B-17G, Our Gal' Sal', *42-31767, in the 351st Bomb Squadron, 100th BG, flown by Lt Robert J. Shoens' crew.* (Thorpe Abbotts Tower Museum.)

B-17s of the 452nd BG flying at 25,000 ft above the overcast en route to Berlin on 9 March. (Sam Young.)

to flak. Cliff Hatcher's crew in the 94th BG completed their 25th and final mission in the *Grand Old Lady*. (On 18 April it was one of eight 94th B-17s shot down over Berlin. Of the 11 aircraft which Cliff Hatcher flew during his tour, nine went down with other crews.)

The 8th was stood down on 10 March, but next day PFF techniques were used by 121 B-17s to bomb Münster, and by 34 Liberators to attack a No-ball site at Wizernes. VI targets were again bombed on 12–13 March. Some 330 bombers hit Brunswick on 15 March, and the following day 679 bombers hit factory and airfield targets in Germany. The Luftwaffe was up in force, and 23 bombers were shot down.

A mission to Frankfurt on 17 March was abandoned, but on the 18th 679 bombers bombed aircraft plant and airfields in south-west Germany and the Dornier works at Friedrichshafen. Starting at 10:00, 28 Liberators began taking off from Wendling. Four returned early with mechanical problems, leaving the remaining aircraft to continue over France. Lt Dalton's crew in 'R for Roger', a Gotha veteran, got caught in prop wash and collided with Lt E. F. Anderson's B-24, slicing off the tail and its turret. Both aircraft collided again as they went down, and exploded in sheets of flame before crashing. As the bombers neared Friedrichshafen, the leading 44th BG at the head of the 14th Wing made an unscheduled 360° turn. The leading elements in the 392nd bombed the target, but the second block, disconcerted by the manouevres ahead, chose to attack the rail yards at Stockach instead. The Liberators became strung out, and heavy Flak dispersed the formation to such an extent that many B-24s flew over Swiss territory on the opposite side of Lake Constance and drew fire from the Swiss guns. The Liberators were running nine minutes late for their rendezvous with P-38 fighter escorts, which was missed, and the 14th Wing was left to fend for itself against an estimated 75 single-engined enemy fighters. They attacked in line abreast, five and six at a time, and harried the Liberators for over 100 miles. Capt Myron Keilman, in the 392nd formation, recalls: 'The lead ship had an engine shot out on the bomb run; then persistent fighter attacks worked the group over all the way to Strasbourg. The lead navigator was blinded by a 20 mm shell.' Even when P-38s came to the rescue, the German pilots continued to press home their attacks. The 392nd was decimated, losing 15 Liberators. The 44th lost eight B-24s.

Col Joseph Miller, CO of the 453rd BG, was leading the 2nd Combat Wing on only his fourth mission. He was in the lead ship with Capt Joseph O'Reilly, the newly appointed Goup Navigator, and Capt Stock in the 733rd Squadron. Jim Kotapish, the co-pilot aboard *Reluctant Dragon*, flying below Stock's B-24, recalls: 'Our astute group navigator had led the group over the harbour and everyone was waiting for us. The first flak burst hit the bomb bay of the lead ship and it immediately burst into flames. All I could think of was, "Please God, don't blow up right now or we'll get the whole 'plane in our nose". It didn't; it banked right in a low spiral and several men baled out of the 'plane, which was streaming flames from the bottom and the waist windows. The second burst hit our left wing. While I heeled over to follow the deputy leader out to sea, Ray Sears, the pilot, was busying himself with number two engine, which had taken the brunt of the burst. I followed the flight of the lead 'plane as long as I could, but it fell behind. The early parachutists were swept out across the lake and drowned before the speedboats could pick them up.'

Col Miller landed in a French field. He was soon in the hands of the French Resistance and, disguised as a priest, made his way across France to Perpignan. He was captured wearing civilian clothing by a German border patrol as he waited to cross into Spain, and handed over to the Gestapo. While in his cell Miller thought back to 1938, when three German officers were attempting to set a new record flying from Berlin to Tokyo. Over the South China Sea their Heinkel

B-17G-35-BO 42-32095 in the 322nd Bomb Squadron, 91st BG in formation over Europe. This aircraft was assigned to the 457th BG on 16 March 1944. (Robert J. Foose.)

developed engine trouble and they were forced to land in the Philippines. Their distress calls had already been picked up by the Army Air Corps in Manila, and a rescue mission led by Col Miller found them. Miller told his Gestapo interrogators of the incident. The Gestapo chief of the Paris region, T. T. Schmidt, conferred with Maj Junge, the deputy commander at Oberusel who, as luck would have it, was the pilot of the record-attempt from Berlin to Tokyo. Junge recounted the rescue and Schmidt casually remarked that he was holding an American colonel by the name of Joe Miller in Paris. Junge was convinced it was the man who had rescued him in 1938. He made

Below *B-24 Liberators in the 466th BG unload their bombs. The Attlebridge outfit made its bombing debut on 22 March 1944.* (USAF.)

Left *A ground launched rocket narrowly misses a B-17 in the 306th BG formation amid flak bursts during the mission to Dijon/Longvic on 28 March 1944.* (Richards.)

Far left *Olive-drab B-17G* Nine-O-Nine, *42-31909, in the 323rd Bomb Squadron, leads other aircraft in the 91st BG.* Nine-O-Nine *completed over 125 missions with out a turnback.* (USAF.)

a positive identification and Miller was sent to Luft III. Meanwhile, Col Ramsey D. Potts assumed command of the 453rd BG.

Altogether, 43 bombers and 13 escorting fighters were lost on the 18 March raids. Next day the bombers carried out 'milk runs' to VI sites in northern France. While 172 heavies unloaded their bombs over the No-ball sites, Bill Rose in the 92nd completed his 25th and final mission to Frankfurt. 'As we entered the flight pattern over Podington,' he remembers, 'we broke away and buzzed the field. Then we partied until our papers came through.' (In 1945 Rose returned to the 92nd BG and flew part of a second tour.)

On 22 March 1944 the heavies again sought the rich industrial targets of 'Big B'. Almost 800 B-17s and B-24s, including the 466th BG, which made its bombing debut, were dispatched. The Attlebridge group lost two B-24s in a mid-air collision. (Two days later the weather was responsible for the loss of two more 466th BG ships which were involved in a second mid-air collision, near Osterburg. On 27 March two more collided, shortly after take-off from Attlebridge.)

Altogether, the 8th dropped 4,800 tons of high explosive on Berlin in five raids during March 1944. The raids cost the 8th scores of experienced crews and valuable aircraft, to say nothing of the mental scars on those who survived. By 19 May 1944 John A. Miller of the 100th BG would have completed six missions to the German capital; the most Berlin missions in one tour by an 8th Air Force member. 'Altogether,' he recalls, 'we started out for Berlin seven times. Twice our co-pilot went nuts and tried to crash us into the sea. These times the crew fought him off the wheel and we aborted. After the second time he didn't return to our crew. He wasn't a coward; he just couldn't go back to Berlin.'

Chapter Eleven

Tumult in the skies

AFTER THE BERLIN raids of early March 1944 the weather closed in over the continent, and shallow penetration missions to VI sites in the Pas de Calais and airfields in France became the order of the day. On 1 April the 8th attempted missions to Germany, but thick cloud grounded the 1st Division while 438 B-17s and B-24s of the 2nd and 3rd Divisions headed for the chemical works at Ludwigshafen. Thick cloud over France forced all 192 B-24s of the 3rd Division to abandon the mission, leaving 246 Liberators to continue to the target. The cloud filled the sky, even at 21,000 ft, and many groups failed to locate their targets. Some 162 B-24s bombed targets of opportunity at Pforzheim and Grafenhausen. Col James Thompson, CO of the 448th BG, was killed when his aircraft ran low on fuel, the crew baled out, and his parachute failed to open. (Col Jerry Mason, an ex-fighter pilot in the CBI Theatre, took over at Seething two weeks later).

Some 38 bombers in the 44th and 392nd BGs veered off course when the command pilot in the PFF lead ship, whose Mickey set had malfunctioned as the formations departed the English coast, decided to carry on to the target. Col Myron Keilman wrote: 'Without visual reference with the terrain, the lead navigator [Capt C. H. Koch] had to rely solely upon prebriefed estimates of winds aloft to carry out his dead-reckoning type of navigation . . . There must have been quite a change in both the direction and velocity of the winds aloft [because] the formations were blown some 120 miles to the right of course and 50 miles further in distance.' It later transpired that 26 B-24s in the 392nd had dropped 1,184 100 lb bombs on a forested area three miles south-east of the Swiss town of Schaffhausen, over 120 miles from Ludwigshafen, and the CO, Col 'Bull' Rendle, had some explaining to do. The mistake led to America paying the Swiss thousands of dollars in reparations. Koch was rebuked and never again allowed to perform the function of lead navigator. Keilman concludes: 'As a personal friend, I felt sorry for Capt Koch. He had flown as my navigator on numerous eight- and ten-hour ocean patrol missions between Ecuador and the Galapogos islands in 1942 . . . When the radar set malfunctioned, the odds were against precision navigation and the command pilot should have recalled (aborted) the mission.' The 1 April mission cost the 2nd Division ten B-24s.

It was not until 8 April that the cloudy conditions abated and allowed the 8th to assemble in force. Some 13 combat wings, consisting of 644 bombers, were dispatched to aircraft depots throughout western Germany, including 192 bombers which attacked Brunswick. Some 34 heavies were shot down during the day's missions, including ten B-24s in the 466th BG. The 445th lead ship, with Lt Col Robert Terrill, the CO, aboard, had two engines knocked out by flak over the target. Despite this, Terrill succeeded in bringing his bomber home on the two remaining engines and was later awarded the DFC by Col Ted Timberlake.

On Easter Sunday, 9 April, 104 Liberators took off from East Anglia for a raid on the aircraft assembly plant at Tutow. At 09:00 two B-24s, belonging to the 389th and 392nd BGs, collided at 8,000 ft while forming up over north Norfolk. Nine men in the 392nd Liberator were killed, and seven men in the forward section of the 389th B-24 were killed instantly when five 500 lb bombs and the full fuel load exploded. The forward section disintegrated and wreckage flew through the air. Incredibly, two men, including Capt (later Col) John Driscoll, the Group Gunnery Officer in the 566th Squadron, who was in the waist position to take strike photographs of the target, survived. Three bombs which failed to explode fell near the bomb dumb at RAF Foulsham, which contained some RDX (high-explosive) bombs.

Meanwhile, the 1st Division was enroute to the Fw 190 plant at Marienburg. Despite the loss of one combat wing and some combat boxes from another, 98 B-17s in the 1st Division placed 71 per cent of their bombs within 1,000 ft of the MPI. Leaving the target, the B-17s received radio orders to join 33 B-17s of the 3rd Division which had bombed the Fw 190 plant at Poznan for mutual protection, but before they could rendezvous the 3rd Division came under heavy fighter

Pistol Packin' Mama, *42-72858, lifts off from Shipdham. It was forced to land at Bulltofta, Sweden, on 9 April 1944 after sustaining damage on the Berlin-Marienburg mission.* Lemon Drop, *the* Eightballs' *assembly ship, can be seen in front of the first hangar.* (Bill Robertie.)

attack. The leading 45th Wing bore the brunt of the attacks, but stout defending by the Fortress gunners kept losses down to just two aircraft. Meanwhile, a further 86 B-17s bombed the Heinkel plant at Warnemünde, while 40 B-17s bombed the airfield at Rahmel and 46 B-17s bombed airfields at Parchim and Rostock. Altogether, the 8th lost 30 bombers.

On the next day, 10 April, 730 crews, including 30 Liberators of the 467th BG at Rackheath, which was making its bombing debut under the leadership of the CO, Col Albert J. Shower, bombed airfield targets in France and the Low Countries. On 11 April well in excess of 900 bombers were dispatched to six Junkers and Focke-Wulf assembly plants in eastern Germany. Some 88 Fortresses of the 1st Division were assigned Cottbus and Sorau. Perry Rudd, who was in the 457th formation, recalls: 'We were knocked out of formation and fell a thousand feet before we recovered. We levelled out just in time to witness a burning B-17 fall off its right wing directly over us. Lt Matterell, the co-pilot, pulled our ship up on the left wing and we fell another 3,000 ft. The burning B-17 missed us by only a few feet. A piece of flak had entered the cockpit before exploding, and had set the nose on fire. The flames spread through the open radio hatch of the doomed ship, leaving a trail of smoke as he spiralled down. Two men got out. The tail gunner went through a wing and a pilot banked his 'plane to let him by. Neither 'chute opened, if indeed either of them had them on.'

At the target the Fortresses were bracketed by more flak. The lead bombardier in the 351st BG was hit in the arm and the limb had to be amputated later. Perry Rudd's B-17, meanwhile, had to salvo its bombs: 'The bomb doors would not close and we headed back to Belgium alone. We received about 20 flak hits on the homeward run. The right aileron was knocked out of position, the rudder was holed, and the right flap was put out of commission. Lt Hovey did a remarkable job of getting us back. We took our crash landing positions, but it was a great landing at Glatton despite the damage, although the 'plane was later declared a sub-depot job.'

Lt Edward Michael and Lt Westberg in the 305th BG brought *Bertie Lee* home to England after it had been devastated by cannon fire and had plummeted into a 3,000-foot dive. Michael crash-landed at an RAF airfield on the south coast, despite his undercarriage and flaps having been put out of operation and the ball turret being stuck in the lowered position with its guns pointing downwards. The airspeed indicator was not working and the bomb bay doors were jammed fully open. Fighting off unconsciousness, Michael skilfully brought *Bertie Lee* down safely on its belly. His miraculous feat earned the second Medal of Honor awarded to a member of the 305th BG.

The 92nd BG, which had been assigned the industrial area of Stettin, also suffered loss. Six aircraft in the 325th Bomb Squadron, flying as the low squadron of the high group, were brought down by vicious and persistent fighter attacks and a concentrated flak barrage. The 13th and 45th Combat Wings in the 3rd Bomb Division force were confronted with bad weather in the Poznan area and were forced to bomb the secondary target at Rostock. Rocket-firing Me 410s and Ju 88s took advantage of a lapse in fighter cover and wrought havoc among the leading groups. The 96th BG was worst hit, losing ten of the 25 bombers shot down this day.

Most of the crews who returned to England had been in the air for more than 11 hours, and tiredness had already begun to take effect during the last stages of the homeward leg. Joe Wroblewski recalls: 'I kept seeing the English coast all the way back across the North Sea. It must have been a mirage. It seemed like we would never get back. I was dead tired when we eventually did get back, and I passed out in the sack and slept like a log.'

On 13th April overall command of the Combined Bomber Offensive and the 8th Air Force officially passed to Gen Dwight D. Eisenhower, the newly appointed Supreme Allied Commander. Col (later Gen) Maurice 'Mo' Preston, CO of the 379th BG, flying at the head of the leading 41st Wing, led the 1st Division to the ball-bearing plants at Schweinfurt, while the 3rd Division went to the Messerschmitt plant at Augsburg. The 2nd Bomb Division was assigned German aircraft manufacturing installations near Munich.

The 1st Division encountered strong fighter opposition, as Col Preston recalls: 'The great majority of attacks were concentrated on a single box, a single element, of the wing formation. The high box (384th BG) was chosen presumably because it was separated some distance from the remaining boxes. I made a determined effort via the radio to induce the element leader [eight aircraft] to get back into formation, but to no avail. He and his entire formation were shot down on a single pass made by the German fighters. I never saw such a thing happen before or since. One pass; scratch one entire formation!'

The 3rd Division was badly mauled by fighters in the bombing of the Messerschmitt plant at Augsburg in southern Germany. Ten Fortresses were forced to head for Switzerland, and many others were either shot down or badly damaged. The B-24s had better luck. One of the returning B-24s in the 453rd BG carried the 2nd Combat Wing Leader, Maj James M. Stewart, who on 31 March had joined the Old Buckenham Group as Operations Officer.

Since 11 April the 94th BG had lost about 14 crews in combat or rotated home. On 17 April ten B-17s in the 94th and nine in the 385th were shot down. Both combat boxes were alone and without fighter cover. Among the replacements sent to the 94th in April was Abe Dolim, an Hawaiian navigator who, three years before, had witnessed at first hand the Japanese bombing of Pearl Harbor. Such was the urgency for replacement crews that Dolim had to wait only until 22 April, 15 days after disembarking from the *Queen Elizabeth* in Scotland, to fly his first combat mission, to the marshalling yards at Hamm. Unfortunately the weather was to play a large part in shaping the mission and was responsible for its ultimate fate.

Crews were apprehensive from the start. They were awakened in the middle of the night because the mission was sheduled for the usual early morning start. It was later postponed for several hours while command waited for the bad weather front over the continent to

B-24 Liberators flying at 22,000 ft pass Magdeburg, covered by a smoke screen, on 18 April 1944. (USAF.)

clear. After several stop-go decisions, final clearance was given in the afternoon. Crews who had been awake since 02:00 had their briefing updated with more recent weather information and began assembling for take-off. The 2nd Bomb Division led the 8th, and began taking off from their Norfolk and Suffolk bases between 16:15 and 16:30. They were followed by the Fortresses from nearby 3rd Division bases and 1st

Crew members of the 453rd BG inspect the damage to their B-24 at Old Buckenham on 20 April after suffering a direct flak hit in the rear of the aircraft which killed the tail gunner on the mission to Wizernes in the Pas-de-Calais. L–R: S/Sgt Bruce P. Prosser, gunner; 1st Lt James S. Munsey, who was an instructor pilot flying with a new crew on its first combat mission; and S/Sgt Walter J. Thomas, waist gunner. Munsey was killed two days later, returning from Hamm. (USAF.)

Division groups further west.

At Bury St Edmunds, Lt Scannel's Fortress lifted off from the rubber-stained runway and climbed to altitude. Abe Dolim recalls: 'We took off in beautiful CAVU (ceiling and visibility unlimited) weather topped with high cirrus clouds. Finally, after more than an hour of forming, we took our place at the lead of the 4th Combat Wing and proceeded at 150 m.p.h. indicated airspeed. Our fighter escort of P-47s and P-38s picked us up just north of Ijmuiden on the Dutch coast. There were no reports of enemy fighters as we turned at the IP and opened our bomb bay doors for the bomb run. From the IP onward there was absolutely no evasive action.

'We saw the flak before we spotted the target. The 88 mm explosions looked like double black mushrooms, as though the shell exploded in the middle and worked itself out at both ends vertically. The railroad marshalling yards at Hamm, the chokepoint to 'Happy Valley', was 3½ miles long, the largest in Germany, so large that we bombed in combat wing formation – three groups abreast. Flak was not too accurate, and we were lucky to be the first over the target. Our bombs blanketed the yard; only a few appeared to go astray.

'As we turned off to the rally point, I looked toward 5 o'clock and saw a sky full of flak with two B-17s in trouble, one in a shallow dive afire and the other exploding after a short vertical dive. I watched several parachutes descend to German soil, then looked for my chest pack – it was not within reach. I made a note to stack it between my position and the emergency hatch against the bulkhead next to my navigation table.'

The 2nd Wing led the 2nd Bomb Division to Hamm, with Lt Col Robert H. Terrill, CO of the 445th, as command pilot. In the clear conditions of late evening the bombers had little difficulty in locating their target – 3½ miles long and nearly a mile wide. Such a large target necessitated bombing in wing formation, but despite the tight wing pattern adopted some bombs fell wide. Strong headwinds and too many short zig-zagging legs to the target took parts of the 2nd Wing over the Ruhr Valley, where they were subjected to intense flak, and delayed the approach to the primary target. Instead of crossing the target on a 135° heading as briefed, the bombers came into the target from 260°. The 2nd Wing missed the IP, and the 445th and part of the 453rd were prevented from bombing the primary target owing to other, incoming groups. The Liberators therefore continued down the Rhine and bombed marshalling yards at Koblenz.

Col Albert J. Shower, CO of the 467th BG, recalls: 'After the target the wing lead told us when over the Channel to break formation and return to base in individual streams of aircraft, due to our inexperience of night flying. We began to let down over France, and some of our gunners began returning ground fire. I told them to cease firing because we could not make out the targets properly and the firing might disclose our position. As we came over the Channel I directed a manouevre to break out into elements and then into single aircraft from a 360° turn. This the group performed. It was not a standard operation as we had never trained for night flying.'

Alvin Skaggs, pilot of *Vadie Raye* in the 448th BG (*Harmful Lil' Armful* having been shot down on 31 December), recalls: 'The ultimate German plan did not begin to unfold until we started back across the English Channel. It was getting dark, and tail gunner Bill Jackson noticed German fighters taking off from bases along the coast. He alerted the crew and I passed the word along to the command pilot, Capt Blum. He had heard no word over the command radio, but listened a while in case any of the commanders ahead of us were reporting this information to Fighter Command in England. After waiting a while he broke radio silence to report this threat and request fighter support.'

The Liberators crossed the French coast between Nieuport and Furnes while German fighters were taking off. The 448th began recrossing the English coast at points from Orford to Southwold, and other Groups were even further north. The skies over England were fairly clear, and although there was no moon the stars were out. Night flying with hundreds of aircraft in the same general area was very hazardous under the best conditions, but the lack of adequate signals by which to identify themselves to British anti-aircraft forces served to increase the difficulties of the American crews. The Luftwaffe pilots soon began switching off their lights, but the Liberators kept theirs on to facilitate formation flying.

The landing procedure required the Liberators to approach a homing beacon near Great Yarmouth at low altitude, go out to sea at about 1,500 ft, make a 180° turn for positive identification and return inland at this height. However, British coastal batteries began opening up, their fire not only embracing the enemy fighters but also the Liberators. Francis X. Sheehan was in the waist position of the *Vadie Raye*. 'Flak was showering all around us,' he wrote, 'and it hit the ship directly to our rear. It exploded in midair, and as I watched this ball of flame fall away I was completely stunned. On board the stricken B-24 had been Lt Cherry Pitts and his crew, among them our closest friends and barrack-mates, including Sgt Arthur Angelo. It was later discovered that the anti-aircraft gunners were firing at every aircraft that had followed us back across the Channel; later identified as Me 410s [of KG 51] which hit us around 1,000 ft.'

Jack Taylor, a member of the Royal Observer Corps at Beccles, was on duty that night. 'I went on duty at 10 o'clock,' he recalls, 'and was told that American bombers would soon be making landfall. Then, in the distance, I saw them coming in low with all their lights on. Suddenly their mighty drone was replaced with a different engine noise. A Ju 88 flew fairly low overhead, quickly followed by an Me 410. Soon, tracer bullets were ripping through the bomber formation over the Beccles area. One Liberator crashed near the school at Barsham [467th], and another fell on the railway line at Worlingham [448th]. I was the first to report to our centre: "Hostile aircraft in the vicinity: sound only." They replied: "There are no hostile aircraft on our chart." I heard other sounds and reported the plots to the centre, but received the same reply. I was very worried, knowing that all these bombers were coming in and being shot at like sitting ducks. I can only assume the German 'planes came in below the radar beams.'

Skaggs broke combat formation after seeing two more aircraft go down in flames, and headed in trail formation back to Seething. He says: 'Several 'planes from other formations had remained at altitude, and we could see some of them going down in flames with the fighters shooting at them. We could see others exploding and burning on the ground. At Seething some were on fire and others were off the runways.'

Hardwick, Bungay and Seething were illuminated by their runway and marker lamps. At just after 21:30 the 20th Wing split into three groups near Southwold to begin their landing patterns. By now the airfields themselves were being bombed and strafed. Some of the hardest hit were those in the Waveney Valley, home of the 20th Wing, where five Liberators were shot down within minutes.

Bill Carleton, Engineering Officer at Thorpe Abbotts, recalls: 'We were a little careless with our blackout, and at least one German saw the lights. He strafed the operations building as well as part of the field, but no-one was hurt. A B-24 flew over and our perimeter defence opened up, along with hundreds of other guns. Fortunately, they were all poor shots and the 'plane was not hit, but it was getting pretty dangerous on the ground. Strafing was one thing, but to have 4,000 "dingalings" shooting into the air was too much. I ran for cover in my newly-dug foxhole, tripped over the mound of dirt and fell into the hole on top of Sgt Spangler, the line chief, who had evidently taken refuge some timer earlier!'

At Rackheath, Joe Ramirez, crew chief of *Witchcraft*, was waiting at dispersal for the 467th BG to return. It was dusk, and he could see smaller aircraft coming in with the formation. He believed them to be escorting P-51s. Col Albert J. Shower was flying in the lead aircraft, piloted by Lt Richard Campbell, which was one of the last to land. He recollects: 'We were very close to landing when control told us to remain airborne. We made three approaches altogether. At one time we were all set to land when the runway lights were turned out and we were ordered to go around once again. Another time the lights were turned on for an approach on a different runway. Then one of the

B-24H Witchcraft *in flight. This was the only original 467th BG Liberator to survive the war with 133 missions to its credit.* (Alan Healy.)

crew reported that someone was on our tail. I told Campbell to turn off even the inside lights to avoid detection. I was quite impatient at the delay in landing, as it seemed every time we lined up we received a wave-off or the lights would be extinguished or the runway switched. The aircraft which were shot down were those that turned on their landing lights.'

As the first few bombers alighted on the runway the German pilots struck, firing their machine guns and dropping bombs. Aircraft veered in all directions, and the normally tranquil Rackheath sky was suddenly turned into a tumult. Anti-aircraft batteries opened up, while some crews manned their .5 calibre guns and blazed away at the intruders. An Me 410 made a pass over the airfield at 50 ft, firing tracers and dropping two bombs. A Liberator undergoing repairs under floodlights at the southern end of the airfield was hit, and Joe Ramirez, standing only one dispersal away, saw Pte Daniel F. Miney killed as he cycled across the concrete. Pte Michael F. Mahoney, a ground crewman working on the B-24, was wounded in the explosion. The other burst destroyed a cottage in the vicinity. Two B-24s were also lost. Lt Stalie C. Reid's Liberator, in the 791st Squadron, went down at Barsham. All the crew perished, trapped in the burning bomber. Lt Roden's B-24 in the 788th Squadron crashed at Mendham.

Col Shower was met by a worried Chaplain, Arthur L. Duhl. The attack passed by Rackheath, to be continued at other bases. A 458th Liberator piloted by Lt T. G. Harris, and Lt R. T. Couch, which crashed in Norwich, was thought to have been brought down by anti-aircraft batteries protecting the city. Russ D. Hayes, serving as an instructor at Horsham St. Faith, who had flown missions with the 389th BG, recalls: 'The sirens began to blow. As I looked into the sky

Col Albert J. Shower, CO of the 467th BG, in the cockpit of Little Pete 2, *a P-47 used by the 'Rackheath Aggies' for monitoring its Liberator formations.* (Alan Healy.)

the huge hulk of a B-24 was skimming the tree-tops with half the gliding plane aflame. I watched it until it was behind the trees, then heard a terrific explosion. As I scanned the skies once more there seemed to be one visible on every horizon of Norwich, and each bomber was trailing fire and smoke. I think the total was seven or more.'

Rick Rokicki, a gunner on *Briney Marlin* at Horsham St Faith, was not flying this day, but recalls the 'utter confusion': 'I know there was much speculation about the anti-aircraft fire and some of our guys were quite bitter about it, but it happened after many tiring hours in the air. Add to that the unfamiliar darkness and a flurry of fierce activity just when everyone figured that it was another mission "in the bag" – then being attacked!'

Liberators were prevented from landing at many bases by enemy fighters which circled like vultures, waiting for bombers to make the attempt. Crews panicked, and many gunners fired thoughtlessly and at random. One Liberator formation dropped flares, which only succeeded in exposing a Fortress formation heading for home. In the chaos *Cee Gee II*, flown by Lt James S. Munsey in the 453rd, which had its formation lights on, was attacked by an intruder aircraft 15 miles from the English coast. Cannon fire knocked Sgt Ralph McClure out of his tail turret and John McKinney, the left waist gunner, was hit in the chest and head on the same pass. The hydraulic system was shot out and the number two engine erupted in flames. It ignited the wing tanks, which exploded, blowing the living and dying through the waist hatch. Munsey and his co-pilot, Lt Robert Crall, managed to keep the B-24 airborne long enough for the five remaining crew to bale out over land. William C. Grady, the radio operator, was killed when his 'chute failed to open. The body of Grover Conway, the top turret gunner, was never found. *Cee Gee II* crashed in flames in soft coastal marshland near Southwold, with Munsey and Crall still in their seats. Munsey was posthumously awarded the DSC for his extraordinary heroism and, months later, at a ceremony in America, the medal was pinned to the coat of his three-year-old daughter, Carole Geane Munsey, for whom her father had christened *Cee Gee II*.

Meanwhile, *Vadie Raye* in the 448th BG was low on fuel, but so close to its home base at Seething that Skaggs decided to try for a landing. 'As we approached the downwind leg with the base just off to our left,' he recalls, 'an Me 110 made a pass at us and riddled our mid-section with hard-nose, soft-nose and .30-calibre tracer bullets. His tracers cut some of our fuel lines and started a fire in the bomb-bay section (later the ground defences shot him down).' Francis Sheehan was struck in the leg and went down on the floor. When he came to he and the nose gunner Eugene Gaskins baled out.

The fire swept from the rear of the bomb bay to the tail section. The rear gunner, Bob Jackson, also baled out and landed close to the MP station near Bungay (Jackson was later killed over Liege on 5 September 1944 by a small piece of flak). Alvin Skaggs remained to try and bring the blasted Liberator down safely: '*Vadie Raye* was now too low for any of the crew in the cockpit and forward section to bale out, so my only alternatives were either to reach a safe altitude for baling out or try to reach the field for a landing. All too soon the engines stopped running. I glanced back at the fire in the bomb bay and could see M/Sgt George Glevanik standing on the catwalk over the bomb bay doors right next to the flaming fuel lines. Seconds later the two outside engines suddenly sprang to life and I was able to climb back to pattern altitude of 1,000 ft. I later learned that George was able to get some fuel to the engines by holding his bare hands very tightly over the breaks in the lines.'

Skaggs was able to bring the burning Liberator down on to the runway at Seething. While it was rolling at 70–80 m.p.h., 1st Lt Don Todt, the navigator, and two others, went up through the top hatch and rolled out over the wing. Miraculously, they all survived. Skaggs and the others scrambled from the wreckage. Glevanik, the brave engineer, was the last to extricate himself. Sheehan and Gaskins had landed safely, and after some help from women at a Land Army hostel, had been returned to Seething by ambulance.

The burning pyre of the bomber illuminated the entire airfield. It served as a beacon for preying twin-engined German fighters, who swarmed towards it like moths to a candle. They strafed the base from every direction. Ground defences hit back with tracer. One intruder attempting to strafe the runway was foiled when someone extinguished the lights. Liberators making their final approach run were forced to circle again as officers in the control tower screamed over the

Capt Elbert Lozes, T/Sgt Ray K. Lee, S/Sgt Frank Sheehan and Capt William G. Blum the command pilot (KIA, 9 September 1944), pose in front of Vadie Raye *before take-off for the marshalling yards at Hamm on 22 April 1944. None could have foreseen their fateful return later that day.* (Sheehan.)

M/Sgt George Glevanik examines the skeletal remains of Vadie Raye *after the aircraft had crashed at Seething following the disastrous mission to Hamm on 22 April 1944.* (Gene Gaskins.)

Capt John Driscoll stands by the nose of Fightin' Sam. *Driscoll was decorated by Gen Jimmy Doolittle for helping rescue four crew members in Lt Edward Foley's crew in* Z-Bar, *which nosed in at Hethel on 22 April 1944 after being hit by flak near Norwich, in the confusion following the raid on Hamm. The crash destroyed a radar shack and killed some civilians inside, but the whole of Foley's crew survived. Gen Ted Timberlake had watched the brave rescue from the control tower.* (Driscoll.)

radio-telephone for them to remain airborne. Crews unable to make contact with traffic control, and with fuel getting low, decided to land. Inexperience was evident as pilots bringing in their B-24s applied the brakes so strongly that they burned out from under them and crews were blinded by flames.

Warnings were given of obstructions at the end of the runway, and when landing lights were momentarily flashed on pilots were horrified to see three wrecked Liberators in their path. They feverishly cut their throttles, but could not prevent their aircraft hurtling towards the wreckage. With collision unavoidable, ignition switches were turned off to lessen the risk of fire. There was a terrific, sickening crash as the bombers hit. Crews scrambled frantically from the upper fuselage, their escape route from underneath blocked because the bombers were embedded in deep mud. Then a fifth and final Liberator hurtled towards the pile and swelled the wreckage. In all, 13 Liberators crashed or crashlanded in east Norfolk on the night of 22 April. Two more were damaged on the ground. Over 60 men were killed and another 23 injured. The fires at Seething were not extinguished until 03:30 the following morning. All this destruction had been wrought by just six Me 410s.

The bombers were stood down, but missions resumed on Monday 24 April, when 750 bombers were despatched to bomb aircraft plants in the Munich area. The 41st Bomb Wing, which bombed the Dornier repair and assembly plant 15 miles south of Munich, bore the brunt of the attacks carried out by an estimated 200 enemy fighters. Of the wing's 15 losses, the 384th BG suffered the worst casualties, losing seven aircraft before the Luftwaffe turned its attention on the 40th Combat Wing. The 92nd BG lost five bombers in the resulting aerial battle, including Lt James E. King's B-17, which tried to reach neutral territory but exploded over Baltenswil, Switzerland. Three days later a funeral service was held for the crew in Berne, and their bodies were interred at the US cemetery at Munsingen. Altogether, 13 B-17s landed in Switzerland this day from the total loss of 39 bombers.

On 25 April almost 300 bombers blasted marshalling yards at

B-17s of the 452nd BG approach the enemy coast on the mission to Friedrickshafen on 24 April 1944. (Sam Young.)

Mannheim and airfields in France. The next day 292 heavies bombed Brunswick after thick cloud prevented bombing at primary targets. Nearly 50 more bombed targets of opportunity in the Hildesheim-Hannover areas. For the first time, on 27 April, when the 8th flew two bombing missions in one day, and the following day, the heavies bombed targets chiefly in France.

On the 28 April raids the 100th BG bombed a No-ball site at Sottevast, near Cherbourg. Col Robert H. Kelly, who had joined the group as CO on 19 April, was killed when his B-17 was hit by flak and disintegrated on the second of two runs over the target. He made the fatal mistake of maintaining the same height and direction as on the first run. John A. Miller, the right waist gunner aboard Lt Townsend's B-17, recalls: 'Lt James W. McGuire's B-17 had its number one engine knocked from its mounting. The engine landed back on the left wing, setting it on fire. As he dived out of formation the left wing snapped off and the 'plane tumbled, a ball of fire, into the clouds below.' Only John Jones, the bombardier, managed to bale out. Every B-17 received hits and was damaged.

On 29 April 579 bombers hit the Freidrichstrasse Bahnhof, the centre of the mainline and underground railway system in Berlin, while 38 other heavies attacked targets of opportunity in the area, including Magdebourg. The bomb groups encountered strong fighter opposition, and Fw 190s shot down or fatally damaged 17 Fortresses in the 4th Combat Wing in 20 minutes. The 385th BG, which was flying its 100th mission this day, lost seven bombers, and the 447th BG lost eleven. The latter group's losses brought its monthly total to 21 aircraft lost. The 94th and 96th BG's losses for April 1944 were also 21 bombers apiece, the 8th's heaviest of the war.

The 2nd Bomb Division, flying 30 minutes behind schedule, brought up the rear of the bomber stream and was met in strength by the Luftwaffe. After leaving Celle airspace the only protection afforded the B-24s was a solitary Mustang group, which was forced to retire just after the Liberators completed their bombing run. At the IP *Play Boy*, piloted by Frank Cotner in the 466th BG, received a direct hit from an 88 which knocked out the No. 3 three engine. Cotner completed the bomb run, but *Play Boy* was attacked by fighters after the target and went down over Holland. Sgt Falk, flying his first mission with the crew as waist gunner, was killed instantly by a shot through the head. Two of the crew evaded capture for the rest of the war, but Cotner was sent to Stalag Luft III.

It was not until the Liberators reached the Dummer Lake on the homeward journey that American fighter escorts reappeared, this time in the shape of P-47 Thunderbolts. German ground controllers, however, seized upon the time lapse and directed over 100 fighters to the Hannover area to intercept. Lt William Moore's B-24 in the 467th BG, which carried Maj Robert Salzarulo, CO of the 788th Bomb Squadron, was shot down over Holland. He and the crew were later reported to be prisoners of war. Lt John L. Low, the Group Bombardier, evaded capture for 296 days in enemy-occupied Holland and was liberated on 29 April 1945. Twenty-five Liberators were lost, including a 458th BG B-24 which was forced to land in Sweden.

During the morning of 1 May more than 500 heavies were despatched to 23 No-ball targets in the Pas de Calais while, in the afternoon, 328 B-17s and B-24s bombed marshalling yards and railway centres in France and Belgium. Both missions were in support of the Pointblank Directive, but bad weather fronts over the continent halted deep-penetration missions like the one to Brunswick and Berlin on 4 May, when 851 B-17s and B-24s were forced to abandon the mission over the Low Countries. The only raid on 5 May was mounted by 33 B-24s which bombed a VI site at Sottevast, and on 6 May 70 Liberators bombed another No-ball site at Siracourt. Over 90 bombers were prevented from bombing other V1 sites by thick overcast. It was hardly an inspiring debut for the 398th BG at Nuthampstead, commanded by Col Frank P. Hunter, which joined the 1st Combat Wing of the 1st Bomb Division.

During the morning of 7 May the B-17s headed for Berlin, joined for the first time by B-24s of the 486th and 487th BGs. These two groups, commanded by Col Glendon P. Overing and Lt Col Beirne Lay (who had been one of Eaker's original staff officers in 1942) at Sudbury (Acton) and Lavenham respectively, had arrived in England in April to join the 92nd Bomb Wing.

John A. Miller in the 100th BG formation recalls: 'Just as we were leaving England Lt Ralph W. Wright's B-17 dived out of formation after the flares, carried in the passageway to the nose, exploded. All the gunners baled out after much trouble, but all of the officers were burned to death.' Bernard Palmquist, the usual ball gunner, was still in hospital recovering treatment for a flak wound in his shoulder, sustained on the 28 April raid on Sottevast. Some 549 B-17s bombed 'Big-B' while 342 heavies bombed Osnabruck, Münster and targets of opportunity. In the afternoon 28 B-24s bombed targets in Belgium.

The next day Berlin was again bombed in the morning, this time by 378 B-17s, while 287 B-24s and 49 B-17s hit aircraft factories in the Brunswick area and 29 other heavies attacked targets of opportunity.

B-24 Liberators of the 486th BG on their bomb run. The Sudbury (Acton) Group made its debut using Liberators on 7 May 1944, and flew its first mission using B-17s on 1 August 1944. (Via Mike Bailey.)

487th BG Liberators taxi out at Lavenham, Suffolk, for the start of another mission. On 11 May 1944 the group lead and deputy lead were shot down. Col Beirne Lay Jr, the CO, baled out and evaded capture. (USAF.)

In the afternoon 81 B-17s bombed No-ball sites, while 56 B-24s bombed marshalling yards at Brussels. The day's raids proved costly; 36 bombers were shot down on the morning raids and five more in the afternoon.

On 9 May 797 bombers were despatched to enemy airfields and transportation targets. The Liberators attacked the railway marshalling yards at Liege, Belgium. Capt Ronald V. Kramer's B-24 in the 448th BG was hit by flak and burst into flames just as it released its bombs. All attempts to control the fire proved futile, and the crew were ordered to bale out. Kramer wrote: 'We were at 18,000 ft. It looked a long way to the ground but I did not hesitate. I jumped and dropped several thousand feet on my back. There was a terrific jerk after pulling the rip cord. Everything seemed very quiet after the terrific noise a few minutes before. I saw the burning pieces of our aircraft falling and tremendous palls of fire and smoke coming from the target. It was a lonely feeling to see our bombers disappearing in the west when in another hour I knew they would be back at Seething.' Kramer was hidden by some Belgian farmers, given a civilian suit and, accompanied by a Belgian who was presumably an underground agent, struck out for France. En route two German soldiers examined the Belgian's papers, but they were not in order and he was later shot. Kramer was taken to Luftwaffe headquarters in Brussels, where he was threatened with execution before being sent to Stalag Luft III.

On 11 May 254 B-24s bombed marshalling yards in France while 549 B-17s bombed marshalling yards in Germany and the Low Countries. Five Liberators, including one carrying Col Beirne Lay Jr, CO of the 487th BG, were shot down. (Lay evaded capture and was eventually returned to England). Eight Fortresses were also lost. Next day the 1st Division sought synthetic oil plants in the Leipzig area, while the 13th and 45th Wings of the 3rd Division went to oil targets in Czechoslovakia and two composite 4th Combat Wing formations attached to a Fw 190 depot at Zwickau.

More than 200 enemy fighters attacked the two composite formations for half an hour, and the 4th Wing lost 11 bombers, including seven from the 447th BG. The Fortresses which won through to the target achieved a highly effective bomb drop. The greatest credit went to the 385th BG, led by Col Vandevanter, the CO. He slowed down his own formation so that other, disorientated, groups could reform on them before starting the bomb run. The 385th stole the bombing honours, placing 97 per cent of its bombs within 2,000 ft of the MPI. This feat earned the group a DUC.

The 13th and 45th Wings, meanwhile, carried out a long and gruelling mission to the oil refinery complex at Brux. Mike Wysocki, in the 94th BG, was flying his 26th mission this day, and was angered by the 10½-hour round trip: 'Gen Doolittle had said missions were now getting shorter and easier! We were under constant fighter attack for 4½ hours, but we weren't so bad off, as the Luftwaffe attacked us from the tail position. They would sit out of range of our gunners and lob rockets at our formation. I had a ringside seat of the 45th Wing who were right in front of us. B-17s, P-51s, 110s and 109s were going down all over the place. I heard that the 452nd really took a beating. While all this was going on, all that was running through my mind was Doolittle telling us missions were getting shorter and easier. Well we finally got back and, after debriefing and cleaning up, I went to the officers' club and proceeded to get gloriously drunk.' Altogether, 46 bombers were shot down.

On 13 May 689 American crews bombed oil refineries at Politz on the Baltic coast and the marshalling yards at Osnabruck. Perry Rudd, in the 457th BG, recalls the trip to Politz: 'Going in over Denmark we were met by about 50 Bf 109s. They passed us and hit a low formation but they did little damage. The closest attacks came from 800 yards. We were lucky though and came through. I only saw one Fort' go down in flames, but quite a few had to leave formation. We had P-51s

A 34th BG B-24 streams smoke at altitude over occupied Europe. (Via Ian McLachlan.)

for escort at the time and there was quite a fright. However, they were forced to drop their tanks and left us as soon as the 109s departed.

'At Politz the clouds were 7 to 9/10ths, so we headed for the secondary target at Stettin instead. The town centre and the docks were hit and our 1,000 lb demolition bombs seemed to wreck the whole works. Flak over the target was light, but they really knew how to use it. Every burst was just off our wing tips at exactly the right altitude. We came off the target with open bomb bay doors which we had to crank down.

'There were no escorts after the target, but we could see Sweden off to our right and it looked really peaceful. Coming back across Denmark there must have been some Danes on the guns, because they fired at us plenty but a mile low and off to the left of us. Two or three guns opened up on a P-51 and gave him a really tough time. It was as if they were showing us they could do it if they wanted to but didn't.' Twelve bombers were lost on the day's raids.

On 14 May the weather grounded all three divisions, but 38 B-17s and 90 B-24s successfully bombed No-ball sites in France on the 15th. No more missions were flown until 19 May, which was frustrating for Joe Wroblewski, who was waiting to fly his 30th and final mission with the 351st BG. The wait was almost unbearable: 'After getting up at 01:00 hours for three straight days each mission was scrubbed. All would have been 'milk runs' or 'easy' raids. Then, at briefing on 19 May, when the weather finally cleared, I sat through briefing and the target was Berlin! What a way to end my tour!

'I cursed the weathermen all the way. He said we could have an overcast at the target with clouds coming up to 25,000 ft. We went in at 27,000 ft with a temperature of about minus 40°C. The clouds were nowhere to be seen, except for a puff here and there. Just before we got to Berlin about 30 enemy fighters came up and made a pass at the group just ahead of us, knocking down two bombers. I broke out in a sweat, and was glad to get into the flak before they could make another pass. Flak was the lesser of the two evils. It was heavy but inaccurate, and we only picked up a few holes and one piece tore away the tail gunner's shoe. He received no injury.

'Bombing was made visually. After "bombs away" the trip back was uneventful. We got a good look at Berlin and saw bombs from the groups ahead exploding in the city. This being our last mission, we shot a green flare upon returning to Polebrook. It sort of upset Colonel Romig, because this was against orders. He threatened us, but all we had to do for penitence was to go on a practice mission two days later.'

Some 493 B-17s had plastered the Friedrichstrasse section of Berlin, and 49 bombed Kiel. Meanwhile, 331 B-24s had set out for the marshalling yards at Brunswick. The mission began badly, and after delays and aborts 291 B-24s finally headed out towards Holland. Over the Zeider Zee a change in wind direction placed the Liberators ahead of schedule, enabling the Luftwaffe ground-controllers to vector 160 fighters against the American formation. The leading 20th Wing bombed at the first attempt and headed for home after almost colliding with the 96th Wing. The 14th Wing, flying behind the 20th Wing, arrived over the target behind schedule after turning late at the IP. Despite valiant efforts by three escorting fighter groups, the Liberators were overwhelmed. Eight ships in the 492nd BG, which had been operational for only eight days, were shot down. Lt Wyman Bridges brought *Lucky Lass* home to North Pickenham, Norfolk, after a collision with a Bf 109. His aircraft had only two engines and had lost half the starboard wing. His miraculous feat earned him the DFC. A total of 273 B-24s bombed successfully, but the day's losses totalled 28 heavies and 20 fighters.

On 20 May 287 bombers hit targets in France, while the second force of 250 heavies scheduled to bomb Liege and Brussels was forced to abort because of thick cloud over the targets. Bomb groups were stood down on the 21st, but the following morning 269 B-17s bombed Kiel and 94 B-24s struck at a No-ball target at Siracourt. This day Abe Dolim flew his 12th mission in the 94th BG. All went well until the group reached the target, as the young Hawaiian recalls: 'At the IP our lead aircraft had trouble withe its bomb bay doors. About five miles from the target it unloaded and, at the same time, most of our group salvoed their bombs. With considerable disgust I watched our bombs plough up same damned Kraut farmer's cabbage patch.

'Large numbers of enemy fighters appeared in the target area and soon we saw several P-38s and 109s in trouble. One P-38 pilot, with a Messerschmitt a bare 50 yards behind, flew under our formation from 12 o'clock but we could not help him. A German fighter pilot dangling from a cream coloured parachute passed within range just under our formation at 1 o'clock. It would have been easy to kill him as he floated past our right wing. Over at 11 o'clock I saw a B-17 straggling and losing altitude, fire sweeping its entire belly while the crew baled out. An airman left the right waist hatch, his open parachute on fire. God! What a miserable way to die.'

On 23 May 804 B-17s and B-24s (including, for the first time, B-24s

Two Liberators in the 754th (Z5) Squadron fly in formation with S.O.L., an Azon Liberator (J4) of the 753rd Squadron, all from the 458th BG. Azon masts can be seen underneath the rear of the aircraft. The first mission using Azon bombs was flown on 23 May 1944, against a bridge spanning the Loire. (Jack Krause.)

of the 34th BG from Mendlesham, commanded by Col Ernest J. Wackwitz), bombed several targets including Hamburg, Saarbrucken and French airfields for the loss of only one bomber; a 458th BG B-24 which collided with a Fortress over Eye, Suffolk, while forming up for the mission to Bourges. Six crewmen were killed. The next day 447 B-17s bombed 'Big-B' while 400 Liberators again bombed airfields in France. Cloud and thick contrails caused the 381st BG to lose contact with other groups in the 1st Wing, and eight B-17s were shot down by fighters. The 'Bloody Hundredth' also suffered badly, losing nine Fortresses from the day's total loss of 33.

The next day crews correctly anticipated a 'milk run' to the Low Countries. Despite perfect weather, some Fortresses in the 390th and 401st BGs bombed using radar. Command needed to know how successful PFF methods could be on D-Day if targets were obscured by cloud. It all served to increase speculation, at Framlingham and Deenthorpe at least, that the invasion of 'Festung Europe' was imminent.

On 27 May 923 B-17s and B-24s pounded the German rail network. Some 24 bombers were lost, including one 458th BG Liberator which collided with another 755th Squadron B-24 north of Cromer in undercast during assembly. One B-24 went into a spin and only one crewman, who left by the waist window, was seen to escape. Two men baled out of the other B-24, but those who remained with the aircraft managed to bring it home safely to Horsham St. Faith.

Col James R. Luper, CO of the 457th, led the Fireball Outfit and the 1st Division to Ludwigshafen in *Rene III*, the 1,000th B-17 built by Douglas, and named after Luper's wife. The flak was heavy, and fighters made head-one attacks that verged on the suicidal. *Rene III* was badly shot up, but Luper nursed her back to Glatton for a crashlanding. She was repaired and flew again. Three other B-17s in the 457th failed to return and 19 were severely mauled.

On the following day three more 457th crews were lost. The 8th despatched a record 1,282 bombers to seven oil targets in Germany. Lt John R. Shaffer, the bombardier in *Naughty Nan* in the 93rd BG, was flying his second mission, to the synthetic oil refinery at Meresburg, the second largest of its type in Germany. 'Flames reaching to 2,000 ft were proof enough that the Liberators had found their mark. Even 200 miles from the target, crews could still see a pall of smoke, which rose 12,000 ft into the air.'

Lt William Bailey's crew, in the 448th BG, were flying their first mission. Ben C. Isgrig, the bombardier, recalls: 'Our particular target was the ammonia section of the plant. We were carrying 48 100 lb GP bombs, and were in the first section over the target. I guess we were all pretty scared and nervous. I watched the lead plane's bombs begin to drop and started to toggle ours out, but, instead of falling clear, seven bombs in the right rear rack hung up. I went back into the bomb bay and was scared to see that the propellers on the fuses of three of the bombs were turning rapidly, which meant they were probably fused and liable to go off at the slightest jolt.

'I got Kovalcheck, a gunner, to help me and were able to get them out by lifting them up one at a time and dropping them out. It was a wonder that one or both of us didn't fall out of the bomb bay. It's no joke to stand on a foot-wide catwalk with no parachute at 22,000 ft in a 20° below zero breeze and no support, and throw out bombs one at a time. Kovalcheck was using our one walkaround oxygen bottle; I had none. As we turned to leave the bomb bay I stumbled and nearly fell from the 'plane, but Kovacheck caught me and pulled me through the door and to the nearest oxygen outlet. The trip home was uneventful.' Altogether, 32 bombers were lost, including seven B-17s in the 401st BG.

On 29 May 881 bombers were despatched to several targets, including the oil plants at Politz and the Junkers Ju 88 plant at Tutow, Ben Isgrig had been assured that the bomb racks had been repaired, but 11 of the 32 100 lb M47 incendiary bombs hung up and, wearing an oxygen mask this time, he salvoed them in the general area of Tutow. Some 34 bombers were lost, including a Liberator in the 492nd BG piloted by Lt William V. Prewitte, which was forced to ditch in the North Sea while returning from Politz. Prewitte's crew was rescued by an ASR launch from Gorleston. Charles Halliday, who was on board the launch, dived into the sea and rescued Lt Elmer W. Clarey, the co-pilot, who had become tangled in his parachute and was being dragged him under. Unfortunately, the bombardier, Lt Henry Muller, drowned after his parachute had failed to open.

On the morning of 30 May 911 heavies, including, for the first time, the B-24s of the 489th BG from Halesworth, were despatched in six forces to attack aircraft targets in Germany, marshalling yards in Belgium and France, and No-ball sites in the Pas de Calais. The 94th BG bombed a rocket storage site at Watten with special loads of six 1,600 lb semi-armour-piercing bombs to penetrate the roof. Mike Wysocki, who was on his 30th and final mission, recalls: 'All I could see was dust in the target area. I was disappointed to think on my last mission that all I dropped was a bunch of duds! (A couple of months later Maj Stevenson, the 410th Bomb Squadron CO, called me over and told me those damn Navy bombs went through the roof right down to the cellar and blew the joint out of operation!) When we came back our B-17 was like a Roman Candle, with all the flares going. It looked like a good old fashioned Fourth of July, only it happened to be Memorial Day!'

On 31 May 371 bombers, including for the first time B-24s of the 490th BG from Eye, Suffolk, led by the CO, Col Lloyd H. Watnee, attacked targets in Germany and Belgium. Meanwhile, four specially equipped Liberators in the 753rd Bomb Squadron in the 458th BG attempted to bomb five bridges at Beautmont-sur-Oise, Melun, and Meulan in France with the revolutionary Azon glider bomb. The device could be released by an aircraft at a distance and then directed on to the target. Basically, it was a conventional 1,000 lb bomb fitted with radio-controlled moveable tail fins. Visibility had to be good to enable the operator in the B-24 to see it right to the target. For this purpose a smoke canister was attached. Each bomber could carry three such bombs, but had to circle the target as many times to release

B-24 Betta Duck *in the 34th BG over the Suffolk countryside in the summer of 1944. This aircraft was transferred to the 466th BG when the Mendlesham outfit converted to the B-17G in September.* (Via Mike Bailey.)

them, which was an obvious disadvantage. The 30 May raid ended in failure, none of the bombs hitting the target. Experimental raids continued in June, with, at most, 15 Liberators being used on any one mission, but results did not improve and Gen Doolittle was forced to abandon the project.

Operation 'Cover' called for raids on coastal defences, mainly in the Pas de Calais, to deceive the Germans as to the area to be invaded by the Allied armies massing in Britain. On 2 June the 8th mounted two strikes on the Pas de Calais. In the first raid, 776 B-17s and B-24s were involved. In the second raid 300 bombers, including, for the first time, B-24s of the 489th and 491st BGs flying the first full 95th Wing mission, struck at airfields and railway targets in France. The two 95th Wing groups bombed Bretigny, Creil and Villeneuve airfields near Paris for the loss of one 491st BG Liberator and four 489th B-24s. Flak also caused varying degrees of damage to 59 other machines. Thirty-five 491st Liberators approached their home base at Metfield, Suffolk, in gathering darkness and landed safely, but at Halesworth three of the returning 37 489th Liberators crashed and had to be written off.

For the next three days hundreds of 8th Air Force bombers flew two missions a day to the Pas de Calais area. On 4 June *Sack Rat*, piloted by Lt Clifford R. Galley in the 491st, developed a high speed stall while forming up and crashed near Sizewell, Suffolk, killing everyone on board.

On Monday 5 June 629 bombers attacked coastal defence installations in the Cherbourg-Caen and Pas de Calais areas, together with three No-ball sites and a railway bridge. Six B-24s, including *Missouri Sue* (a 44th BG PFF ship), which carried the 489th BG deputy Commander Lt Col Leon R. Vance, were lost. A malfunction prevented bomb release on the target, a V1 site near Wimereaux and, despite protests, Vance ordered the crew to go around again. This time the bomb drop was made by hand but two bombs hung up. Now the flak had increased in intensity and an 88 mm salvo burst directly

Lt Col Leon Vance (left) with the 489th BG CO, Col Ezekiel W. Napier, at Wendover Field, Utah, in December 1943. Vance was awarded the Medal of Honor for his actions on 5 June 1944. (Charlie Freudenthal.)

under the port wing. Capt Louis A. Mazure, the pilot, was killed instantly when he was hit in the temple, and Earl L. Carper, the co-pilot, was seriously wounded. Three engines were put out of action and *Missouri Sue* rose menacingly on the verge of a stall.

The tall, rangy, colonel, who was standing behind the pilots' seats, looked down to see that his right foot had been virtually severed from his leg and was attached only by the Achilles tendon, which was jammed behind the co-pilot's seat. Despite his terrible injury, Vance managed to reach the panel and feather the three useless engines. Carper cut all four engines and turned the B-24 towards England. When the shoreline came into view Lt Bernard W. Bail, the radar navigator, ordered the crew to evacuate the B-24.

Although he was suffering from shock, Bail managed to get the colonel down into his navigator's seat. He took off his belt and wound it around Vance's thigh to stop the blood spurting. His quick thinking undoubtedly saved Vance's life. Bail told him they would have to jump because there was no way they could land the B-24, especially since the two bombs were ready to go off on impact. The colonel shook his head and said he would not jump. Bail knew that he could not possibly drag Vance to the bomb bay and push him out, and he was also aware that the aircraft was rapidly losing altitude. There was little time left to save himself. Bail checked the tourniquet one last time, shook Vance's hand, and jumped from the open bomb bay. Vance managed to get into the cockpit, and succeeded in ditching within reach of the English coast. The impact blew him clear of the aircraft, and he was quickly picked up by ASR, who gave him immediate medical attention.

Vance was awarded the Medal of Honor. He was the fifth and final airman in the 2nd Bomb Division to receive the award (the other four all being awarded for actions at Ploesti in August 1943). He underwent amputation of his right foot, and was later invalided home in a C-54. Somewhere between Iceland and Newfoundland the Skymaster with its crew and patients disappeared without trace. (Bail was later shot down, on a mission to Stüttgart, his 25th operation, and made a Pow).

Meanwhile, on the night of Monday 5 June Abe Dolim recorded in his diary: 'There have been all sorts of rumours about an imminent invasion of the enemy coast'. Ben Smith in the 303rd BG at Molesworth, wrote: 'We saw RAF aircraft and gliders coming over, wave after wave. We knew we would be going in the morning and thought there would be hell to pay. We didn't sleep much that night.'

Chapter Twelve

D-Day and beyond

COMBAT CREWS IN the 446th BG at Bungay (Flixton) airfield were tumbled out of their bunks during the night of 5 June, and the Tannoy system summoned them to a main briefing at 22:30. Top brass from both 2nd Bomb Division and Wing headquarters had descended on the base, and senior officers had quickly disappeared behind locked doors for a hastily convened conference. Field Order No 328 came in over the teletape machines throughout the three Divisions. At Flixton, flying control was the first to receive the news. To almost everyone's surprise and delight, the Bungay Buckeroos had been selected to lead the entire 8th Air Force over the invasion coast of France on D-Day.

Four more briefings followed into the small hours of 6 June. The briefings, given by Capt Hurr, were the longest and most detailed the group had ever received. Crews were advised that six Liberator elements would take off at ten-minute intervals. Maj Stahl concluded the briefing: 'You are to strike the beach defences at Point de la Percèe, dropping your bombs not later than two minutes before zero hour [06:30]. Landing craft and troops will be 400 yards to one mile offshore as we attack, and naval ships may be shelling our targets onshore. Deadline on our primary target is zero hour minus two [06:38]. After that, bomb the secondary target, which is the road junction in the Forest of Cerissy, or the target of last resort, which is the choke point in the town of Vire.'

Squadron operations were notified that the mission was to be a maximum effort, so that ground crews would have to pull out all the stops. Orders for bomb loading and fuelling were issued earlier than usual, and no one a permitted to leave the base. At nearby Seething the 448th crews were called to the briefing room at 23:00 and Col Jerry Mason said: 'This is it'. Their target was Omaha Beach. The first mission was primarily concerned with the neutralizing of enemy coastal defences and front-line troops. Subsequent missions would be directed against lines of communication leading to the bridgehead. The Liberators would be in good company, with no fewer than 36 squadrons of Mustangs and Thunderbolts patrolling the area. Initially, they would protect the bombers, but would later break off and strafe ground targets. It was evident that there could be no delay, and that stragglers would be left to their fate. Any aborts were to drop out of the formation before leaving the English coast and then fly back to base at below 14,000 ft. It was a one-way aerial corridor, and the traffic flow would be intense. If a B-24 had to be ditched, only those ships returning to England from the beachhead would stop to pick up crews. Gen Doolittle, in a message read out to the men at all bases, said: 'The 8th Air Force is currently charged with a most solemn obligation in support of the most vital operation ever undertaken by our armed forces . . .'

The briefing over, a line of trucks was assembled to take the crews to their waiting Liberators. At 01:30 the slumbering cathedral city of Norwich and the pre-dawn calm of the surrounding countryside were shattered by the roar of hundreds of Twin Wasps and Wright Cyclones being pre-flighted at all points of the compass. Overhead, the moon shone through thick black undercast. By 02:00 the Liberators at Flixton were formed in two lines, converging at the head of the runway. This avoided the problem of anyone leaving a revetment, going off the runway, and ruining the timetable. Col Joe Brogger, the air commander, sat in the cockpit of *Red Ass*, referred to (for public relations purposes) *The Buckeroo*, piloted by Lt Charlie Ryan of the 704th Bomb Squadron. All aircraft had their navigational lights on, with the yellow-orange assembly ship, *Fearless Freddie*, completing the picturesque spectacle.

Just on 02:20 Capt Smith in the control tower, told the crew of the chequered caravan at the edge of the runway to: 'Give 'em the green light,' and the B-24s thundered down the runway. The first to arrive in the assembly area was *Liberty Run*, a PFF ship in the 564th Squadron of the 389th BG, which Lt L. J. Litwiller of the 93rd BG and his crew had flown over specially from Hethel the previous afternoon. The dead-reckoning Navigator, Robert A. Jacobs, recalls: 'At this time the 564th Squadron was composed of selected lead crews from 2nd Bomb Division units who were given additional training in PFF techniques, which included bombing through undercasts using H2X radar'. Col Brogger and the other 446th aircraft in the lead

B-24 Red Ass *in the 704th BS, 446th BG.* (USAF.)

section formed on *Liberty Run* and headed for France. There was a solid undercast, and the 446th released its bombs on the H2X aircraft's smoke markers.

Ben Isgrig in the 448th recalls: 'It was just getting light as our formation left the English coast, and the clouds broke enough for us to see the hundreds of ships in the Channel heading for France. We could plainly see the heavy warships shelling the coast, which was shrouded in smoke. Beside seeing more ships than I had ever seen before, there were also more heavy bombers in the air than I thought possible to put up in one area.'

In all, 1,361 bombers were despatched on the first of the four missions flown on D-Day. Bob Shaffer, the bombardier in *Naughty Nan* of the 93rd BG, flown by Lt Sneddon, wrote: 'I saw battleships firing at gun emplacements. It was quite a sight – quite a show. The flak was light and the mission successful.' Isgrig, however, recorded: 'The coast itself was covered in clouds. We didn't see our target at all; neither did we see flak or fighters.' Some 1,015 heavies bombed coastal installations, while 47 hit transportation choke points in Caen and 21 more hit alternative targets.

There was no sleep for those left behind, who would fly the second and successive missions to Normany. Henry Tarcza, the navigator in *El's Bells*, piloted by Matthew McEntee, was at the 95th BG's base at Horham, Suffolk. He recalls: 'The red streamers on the map ran from every airbase in England and crossed the Channel, converging on one tiny spot near Cherbourg. The briefing colonel pointed towards that area with what happened to be an old billiard cue and said: "Yes gentlemen, this is the day you've been waiting for and this is the spot that has been selected." It was a relatively short briefing because the navigators had already been given separate instructions. Before unlocking the exit doors the briefing officer smiled and said: "Good luck gentlemen and give 'em Hell!"'

Perhaps it was the tension brought on by the big occasion, but not

S/Sgt Hugh R. McLaren, ball-turret gunner in the 565th Bomb Squadron, 389th BG, poses in front of the B-24 at Hethel which was originally just called Patches. *On 6 June 1944* Patches *was almost cut in half by the premature explosion of a fragmentation bomb. It was repaired and the name changed to* D-Day Patches. (McLaren.)

Tar Hell Baby, 41-29125, *in the 446th BG, overflies Portland Harbour, Dorset, on D-Day, 6 June 1944.* (USAF.)

all crewmen were impressed with the message from Gen Eisenhower, which was read out at all bases. Ben Smith recalls: 'At briefing we heard Eisenhower's inspirational message to the departing troops. At least it was supposed to inspire. I remember thinking that Churchill could have done it with a lot more class.'

Lt Franklin L. Betz, a navigator in Capt Douglas H. Buskey's crew in the 379th BG, lifted off from Kimbolton at 04:45. 'The lead 'plane roared down the runway, lifting gracefully into the grey light of the early morning,' he remembers. 'The remaining Fortresses, lined up like dancers in a conga line, swung on to the runway in turn and followed. My heart raced from the excitement of knowing that I was involved in an undertaking that, if successful, would be a major turning point of the war.

'The fluffy layer of clouds below hampered visibility, but there were some breaks on them and I could see the choppy dark waters of the English Channel. As we droned steadily toward the continent, I gasped when a huge opening in the clouds revealed ships and boats of all sizes dotting the water as far as I could see. Hundreds – no, there must be thousands, I thought. Although no one type of ship could be identified from nearly three miles high, I was to learn later practically the whole spectrum of powered vessels from battleships to motor launches made up the invasion fleet.

'More holes appeared in the clouds and the awesome spectacle continued to unfold. I arose from my seat in the navigator's cramped work area in the left rear of the B-17G's nose to get a better view from the right waist window. Fascinated, I saw puffs of white smoke snort

Baby Doll *and other Liberators in the Debach based 493rd BG in formation. (Via Mike Bailey.)*

from the huge guns of battleships and cruisers aimed toward the mainland, and a moment later massive explosions could be seen a short distance inland where the shells landed, kicking up a fountain of dirt and debris that, I reflected, must be a mixture of steel and stones, flesh and bones when the targets were hit.'

Henry Tarcza gazed in awe at the hundreds of ships and boats off Omaha Beach below: 'All were headed toward the beach landing site, and it appeared from our altitude that one could almost step from one vessel to another and walk between England and France.

'Our group of about 40 B-17s in close formation began to ease its way into the narrow corridor for the bomb run. As we reached Omaha Beach the lead 'plane released a smoke bomb, which was a signal for all 40 aircraft in to drop their bombs simultaneously. Thus, more than 100 tons of bombs exploded in a matter of a few seconds. This was the only mission over Europe when I actually felt the concussion of our own bombs. The explosions caused our aircraft to bounce and vibrate. Obviously, the long-planned invasion had remained a well guarded secret. We encountered no German aircraft in the target area and enemy gunfire was very light and inaccurate.' Altogether, 528 bombers were despatched on the second strike. Most crews returned with their bombs because their targets were covered by cloud, though some 37 bombers did manage to bomb Argentan.

Meanwhile, groups in the 1st Task Force of the 1st Bomb Division prepared to bomb their allotted targets in the Cherbourg peninsula. Perry Rudd's B-17 was one of a record 48 despatched by the 457th BG that day: 'We flew over our target in the Cherbourg Peninsula at 16,400 ft and dropped 38 100 lb demolition bombs through overcast. The landing troops hit the beach 14 minutes after we dropped our bombs. There were reports that some of our bombs were still exploding as the boys went in.'

Frank Betz, in the 379th, dropped his bombs at 07:07 from 14,750

A 486th BG Liberator passes over Allied shipping off the Normandy beach-head near Caen on D-Day, 6 June 1944. (USAF.)

ft. He recalls: 'The return to Kimbolton was uneventful, and was indeed a "milk run" from the standpoint of no enemy fighter attacks and no flak. We touched down at 09:26 and I could sense an air of excitement on the base when I dropped to the ground from the 'plane after the pilot parked it in the dispersal area. What I had seen through the breaks in clouds was an unforgettable sight.'

Excited crews touched down at their bases and poured out their stories to receptive ground crews and newsmen. Perry Rudd recalls: 'Coming back across the Channel we could see more ships than you could count. It really was a sight to see the invasion fleet at a port in England ready to set out. They must have been part of the second wave to go over. The boys wanted to go in low for a look, but they made us stay up.'

Back at Horham, Henry Tarcza and the rest of the crew told an Associated Press reporter their views on the historic mission. 'Emotions varied among our crewmembers,' says Tarcza. 'Many of our thoughts, feelings and opinions we kept to ourselves. As we all parted for our respective quarters Matthew McEntee said: "Thank you, men, for your fine co-operation as a combat crew. It is doubtful if any of us will ever in our lifetime, participate in a historic undertaking of this magnitude." So far, nobody has.'

Ironically, amid all this activity, the German radio station at Calais was on the air playing a song called *Invasion Day*. The third mission involved bombing the important communication centre at Caen, and 56 Liberators managed to bomb through overcast skies. Not all of the Fortress groups made it, as Perry Rudd recalls: 'We were briefed for two more raids in the afternoon, but the weather was too bad for us to fly. I really wanted to make both of them, but we'd probably have lost more ships because of the weather than by the Jerries.'

Ben Smith, in the 303rd BG, was one who did get a second look, when 553 bombers hit transportation chokepoints in towns imme-

B-17 D-Day Doll *in the 447th BG reveals two sides to its nature.* (Robert E. Foose.)

diately south and east of the invasion beaches. 'We flew two missions on D-Day,' he says, 'and did not see a single German fighter or even a burst of flak. Amazing! I could see a battleship out in the Channel; I believe it was the *Texas*, firing at shore targets. There was a solid mass of ships offshore, and we could see the beach head landing craft and others streaking in with their precious burdens. At least, we knew we had made a beach head.'

A total of 2,362 bomber sorties, involving 1,729 B-17s and B-24s, was flown on D-Day, dropping 3,596 tons of bombs for the loss of only three Liberators. One belonging to the 487th BG at Lavenham was

B-24H Liberator Fords' Folly *in the 578th Bomb Squadron, 392nd BG, is loaded up with ammo for its 100th mission, on 6 June 1944. The B-24 was hit over Koblenz on 11 September 1944 by fighters which set the No.3 engine on fire. The aircraft was engulfed in flames, and was last seen spinning in and crashing with the loss of Lt C. A. Rudd's entire crew.* (USAF.)

shot down, and two others collided. (The Liberators of the 493rd BG from Debach, commanded by Col Elbert Helton, made their debut. VIII Fighter Command flew 1,880 sorties and claimed 28 enemy fighters shot down.

Ground crews worked throughout the night of 6 June and all day on the 7th so that two missions could be flown. On 8 June 1,135 bombers were despatched to communication targets in France. Bad weather prevented 400 heavies from bombing, and next day cancelled out any bomber strikes at all. It also severely curtailed operations on 10 June. Of the 873 bombers airborne, over 200 were forced to abort because of

B-24J Lucky Penny, *42-220169, in the 853rd Bomb Squadron, 491st BG, piloted by Lt Fletcher Sharp, on his fourth mission, suffered a crucial power failure on take-off from Metfield on 8 June 1944. It veered off course and, as a wing dragged, slewed into the ground. Two of the 1,000 lb bombs exploded, killing all the crew and damaging several B-24s nearby.* (Dan Winston.)

cloud conditions. Some 589 bombers, including 31 Pathfinders, attacked eight airfields in France and nine coastal installations in the Pas de Calais. A 448th BG Liberator, shot down by flak just east of Evereux, was the only bomber lost on 10 June. Ben Isgrig recalls: 'The ship directly behind us caught fire in the bomb bay and fell apart just as it dropped its bombs. Seven 'chutes were seen over the target; a hell of a place to have to bale out. Our left wing ship had its right waist window shot out and some men wounded. We dropped our bombs through clouds.'

On 11 and 12 June bad weather ruled out targets in Germany, and the 8th despatched its bombers to France. On the 11th the 96th Wing was prepared for a strike on the highly important railway bridge at Blois-Saint-Denis on the Loire, about halfway between Tours and Orleans. After the briefings at Horsham St. Faith, Attlebridge and Rackheath, crews were in no doubt as to what must be the final outcome of the attack on the bridge which the Germans were using to supply troops attacking the Allied bridgehead. The Field Order called for the destruction of the bridge at all costs. There was to be no minimum altitude established for the bombing, which was to be made through the clouds in three-ship elements if overcast obscured the target.

Lt Col Harlan Oakes was one of those who flew in the 466th. 'I was not authorized to go on the raid,' he says, 'being in A-2 Section and working with British Intelligence. Warren K. Burt, pilot of the ship I flew in, agreed to say nothing of the matter. We proceeded to the hardstand after a briefing which was short, being told that we would be more fully briefed when we were airborne. Had I known, coward that I am, I would not have picked this mission for a "joy ride". I should have had an inkling that something was amiss as we were loading bombs at the hardstand in the darkness. One 2,000 lb GP bomb out of a total of three dropped on the hardstand: deathly silence, and Burt's voice roared out: "What the hell are you trying to do, kill us all?"'

The 458th BG, with 12 Liberators from the special 753rd Azon Squadron, led the mission with 15 Liberators of the 467th and 19 B-24s of the 466th. Harlan Oakes continues: 'We were advised in the air that our rendezvous was with the 467th, and were given a diversionary support unit which faked a flight towards Paris. We were also advised to bomb visually, no matter how low we had to fly. Our cameras and intervalometers for photos were set for 20,000 to 25,000 ft, the normal altitude. As a former photographer for the Air National Guard, I realized that the automatic cameras were going to leave a lot of blank spot on film and the results could not be ascertained.

'We maintained strict radio silence until we turned on the bomb run. By this time we were down to about 6,000 ft, as the cloud cover had lowered. On the actual drop the altimeter reading was approximately 5,500 ft according to Capt Burt. Our group lead navigator, Capt Leeds, had us dead on target and our lead bombardier, Capt Gerald Merket, had us dead on with bomb-sights. There was a lot of chatter on the intercoms during the run. Most of us were a little concerned over automatic flak at that altitude. We were certainly sitting ducks, lumbering along at about 155 m.p.h. indicated air speed. But the Lord takes care of fools and drunks and babies. Although no-one had been drinking we certainly were thankful for his consideration of the other two categories.

'I had to open the escape hatch in the rear to get a shot of the run, and was glad when Sgt "Pop" Julian said he would hold on to my 'chute harness while I leaned out of the hatch to take the pictures. We had not one shot fired at us in anger, although we did see a convoy of Germans off to our right after the drop. Significantly, there were a couple of French farmwomen near the bridge, waving white cloths at us as we flew over. I should guess the most danger we were in on this raid was at the bombing time and when the lead pilot started to fly over a convoy in the Channel when we were returning to England. We bombed about 09:00 hours and made landfall about 10:00 hours in the West Country.' This was the first low-altitude bombing ever performed by heavy bombers operating from England, and the result was decisive. The bridge was completely destroyed in the hail of bombs dropped by the 96th Wing, and the 458th received a 2nd Bomb Division citation.

On the next day, 12 June, William Bailey's crew in the 448th taxied out for their ninth mission, to Rennes, but their B-24 developed electrical trouble and they were given a replacement ship called *Squat 'n' Droppit*. Durwood Stanley, the regular ball-turret gunner, had already been withdrawn and the crew was reduced to nine members. Bailey took off late and tagged on to the 446th BG. At the IP the mission turned to a disaster. No fewer than four bomb runs were attempted, and on the fourth *Squat 'n' Droppit* was hit by flak. Enemy fighters attacked the lone 448th aircraft, and Isgrig heard Ken Zierdt, the radio operator, repeat over and over in a steady voice: 'Fire in the bomb bay, Fire in the bomb bay!' In a few more seconds someone said: 'Get the hell out of here'.

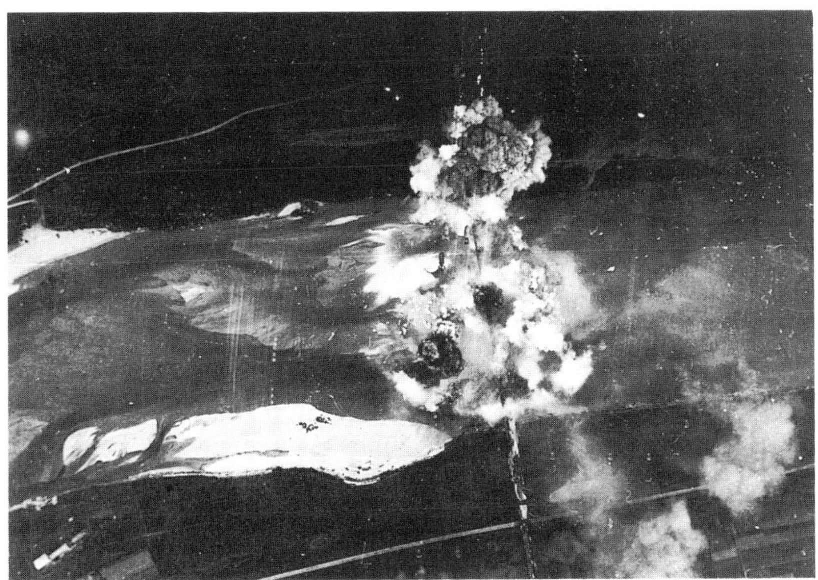

Bombs from Liberators of the 96th Bomb Wing hurtle down on the railway bridge at Blois-St Denis, France, on 11 June 1944. This photograph was taken by Harlan Oakes of the 466th BG, at 5,500 ft while suspended half out of the camera hatch! (Oakes.)

Vic Fleishman, the navigator, and Leslie Fischer, the engineer, baled out, and Isgrig quickly followed. Meanwhile, George Cooksey and Zierdt had opened the bomb bay doors and had baled out. Zierdt was hit by machine gun fire from a Bf 109 and died later on the ground. Isgrig continues: 'A Mustang circled lazily above me while another followed the German down. The Bf 109 cut to the left; passing within fifty yards of me, and began to climb. The P-51 was right on his tail. I screamed and cursed the German, waving and offering all my moral support to the American as he passed. The German didn't have a chance. Within ten seconds his ship began to fall apart and burn. The German baled out and he landed three hundred yards from me.'

After shooting down the Bf 109, the P-51 climbed toward Fischer, circled him, and waggled his wings before roaring away. (Long after the war Isgrig and Fischer discovered that their saviour had been Maj George Preddy of the 352nd Fighter Group. Preddy, who was killed on Christmas Day 1944, finished the war as the number two American air ace in Europe). Bailey's crew were rescued by the French resistance and were returned safely to England after D-Day.

Tactical targets in France continued to be attacked until 15 June, when the 40th Combat Wing was despatched to Nantes to finish off the railway bridge and 1,225 bombers attacked an oil refinery at Misburg. The 1st Division, meanwhile, struck at targets in northern France – mostly airfields which could be used to launch Luftwaffe attacks on the Normandy bridgehead. At the Le Bourget and Melum airfields, near Paris, five B-17s in the 457th BG, including the lead ship flown by the Lt Malcom Johnson and which carried Col Cobb of the 94th Wing, were brought down by flak. One of them ditched in the Channel, and five of the crew drowned before ASR could reach them.

B-24 Liberators over the burning oil refineries at Politz on 20 June 1944. (USAF.)

After the D-Day missions raids were made on oil and tactical targets. On 20 June a record 1,402 bombers were despatched on two missions against oil and No-ball targets. In the morning's mission 1,257 B-17s and B-24s of the 1st and 3rd Bomb Divisions made for Hamburg and the Hannover and Magdeburg areas respectively. The 2nd Division made a 9¼-hour round trip to Politz and Ostermoor. Some 760 fighters escorted the three Divisions to their targets, while 130 Liberators bombed ten No-ball targets in the Pas de Calais, escorted by 42 P-47s.

The Luftwaffe intercepted the 2nd Division while it was temporarily without adequate fighter cover. The Steeple Morden based 355th Fighter Group had been delayed by its new-type drop tanks, which failed to jettison, leaving only the 339th Fighter Group from Fowlmere to protect the entire 2nd Bomb Division. To make matters worse, the Mustangs were forced to escort a strung-out formation. The 14th Wing in the van was six minutes behind schedule, while the last wing was two minutes behind.

Messerschmitt Me 110s and Me 410s ripped through the formations over the Baltic with rockets firing and cannon blazing. Lt Keller in the 44th BG was forced to make for Sweden after sustaining damage, while five B-24s in the 492nd formation were shot down. Flak was also heavy and *Heavenly Body*, piloted by Lt Dudley Friday in the 491st formation, was hit by a shell which tore through the floor of the flightdeck and ripped through the roof of the fuselage, taking the radio-operator's seat with it. Fortunately, no-one was injured. Another flak burst rocked Lt Charles Stevens' B-24 and shot away the nose section. The bombardier and navigator were killed, but Stevens nursed the bomber back to England and made a superb one-engined landing on Dover beach. Two crewmen were killed when they decided to chance jumping from the B-24. They delayed pulling their ripcords and their parachutes failed to deploy fully.

Anxious eyes scanned the skies over East Anglia when it was realized that 34 bombers were missing. The severest blow was felt at North Pickenham, home of the 492nd, where 14 B-24s failed to return. Lt Velarde's B-24, in the 856th Squadron, which returned early with engine trouble, was the only Liberator in the squadron to survive the mission. Five of the 18 B-24s that put down at Bulltofta airfield, at Malmo in Sweden, came from the 492nd. In all, 50 heavies and seven fighters were lost this day. There was some consolation in the news that synthetic oil production at the Politz plant had been severely reduced.

On 21 June the 8th flew its second shuttle mission from England. The operation, code-named 'Frantic', employed 1,311 bombers. Some 163 B-17s of the 13th and 45th Wings of the 3rd Division, each equipped with a long-range bomb bay tank, bombed the Rhurland-Elsterwerda synthetic oil plant 50 miles south of Berlin and then flew on to Russia, escorted all the way by 70 Mustangs of the 4th and 352nd Fighter Groups. Near Cuxhaven, four aircraft in the 452nd BG were involved in a mid-air collision. A second formation, made up of the rest of the 3rd Bomb Division, the 1st Bomb Division and the 2nd

Bomb Division, bombed Berlin and returned to England. Despite the intense fighter cover near Berlin, Me 410s swooped on the rear of the 1st Division formation and made several attacks on the B-17s. Altogether, 44 Fortresses and Liberators were shot down.

The shuttle force touched down at Poltava, where a Heinkel He 177 high-altitude reconnaissance aircraft which had shadowed the formation for about 400 miles into Russian territory flew off to report its findings. A few hours later 60 Luftwaffe bombers bombed Poltava, destroying 44 of the 72 bombers and severely damaging 26 more. Luckily, further losses to the 13th Wing Fortresses at Mirgorod and to the Mustangs at Piryatin were avoided by their flying 150 miles to safety to Zaporpozhe. Gen Carl Spaatz was to concede later that the Poltava raid was the '. . . best attack the Luftwaffe ever made on the AAF'.

In England, meanwhile, the 8th continued to bomb No-ball targets and airfields in France. On 23 June two missions were again flown. At midday 211 bombers attacked 12 V1 sites, escorted by four Mustang groups which broke away after the strikes and strafed transport targets in the Paris area. In the late afternoon 196 bombers attacked airfield targets in France. Henry A. DeKeyser, the 24-year-old left waist gunner in Lt Bob Reese's crew in the 392nd BG, which was part of the B-24 force which bombed Leon/Athies airfield, recalls: 'We were number four in the lead flight, flying in our B-24 in the 576th Bomb Squadron, directly behind the command ship [piloted by Lt W. T. Whittemore with Capt M. H. Graper, Operations Officer of the 577th Squadron]. Three Me's made a head-on attack and kept on going. They must have radioed our altitude because the flak guns opened up almost immediately.

Second Lieutenant John Walters, the nose gunner, said on intercom: "Oh my God!" He saw the command ship explode from a direct hit, and No.2 and No.3 ships had also blown apart. I saw large pieces of B-24 going by and a body curled up in a ball and was gone. We watched for parachutes and saw none. Reese threw our 'plane into a dive. The rest of the 'planes were turning to one side or the other and diving. Four more black bursts of flak burst directly above us, just about in the place we had been in. Reese got on the radio and told the rest of the formation that had scattered to form on him. The flak was still coming up in four bursts in the track we would have been in if we had stayed on the same heading.

'God was our co-pilot. It was solid cloud below, so the gunners on the ground could not see us without their radar. As we flew on we threw out chaff. By the time Flt Off Bill Minzenberg got us back on course we came off the French coast heading for London, and flying over London was a no-no. We fired colours of the day and T/Sgt Ralph Buttzman, the radio operator, was in touch with a ground station and we were cleared to fly over London as long as we stayed at about 20,000 ft. The clouds were gone over England and we got a beautiful view of London and the countryside.' (Bob Reese; Joe Ionnata, the co-pilot; Bill Minzenberg; Gus Thornton, the top turret gunner and Ralph Buttzman, were all killed over the village of Foxly, Norfolk, on

B-17 Flying Fortresses in the 94th BG lower their undercarriages to make a more accurate drop to the French forces in the Ain and Haute Savoie on 25 June 1944. Some 2,088 supply containers were dropped by 176 B-17s of the 3rd Division to the FFI (Forces Françaises de l'Intèrieur, *or French Forces of the Interior) in 'Operation Zebra'. A large fighter escort protected the B-17s, and only two were shot down. Two other B-17s turned back with mechanical problems. The 3rd Division carried out further large-scale supply drops in July, August and September.* (USAF via Cliff Hall.)

5 July 1944 on a practice mission).

Meanwhile, in Russia, at around 12:15 hours on 26 June, the surviving Fortresses took off on the next stage of the shuttle to Foggia, Italy, with a raid on a Rumanian oil refinery en route. Crews reported

A badly wounded gunner in the 379th BG at Kimbolton has his wounds treated following the mission to Bremen on 24 June 1944. (Richards.)

seeing a large column of smoke and flames shooting skywards after the attack. At Foggia Main repairs were carried out to aircraft damaged in Russia and during the raid on the oil refinery. Some aircraft were too badly damaged for further combat, and had to be sent back to England by the much coveted ATC route via Cairo and Casablanca. The appropriately named *Belle of the Brawl* belonging to the 388th BG, touched down at Payne Field, Cairo, with over 100 linen patches glued over holes in her fuselage. On 5 July the 13th and 45th Wings took off from Foggia on the final leg of their shuttle. Crews flew quite low over Rome and then headed for the marshalling yards at Beziers in France. Some Bf 109s approached the bombers, but the P-51 escort took good care of them.

During the shuttle force's absence tours had been raised from 30 to 35 missions. Headquarters also announced that deep-penetration missions would rank equally with the short-haul raids in the table of missions per tour. On 7 July the 2nd Division was despatched on an 8¼-hour round trip to the Junkers factory at Bernberg when more than 1,000 heavies bombed three synthetic oil plants as well as eight aircraft assembly plants and other targets, all in Germany. Tactics directed that all three Division leave the English coast at different points, with the 1st and 3rd Divisions converging about 100 miles west of Berlin, leaving the B-24s to fly farther north and parallel with the Fortresses.

Unfortunately the massive deception plan was ruined when the B-17s arrived behind schedule, and the Luftwaffe concentrated its attacks on the luckless Liberators. Over 200 German fighters rode into the battle, throwing the 2nd Division into confusion. The 44th was forced to veer to the right to avoid a collision with the four incoming Liberator groups, and the fighter escort went with them. Lt Pete Henry in the 44th formation noted that: '75 Me 410s attacked the Eightballs in mass formation, getting four ships in the low Squadron'. The unfortunate 492nd BG was left completely exposed. Only the day

B-17G Happy Bottom, *532nd Bomb Squadron, 381st BG, on 1 July 1944. At a ceremony at Ridgewell, film star Edward G. Robinson christened it in honour of his wife Gladys ('Glad-ass'!). (USAF.)*

before *Boulder Buff* had been forced to land in Sweden, but this time there was no escape for the hapless unit, and 11 B-24s were shot down in quick succession.

The 8th continued its bombardment of V1 sites in the Pas de Calais, and on 14 July, 'Bastille Day,' the B-17s dropped much needed replacement arms and ammunition to gallant groups in the French Resistance movement at 'Area 9' near Limoges. The Maquis had gained control of an area of 100 square miles since the B-17s' last drop, only three weeks before.

For three successive days, beginning 11 July, the heavies blasted industrial sections of Munich. Jet aircraft and experimental works dotted the vicinity. The hub of the complex was the massive Allach aero engine works, which, with assembly plants and Luftwaffe airfields close by, made Munich a top-priority target. On the 16 July mission to Munich, the 1st Scouting Force of Mustangs and Mosquitoes, developed and led by 42-year-old Col Budd J. Peaslee, was used for the first time. Peaslee's scouting force flew just ahead of the main bombing force, transmitting up-to-the-minute weather reports back to the task force commander to prevent him leading his bombers into heavy weather front which could disrupt the mission and, in some instances, lead to its cancellation.

Peaslee's weather scouts also proved effective on the 18 July mission to the principal German research and development centre at Peenemünde, on the Baltic coast, where German scientists were trying to create the atomic bomb. The MPI was well covered with bomb hits and smoke was reported rising to 12,000 ft. The bomb pattern brought acclaim from Gen Spaatz, among others, who described it as '. . . one of the finest examples of precision bombing I have seen'.

On 19 July some 1,200 bombers attacked targets in south-central Germany again, and two days later the 8th went to Schweinfurt. Peaslee's weather scouts were instrumental in preventing the 1st Bomb

A bemused S/Sgt Virgil R. Heddleston of the 446th Bomb Group 704th Bomb Squadron, is photographed shortly after capture on Monday 31 July 1944 after baling out of his Liberator Hula Wahinna II *on the mission to Ludwigshafen. The pilot, co-pilot and tail gunner were murdered by German civilians.* (Rudy Heddleston.)

SUPER RABBIT

Far left *B-17G 42-102598,* Super Rabbit, *in the 351st Bomb Squadron, 100th BG, crash-landed at Thorpe Abbotts following the mission to Merseburg on 28 July 1944. (Via Mike Bailey.)*

Far left, below B-17G-90-BO Never Had It So Good, *43-38513, in the 339th Bomb Squadron, 96th BG, in flight. This aircraft survived the war. (Via Mike Bailey.)*

This page Aries *and* Libra *Liberators of the 834th 'Zodiacs' Bomb Squadron of the 486th BG, some of which were transferred to the 492nd Carpetbaggers' spy dropping outfit at Harrington when the Sudbury outfit converted to the B-17G in July 1944. Even when the aircraft were painted black for missions at night the distinctive artwork was carefully preserved. (Dick Bagg.)*

Division entering a cloud belt which towered to 28,000 ft. Unfortunately, the 2nd Bomb Division did not receive the radio signal, and 26 Liberators failed to return as a result of collisions and enemy action. In sharp contrast, the 1st Division lost only three bombers, and the 2nd and 3rd Divisions wasted no further time in forming their own scouting units.

During July the 8th flew seven tactical missions in support of the Allied armies in northern France. On 24 July Operation Cobra was scheduled to penetrate German defences west of St. Lô and secure Coutances, but bad weather prevented all but 352 of the 1,586 bombers from bombing the primary for fear of hitting their own troops. On 25 July 1,495 heavies dropped thousands of fragmentation bombs and 100 lb GP bombs on German positions in the Marigny-St Gilles region to the west of St. Lô, just ahead of advancing US 1st Army troops. Some groups bombed short when smoke-markers dropped by the lead ships on bomb release were blown slowly back towards the American lines. Bombs from the last few B-24s in the Division hurtled into American forward positions, killing 102 men and wounding 380. Among the dead was Gen McNair. Five bombers were shot down.

Late in July the ball turrets were removed from many Liberators to improve stability and altitude performance. During the last week of July Gen Doolittle carried out the first stage of his plan to convert his Liberator groups to Fortresses. The 486th and 487th BGs in the 92nd Wing were taken off operations and by the end of the month were ready to begin combat missions in Fortresses. Between the end of August and mid-September the 34th, 490th and 493rd Groups in the 93rd Wing also changed over to the B-17. Meanwhile, on 7 August, the 492nd BG was withdrawn from combat after losing 54 aircraft between May and July 1944. This was the heaviest loss for any B-24 group for a three-month period. The 2nd Bomb Division now totalled an unlucky 13 groups, with the 491st BG moving from the 95th Combat Wing to the 14th Wing. The 95th Wing, which had begun with only two groups, ceased to exist on 14 August, when the 489th was transferred to the 20th Wing as a fourth group. It was the end of another era for the Liberator groups of the 8th Air Force.

Chapter Thirteen

Wings of silver

AUGUST FOLLOWED THE same operational pattern as July, with bombing raids on airfields in France and strategic targets in Germany. On 1 August, while heavy bomb groups struck at airfields in France, 191 B-17s dropped supplies to the French Underground movement. On 4 August the 8th returned to strategic targets, 1,250 heavies bombing oil refineries, aircraft factories, airfields and the experimental establishment at Peenemünde in two raids that day. The pattern continued on the 5th, when 1,062 bombers attacked 11 separate oil producing centres in central Germany without loss.

Next day 953 bombers struck at Berlin and oil and manufacturing centres in the Reich, for the loss of 25 bombers. Some 75 Fortresses in the 95th and 390th BGs hit the Focke-Wulfe plant at Rahmel in Poland. After the raid the two groups flew on to their shuttle base at Mirgorod in Russia, the scene of such devastation two months before. During their stay they flew a raid to the Trzebinia synthetic oil refinery and returned to Russia before flying to Italy on 8 August, bombing two Rumanian airfields en route. Four days later they flew back to Britain on the last stage of their shuttle, bombing Toulouse-Francaal airfield as they passed over France. This third shuttle proved more successful than the disastrous shuttle of June 1944, not a single Fortress being lost.

On 9 August bomber crews were summoned to the usual daily briefing. Bob Maag of the 94th BG flew his 20th mission this day, to Stuttgart, in *Skinny*: 'We didn't know that she was something of a legend (the first B-17 in the 94th to complete 100 missions), but realized that she was a venerable veteran. We assumed she got her name from the fact that she was an anomaly – a B-17G with no chin turret. Her missing chin turret gave us lower fuel consumption.

Take-off was delayed one hour, then two, before the B-17s headed for Stuttgart: 'In Luxembourg we were led over some flak guns mounted on railroad cars, and all hell broke loose. *Skinny* took a hit through the Plexiglas which caught me on the left side of the face and wounded George Byczkowski, the top turret gunner, in the leg. I lost my left eye and the co-pilot, Ivan Walker, had to take over the controls. Lyle Haines and Smitty, the bombardier and navigator, somehow managed to get me into the nose of the 'plane, where they

B-17F Royal Flush *in the 100th BG was shot down on its 75th mission, to Villacoublay airfield, France, on 11 August 1944, and the wreckage landed on the Pleine de Clamart. This photo was taken on 13 August by city of Clamart historian, the late Leopold Morehoisne.* (Via Chuck Nekvasil.)

did what they could to keep me alive. Ivan got us down safely and made sure that *Skinny* was the first to land, thus ensuring that George and I would get medical attention at the earliest possible moment.' For their actions, Walker, Smith and Haines were awarded the DFC.

On 29 August the 93rd, 446th and 448th BGs in the 20th Wing began 'trucking' missions to the troops in France, who were in urgent need of fuel and supplies. The bulk of the operation was completed using Liberators, whose cavernous fuselages were ideal for the task. Crew chiefs stopped painting bomb symbols on the Liberators and instead stencilled flour sacks and freight cars. The aircraft flew empty to the depot in southern England, where Royal Artillerymen loaded them with urgently needed foodstuffs and medical supplies, and they then flew over the Channel, dropping down to tree-top level to Orlèans-Bricy airfield, about 70 miles south of Paris.

On 11 September the 96th Wing went off operations and the 458th, 466th and 467th began 'Trucking' operations. Philip G. Day, co-pilot

B-17Gs in the 490th BG ride through flak. The 490th was one of five units which converted to the B-17 from the B-24, and first used B-17s on 27 August 1944. (Via Mike Bailey.)

of *Lil' Peach* in the 467th BG, recalls: 'We hauled boxed goods and five-gallon Jerry cans of gasoline initially, but soon we were hauling 80-octane gas only, in our 'plane's outer wing 'Tokyo' tanks, in tanks installed in the bomb bays and in fighter drop tanks carried in the waist area of the ship. These loads were about 2,700 gallons, which were pumped off at the landing fields in France. In addition, we carried enough 100-octane in our wing tanks for the approximate five hours round trip. At the height of the operation there were 150 airplanes at Rackheath. All armament was taken from the 'planes except the Martin upper turret guns and ammunition, and we flew at altitudes of 1,000 ft or less, ready to go "on the deck" if attack by enemy fighters occurred.' On 12 September the 458th BG alone delivered just over 13,000 gal of fuel to units in France.

Meanwhile, on 9 September the Allies had launched Operation 'Market Garden', using British and American airborne divisions against German-held Dutch towns on the Rhine. On 17 September the Liberators flew practice trucking missions over Norfolk. That night motor trucks brought supplies to the bases in the region and men loaded each Liberator with about 6,000 lb of perishables and fuel supplies for the armies in Holland. The next day six specially modified Liberators in the 458th delivered over 9,000 gal of fuel to Gen Patton's forces in France while 252 supply-carrying B-24s took off for LZ.N Knapheide-Klein Amerika (Little America) near Groesbeek on the first full divisional 'trucking' mission. Unfortunately some Liberators and C-47s got in each others' way over the sea and were forced to abort, while others experienced navigational difficulties. The remaining Liberators dropped to 400 ft over the drop zone.

'Dusty' Worthen, the bombardier in Joe Rosacker's crew in the 93rd BG, recalls: 'The view along the route to the drop zone was incredible. Crashed C-47s, burned outlines of crashed gliders, gliders nosed up or on their back – a general mess. Our flight was over farming area. We

B-17Gs in the 34th BG amid flak filled skies over the cloudy landscape of occupied Europe. The Mendlesham Group flew its first B-17 mission, after converting from the B-24, on 17 September 1944. (Via Mike Bailey.)

A B-24 Liberator some miles west of Breda, Holland, on 18 September, photographed by Jaap Beynes, who risked his life taking this picture. The Dutchman was saving his precious film for the liberation, but felt compelled to take this remarkable photo. (Jaap Beynes via Father G. Thuring.)

could nearly see the flying feathers of the fluttering chickens; the cows were in full gallop – right through fences and bushes. The Dutch farmers were waving happily. It was certainly a different sight than we would see at our usual 22,000 ft altitude. As we neared the target the small-arms fire became intense. We were hit several times. One slug stopped in the back pack parachute of our tail gunner.' The First Allied Airborne Army recovered 80 per cent of all supplies dropped by the 20th Wing at Groesbeek.

Meanwhile, the 14th Wing dropped their supplies to the 101st

Parachutes attached to supply canisters billow out over Best, Holland, during the 44th BG's contribution to Operation 'Market Garden' on 18 September 1944. The middle aircraft is Corky.

A B-24 of the 855th Bomb Squadron, 491st BG, drops supplies to the Allied armies on 18 September 1944. (Dan Winston.)

American Airborne at Best. Ted Parker, a waist gunner in the 491st Bomb Group, recalls: 'At the target I opened the hatch in the floor and had to work quickly because we would be passing the dropping zone fast and at low altitude. In my haste my leg became entangled in the parachute straps attached to the ammunition track, and I was pulled out of the hole when the last bundle went out. I just managed to cling to the track, but my legs were dangling out of the hatch. The Quartermaster [who had 'frozen' since take-off] ignored my calls for help. Finally the tail gunner, David Slade, heard me and came to my assistance.'

The 14th Wing Liberators flew over a small town and came under small-arms fire from some Germans who could quite easily be seen in the streets. One bullet, well spent by the time it reached the B-24, hit Ted Parker in the cheek. He watched helplessly as the lead aircraft, flown by Capt Jim Hunter and carrying Capt Anthony Mitchell, the air commander, was shot down. 'She took one bounce and struck some haystacks, exploding in a large orange flame,' he says. 'Our altitude was about a hundred feet at the time. The tail gunner was the only survivor. He was hidden by some Dutch monks until liberated.' The 491st lost four B-24s on the mission.

In the 44th BG formation Pete Henry, flying deputy lead of the third squadron in an ex-490th BG B-24J, later named *Henry* after the King Features cartoon character, received hits in the leading edge of his port wing. A .30-calibre shell cut the line supplying manifold pressure and also holed the fuel tank. Petrol began leaking into the bomb bays. Henry got his aircraft home, but one Liberator was forced to ditch in the North Sea. Only three crewmen were seen scrambling from the sinking bomber. Two groups of P-47s had failed to nullify the almost constant small-arms fire, and the 2nd Bomb Division lost 16 Liberators and 70 more were damaged, while 21 fighters were shot down.

On the following day, 19 September, the 458th despatched 24 Liberators to France, carrying 38,016 gal of fuel for the troops. Col Albert J. Shower's 467th was also involved in the 'trucking' opera-

B-24J-155-CO Henry, *44-40279 in the 66th Bomb Squadron, 44th BG, was an ex-490th BG machine which was transferred to Shipdham when the Eye Group converted to the B-17G in August 1944. It returned to the ZI in 1945.* (Pete Henry.)

tions. He recalls: 'From 19 September until 3 October the 96th Wing flew no combat missions, but established a forward base at the airfield at Clastres, near St Quentin, France. We ferried gasoline for Patton's tanks and motorized units.' During its 14 days of 'trucking' the 467th delivered 646,070 gal of 80 octane fuel to the Allied armies. In 13 days of 'trucking' missions, the 458th also delivered 727,160 gal of fuel to the tank units.

In mid-September Fortress pilots had to call upon all their experience to fly a mercy drop to beleagured Poles of the Polish Home Army in the ruins of Warsaw. The Polish capital was cut off from the outside world, with the Germans on one side and the Russians on the other. Russia had asked Gen Bor to rise against the German occupiers, but had then stood by while the gallant Poles were gradually annihilated. Some RAF flights operating from Italy supplied the Poles in August, but then ceased because of the danger to crews. It was not until early September that the Russians finally agreed to co-operate and allow the B-17s to fly on to Russia after the drops.

An attempt to reach Warsaw on 15 September was aborted because of bad weather, and it was not until the 18th that the 13th Wing was able to fly all the way. Col Karl Truesdell of the 95th BG led the B-17s over Warsaw, and the supply drop was made from between 13,000 and 18,000 ft amid limited but accurate flak. The strong American fighter escort was unable to prevent the Luftwaffe attacking the 390th BG, which was flying as the low group, during the dropping run. One Fortress was shot down and another landed at Brest-Litovsk. However, the remaining aircraft succeeded in reaching their shuttle bases at Mirgorod and Poltava. On 19 September they took off again for the now-familiar return flight via Italy and France, but this time without bombing because all French territory had been overrun.

Bad weather throughout the rest of September severely limited missions, and only 14 were flown that month. On the mission to oil refineries at Merseberg on 11 September savage fighter attacks cost the

B-17Gs in the 96th BG taxi out at Snetterton Heath in 1944. The nearest aircraft is 43-37794, AW-T in the 337th Bomb Squadron, which was shot down by flak over Wiesbaden on 19 September 1944. Lt Raymond Bauman's crew were all made PoWs. (Robert E. Foose.)

92nd BG 12 B-17s. Next day the 3rd Division bombed the Magdeburg oil refinery and marshalling yards at Fulda, while the 1st Division hit oil targets at Brux in Czechoslovakia. About 450 fighters attacked the formations and 45 heavies were shot down.

On 27 September the B-17s bombed oil targets, and engineering centres at Cologne, Ludwigshafen and Mainz. Meanwhile, 160 Liberators in the 96th Combat Wing transported fuel to France while 315 B-24s were despatched to the Henschel engine and vehicle assembly plants at Kassel in central Germany. The leading 445th BG, navigating by Gee, made a miscalculation at the IP and headed for Gôttingen, about 30 miles to the north-east of Kassel. The 445th dropped its bombs through solid cloud over, and they fell half a mile short of Gôttingen. The group then flew further to the east, placing them well behind the main force and in an area where the Luftwaffe was forming for an attack. The mistakes cost the 445th BG dearly, and 25 of its 37 B-24s were shot down in fierce fighter attacks. Two of the B-24s crash-landed in France, a third managed to cross the Channel only to crash in Kent, and a fourth crashed near Tibenham. Only seven aircraft returned to the airfield, and they carried one dead crewmen and 13 wounded.

The heavies bombed Magdeburg, Kassel and Merseburg on 28 September for the loss of 30 bombers, including 11 Fortresses in the 303rd BG. The tragedy was repeated eight days later, when the 385th BG also lost 11 B-17s, most from the 549th Squadron, when the 8th ventured to Berlin. Only the arrival of the P-51 escort prevented further carnage. Despite mounting losses, there was inceasing evidence that the 8th's bombing offensive, particularly against oil targets, was reaping rewards, and Doolittle continued to apply pressure on Germany's oil manufacturing industry. On 7 October over 1,300 B-17s and B-24s bombed five synthetic oil plants in Germany for the loss of 52 heavies. The 1st and 3rd Bomb Division were assigned refineries at Politz and Merseberg respectively. S/Sgt Adolph J.

A formation of 445th BG Liberators en route to Glinde, Germany, on 6 October 1944. (USAF.)

Smetana, a tail gunner with the 351st BG at Polebrook, recalls the mission to Politz: 'Nearing the target I saw this "boiling mass" of flak. We started to make a 360° turn and I thought: "Thank God we don't have to fly through it". However, I was soon to discover that another group had cut us off and we were only waiting our turn. God, it was awful. I could see 'planes falling from all over the sky. When the first flak burst was at our altitude I knew we had just "bought the farm". It was a hell of a ride through that stuff. Our group just simply disolved.

'We finally got through after what seemed an eternity. We found ourselves flying in formation with only one other 'plane, and that was all in flames. If it had exploded we would have gone up with it. I was so scared I couldn't even tell the pilot to get the hell out of here. (We were breaking in a new officer crew that day, flying their first mission.) Finally "Pops", the top turret gunner, screamed over the interphone to ". . . get his bloody arse out of it or we would never see Polebrook again". He shouted many other choice words over the interphone, but our pilot did what "Pops" said and broke off.

'Out of the corner of my eye I saw cripples heading for Sweden, but mostly my eyes were focused on the flying coffin in front of us. It finally went out of control and started down. Tears welled up in my eyes, and I prayed that nine spots would come out of that 'plane. One who didn't was our usual waist gunner, who had been with us since we had been grouped together at Ardmore AFB, Oklahoma. It was his very first mission in action.'

Four bombers in the 457th BG, including *Rene III*, flown by Col James R. Luper, CO of the Fireball Outfit, were lost over the target. Luper and Capt Norman Kriehn, the Group Navigator, survived and were made PoWs. A short time later Col Harris E. Rogner assumed command of the Fireball Outfit.

On 14 October 1, 100 B-17s and B-24s bombed marshalling yards and targets in the Cologne area. *Jolly Roger*, piloted by Lt Klusmeyer in the 458th BG, took a direct flak hit in the nose. Lt Robert L. Ferrell, the lead navigator, recalls: 'With his eye glued to the Norden sight, Ernest Sands, the bombardier, shouted, "Bombs Aw . . ." The Plexiglas of the Emerson nose turret turned red with blood, and the bombardier was blown from over the bombsight back into the nosewheel well. My left hand showed blood through my gloves from three shrapnel piercings, and the smell of cordite seeped through my oxygen mask.' Ferrell went to the aid of the second navigator, Millard C. Miller: 'I slipped my hands under his armpits and pulled on him. His head fell back against my right shoulder. I looked at Miller and vomited into my oxygen mask, and nearly drowned from it. I had never seen a human head hit by a shell. I laid him on the floor of the navigator's compartment. Sgt Pohler, the engineer/upper turret gunner, dragged Miller through the tunnel and toward the flightdeck, where he was thrown out the bomb strike camera hatch opening after Pohler secured a 25-foot static line clip to his "D" ring.'

With a macabre touch, Ferrell made an entry into his navigation log using the blood lying on his table. Three rings on the bale-out bell ordered the crew to abandon the aircraft. A raging fire in the bomb bay forced the men back to the front compartment. Ferrell pulled the emergency handle on the nosewheel doors, but they failed to open. 'This was our only way out now,' he continues. 'Sands stooped over and jumped up and down on the nosewheel doors. They began to part and fly away. He dropped through the opening until his outstretched arms held him momentarily. He looked at me and shouted: "This sure as hell pisses me off!", then he dropped out and away.' Ferrell quickly followed. Klusmeyer, co-pilot Fred Wright and Ferrell landed in Boppard, Germany, near the same farmhouse and were taken prisoner. Miller also survived but although one or two of the enlisted men initially managed to avoid capture, they were eventually caught.

Bad weather throughout November slowed down the Allies' advance all along the western front and severely hampered missions. When they were flown they were usually against oil targets. On 2 November approximately 1,100 heavies bombed four large German synthetic oil refineries. The force which attacked the vast I.G. Farbenindustrie's synthetic oil refinery at Leuna, three miles south of Merseburg, came in for particularly heavy punishment by an estimated 500 fighters. Forty heavies were shot down, including 12 91st BG Fortresses and nine in the 457the BG.

It was for his actions this day that Lt Robert Feymoyer, a navigator in the 447th BG, was posthumously awarded the Medal of Honor. His B-17 was rocked by three flak bursts which showered it with shrapnel. Feymoyer was hit in the back and the side of his body, but he refused all aid despite his terrible wounds so that he might navigate the Fortress back to Rattlesden. He was propped up in his seat to enable him to read his charts, and the crew did what they could for him. It is not until they reached the North Sea that Feymoyer agreed to an injection of morphine. He died shortly after the aircraft landed at Rattlesden.

Losses were so bad on this mission that groups were stood down for two days following the raid. On 9 November the heavies returned to tactical missions in support of Gen George Patton's 3rd Army, which was halted at the fortress city of Metz. The 8th was called in to bomb German lines of communication at Sarbrucken, and also enemy gun emplacements to the east and south of Metz to enable the advance through Belgium to continue. The mission was assigned top priority, and at bases throughout East Anglia Fortresses taxied out in the mist and bad visibility. The conditions contributed to the loss of eight bombers during take-offs and landings, and further disasters befell some groups as the mission progressed.

Lady Janet, flown by Lt Donald Gott and Lt William E. Metzger in the 452nd BG, was severely damaged by flak. The engineer was wounded in the leg, and a shell fragment severed the radio operator's arm below the elbow. While Metzger attended to the crew, Gott flew on to Allied territory, salvoing the bombs over enemy territory en route, Metzger selflessly gave his parachute to a gunner whose own had been damaged in the fire, and all except the radio operator were told to bale out. Metzger and Gott prepared for a crash landing with only one engine still functioning and the other three on fire. Gott brought *Lady Janet* in, but at about 100 feet the fire took hold of the fuel tanks and the bomber exploded, killing Gott, Metzer and the radio operator instantly. Both pilots were awarded posthumous Medals of Honor.

On 16 November the 8th provided support for the advancing US

706th BS, 446th BG Liberators in formation on a 13 November 1944, practice mission led by a PFF ship. (USAF.)

and British armies. The mission was very carefully planned to avoid bombing friendly troops near the targets, just east of Aachen. The Allied artillery fired red smoke shells every 500 yards along the front, and barrage balloons were placed along the edge of the area. The use of radio signals was especially worthwhile when 8/10ths cloud covered the front lines, and helped ensure accurate bombing. Worsening weather conditions forced some groups to fly to the north of Britain to escape the conditions, and they were unable to return to their home bases for a few days.

On 21 November the 8th returned to Merseburg for the first of three more raids on the refineries in a week. Merseberg had become synonymous with flak, and crews hated all missions to the city. Herman L. Hager, a radio-operator in *Nutty Hussy*, piloted by Lt Wismer in the 603rd Bomb Squadron of the 398th BG, had already been there on two previous occasions, and knew what to expect: 'To say the least, shivers always ran up and down our spines to see this mission on the map. Like Schweinfurt and others, this was one mission [on which] one could count your blessings if you returned unharmed.'

The 398th BG despatched 37 Fortresses this day, but ten Fw 190s shot out from the clouds and made a frontal attack on the 603rd Squadron, shooting down seven Fortresses, including *Nutty Hussy*. Herman Hager enjoyed only the briefest freedom before being sent to Stalag Luft IVA.

On 25 November more than 900 bombers were despatched to oil and marshalling yard targets in Germany. The 2nd Bomb Division, including 31 Liberators in the 491st BG, flew to the oil refineries at Misburg, a target that had been partially destroyed three weeks before. By the time the IP was reached at Wittengen, three 491st machines had aborted. Three Me 262s observed the group over the Dummer Lake area and charted their strength, route and speed. Shortly afterwards between 150 and 200 German fighters were observed high above the bombers. They made no attempt to attack the B-24s, but invited combat with the American fighter shield of some 245 aircraft. The American fighters engaged the Luftwaffe, leaving the bombers to continue to the target unescorted.

Lt Col Charles C. Parmele, CO of the 854th Squadron, flying as Air Commander, led 27 B-24s to the target, where they split up. The German anti-aircraft guns ceased firing, and over a hundred fighters bore in for the kill. They hit all three squadrons in turn, and downed 16 Liberators in 15 minutes. Only the timely arrival of eight P-51 weather scouts saved the remaining 12 B-24s. They held off the attack until reinforcements arrived, and the tattered remnants reassembled into one formation and headed for home. Only three Liberators survived from the ten in the 854th Squadron, while all nine in the 853rd, which had been bringing up the rear as the high squadron, were shot down. On the evening of 27 November 16 replacement crews arrived from Stansted. For its action over Misburg the 491st was awarded a Divisional Unit Citation.

On 30 November about 1,200 heavies bombed four synthetic-oil

B-17Gs in the 100th BG take evasive action from enemy flak. The nearest aircraft is 43-38945 in the 418th Bomb Squadron. (Thorpe Abbotts Tower Museum.)

B-17G-70-BO Lassie Come Home, *43-37715, of the 306th BG, in formation with B-17G-55-BO 42-10257? and other 306th aircraft.* (Richards.)

refineries in Germany. The leading 1st Division force attacked Zeitz, while the 3rd Division bombed Merseburg itself, 20 miles to the north, and the Liberators bombed Lutzkendorf. Appalling losses were suffered by the 8th Air Force, which lost 29 heavy bombers, but Merseburg had suffered its greatest damage, too. By the end of November 1944 more than 43 refineries, processing both crude and synthetic oil, had been destroyed.

Chapter Fourteen

The Ardennes Offensive

DECEMBER 1944 BROUGHT the worst winter weather in England for 54 years. Water froze in the pipes and a thin film of ice coated runways at bases throughut eastern England. The temperature dropped to as low as −18°C, but the greatest problem was lack of visibility during missions. The 489th BG at Halesworth was spared the English winter when it returned to the USA to be retrained as a B-29 unit and redeployed to the Pacific.

Eastern England was still in the grip of a particularly bleak December when, on the 16th, Field Marshal Karl von Rundstedt and his Panzer colums punched a hole in the American lines in the forests of the Ardennes. The operation was similar to his advance into France in 1940, and created a salient or 'bulge' in the Allied front lines. In England the bombing force was grounded by fog, just as Hitler had hoped, and was unable to intervene. The German advance caught almost everyone by surprise, not least the briefing officers at some of the bomber bases. At Shipdham the briefing did not allow for the Germans advancing so far into Belgium. Pete Henry was leading the second squadron, low left of the 392nd, using GH. No fighters appeared, but the formation received a rude shock when German guns opened up eight minutes earlier than expected. The barrage continued for 27 minutes, but the Eightballs managed to get to Ahreweiler, Germany, where they bombed communications and troop transports with 500-pounders. The results were described as 'excellent', and Pete Henry's bombardiers, Lt Albert E. Jones and Lt Lee, received citations from Gen Johnson for their GH-visual over the target.

It was not until 23 December, when traces of fog still shrouded the bases, that B-17s managed to take off and offer some hope to the hard pressed infantry divisions in the 'Bulge'. Some 400 B-17s of the First Bomb Division attacked the marshalling yards at Ehrang, Germany, and earned a commendation from Brig Gen Howard M. Turner.

On Christmas Eve traces of overcast still hung in the air, but the fog lifted sufficiently for a record 2,034 heavies, including war-weary hacks and even assembly ships, to be despatched to bomb Luftwaffe airfields in the vicinity of the Ardennes. At Rackheath a record 61 Liberators, including *Pete The POM Inspector* (the Group's unarmed Assembly Ship), were airborne in only 30 minutes. *Pete* was flown by

B-17Gs in the 613th Bomb Squadron, 401st BG, drop their bombs. (Via Mike Bailey.)

Lt Charles McMahon, a 'Happy Warrior' pilot now on the Group Operations' Staff who had decided to risk one last mission. He came through safely though his aircraft was armed only with carbines in the waist positions.

Visibility was still poor, and led to many accidents during take-off. At Podington, for instance, Lt Robert K. Seeber's Fortress crashed into a wood about 200 yards to the left of the runway. The wood had not been visible during take-off because of the thick fog. About two minutes later Seeber's B-17 exploded, killing six of the crew. At Glatton the 457th managed to get six aircraft off in reduced visibility, but the seventh crashed at the end of the runway and operations were halted for a time.

The 1st Division bombed airfields in the Frankfurt area and lines of communication immediately behind the German 'Bulge'. Crews were told that their route was deliberately planned to go over the ground troops' positions for morale purposes. Brig Gen Fred Castle, former CO of the 94th BG and now commander of the 4th Wing, drove to Lavenham airfield and elected to fly in the 487th formation, even though he carried a 30-day leave order in his pocket, and lead the 3rd Division on what was his 30th mission. Soon Castle was in the air, and all went well until the formation was over Belgium about 35 miles from Liege, when his aircraft's starboard outer engine burst into flames and its propeller had to be feathered. The deputy lead ship took over and Castle dropped down to 20,000 ft, but at this height the aircraft began vibrating badly and he was forced to take it down another 3,000 ft before levelling out. The Fortress was now down to 180 m.p.h. indicated air speed and being pursued by seven Bf 109s. They attacked, wounding the tail gunner and leaving the radar navigator nursing bad wounds in his neck and shoulders. Castle could not perform any evasive manouevres with the full bomb load still aboard, and he could not release it for fear of hitting Allied troops on the ground.

Successive fighter attacks put another two engines out of action and the B-17 lost altitude. As Castle fought the controls in a vain effort to keep the stricken bomber level, he ordered the crew to jump. Some of the crew baled out, and then the bomber was hit in the fuel tanks and oxygen systems, which set the aircraft on fire. Castle attempted to land the flaming bomber in an open field near the Allied lines, but as it neared the ground it went into a spin and exploded on impact. Brig Gen Castle was posthumously awarded the Medal of Honor; he was the highest ranking officer in the 8th Air Force to receive the award.

Overall, the Christmas Eve raids were effective and severely disrupted von Rundstedt's lines of communication. The cost in aircraft, though, was high. Many crashed during their return over England as drizzle and overcast played havoc with landing patterns. Tired crews put down where they could. Any who felt inclined to join in the festive spirit on the base were disappointed, because another strike was ordered for Christmas Day. However, a number of Fortresses from the 1st Division were still reposing at other bases in the region after their own bases had been 'socked in' by the prevailing mists in the east Midlands. It was a much smaller force, therefore, which was despatched from the 2nd and 3rd Division bases. Some 350 heavies bombed 18 targets, mostly railway bridges and communication centres west of the Rhine.

On 26 December most bases were foggy and snowbound, and visibility was sor poor that only just over 100 bombers attacked their targets. Eighth Air Force headquarters was only too aware of the problems confronting the bomber groups, but, despite the dangerous conditions, the mission of 29 December had to go ahead. At 08:40 a 390th BG Fortress crashed on take-off from Framlingham and plummeted into the centre of nearby Parham village. The crew perished in the explosion, which shattered the windows of every home in the vicinity, but miraculously no inhabitants were harmed. At Rackheath, a ground fog came in over the base at take-off time and reduced visibility to a few feet. Lt Col James J. Mahoney recalls the tragic events which followed: 'Col Walter Smith called up Division headquarters and asked for permission to cancel or postpone the missions, but Division refused. They said it was top priority, and that the mission must be flown. Smith woke me for advice, and I called Division and told them it was impossible to take off. But they told us to get airborne. I then woke Col Shower; the Division officer who was causing the trouble had been a classmate of his at West Point, so we hoped he could influence him. But the officer was adamant that the mission should go ahead, as it was in support of Gen Patton's forces near Metz.

'Col Shower decided to let the lead and deputy lead aircraft from each squadron go. These six 'planes would take off first and climb to form a skeleton formation and then fire flares. As the others came up it was hoped they would spot the flares and take up a prearranged position in the formation. Col Al Wallace, CO of the 791st

Squadron, who thought it suicide to take off, flew the first B-24. It would be a take-off using instruments. We figured the lead crew pilots would be experienced enough to take off on instruments, but we had been having problems with faulty equipment sent by a subcontractor in the States. Wallace took off, and within minutes called over the radio, warning us not to let anybody else take off. They had made it – but only just.

'The second B-24 – deputy lead of the first squadron – taxied out. You couldn't see more than 20 ft. We heard him go on emergency power. The engines really whined, and it was obvious he was in trouble. We heard a crack, but nothing else happened and we kept waiting for explosions. The third B-24 touched a tree on take-off and landed minutes later at Attlebridge. The fourth aircraft took off and really whacked the trees. As soon as we heard this, Col Shower cancelled the mission. He didn't care what Division said; he wasn't goint to let any more 'planes leave Rackheath. He told crews to turn off their engines and stay where they were. It was too foggy even to taxi, and we had jeeps leading them out.'

The second B-24 had taken off, hit the trees, and had made a wheels-up belly landing in the field. The fourth Liberator had done exactly the same, and had landed right on top of the crashed aircraft. The first crew were just freeing themselves from their burning aircraft when the other had plummeted down on top of them. Fire crews found only the charred remains of their bodies. In all, 15 men were killed and four injured in this fiasco in the fog. The crew of the other Liberator baled out after heading their bomber out to sea.

On 30 December more than 1,000 heavies again bombed lines of communication, and on the 31st the bombers struck at tactical targets while 3rd Division crews returned to oil production centres. The 100th BG, which was assigned Hamburg, flew out over the North Sea only to encounter strong winds which reduced the ground speed of its Fortresses to just 100 m.p.h. At 11:33 the lead ship dropped his smoke bombs to signal the rest of the group to drop their bombs. The sky over Hamburg was filled with accurate bursts of flak, and *Fools Rush In*, flown by Lt Floyd Henderson was struck while on the bomb run and dropped sharply, crashing into the B-17 flown by Lt Clifton Williams, which was cleaved in two. Both aircraft fell in flames. Lt Billy R. Blackman's Fortress had two engines knocked out and fighters set it on fire. Blackman, navigator William B. Sterret and some of the crew managed to bale out before it exploded. Bob Freshour's 'chute opened, but he was dead when he hit the ground. Basil Numack, one of the waist gunners, and Joe Pearl were killed by fighters. Carson, the ball-turret gunner, was unable to get out of his turret and Bob Fortney, the radio-operator, did not have his parachute on. Andy Herbert, the tail gunner, and Tom Pace, who was also blown out in the explosion, survived and were made PoWs. Altogether, the 100th BG lost 12 Fortresses – half of the total borne by the entire 3rd Division.

On 1 January the 1st Air Division (on this day the prefix 'Bomb' was officially changed to 'Air') encountered enemy fighters in some strength during raids on the tank factory at Kassel, an oil refinery at

B-17G-1-BO Fools Rush In, *42-31066, in the 351st Bomb Squadron, 100th BG, piloted by Floyd Henderson, was one of four aircraft lost in two collisions on New Year's Eve 1944, during the mission to Hamburg. Only three men survived.* (Thorpe Abbotts Tower Museum.*)*

Magdeburg, and marshalling yards at Dillenburg. The Magdeburg force came under heavy fighter attack, while the Kassel force was badly hit by flak. Next day the heavies once again pounded lines of communication, and raids of this nature continued until the position in the Ardennes gradually swung in the Allies' favour. For once the general 'bitching' on the bases ceased when it was learned that ground personnel would be drawn from the bomb groups as replacement infantry for invalided men who fought in the Bulge. The 'ground pounders' began to realize that life in a bomb group was not so bad after all.

On 5 January the severe wintry weather over England was responsible for several fatal accidents during take-off for a mission to Frankfurt. Snow flurries swirled around the runways, and at Mendlesham a 34th BG Fortress came to grief while attempting take-off. The conditions were also responsible for a mid-air collision in the vicinity of Thorpe Abbotts.

A period of fine weather, beginning on 6 January, enabled the heavies to fly missions in support of the ground troops once more. These were mostly against lines of communication, airfields and marshalling yards. Finally, the German advance in the Ardennes came to a halt and ultimately petered out, allowing the heavies to resume deep penetration missions. On Sunday 14 January the 467th BG went to the Hallendorf steelworks west of Berlin. For *Witchcraft*, one of the most famous of all Liberators, it was her 100th mission, all without once turning back. A newspaper reporter flew in *Witchcraft* to cover the unique event. The Liberator went on to fly 30 more missions, and no crew members were killed or wounded and the aircraft never returned to Rackheath without first bombing its target.

A B-17G of the 95th BG overflies the 486th BG base at Sudbury (Acton) en route to Horham in 1945. (USAF.)

By the same token *Lassie Come Home*, a Liberator in the 458th BG at nearby Horsham St. Faith, was an unlucky ship. It returned from the 14 January mission to the Hermann Goering Works at Halle with one engine stopped and its landing gear down. The pilot, who was on only his third mission, banked into his dead engine. He lost a second engine and crashed upside down on gardens at Spynke Road, just short of the base. Earl Zimmerman, who was stationed at Hethel, had cycled over to Spynke Road that day to visit his future wife, June Courtney. He recalls: 'We were sitting around the fire at tea time when we heard the 'plane coming over. Suddenly it happened – the sound of engines turning over at high r.p.m.; a loud crash as the 'plane took off the top of our house, and a huge shadow passing by the window. I ran out of the back door and there was a lot of gasoline all over the place, so I ran to all the neighbours telling them to put out all their fires.

'The aircraft was such a tangled mess it was difficult to know where to look to find any survivors. About the only recognizable portion was a piece of the fuselage from the waist window to the tail. It was so mangled that I could not get inside, but some neighbours came running over and we eventually managed to get two boys out alive. We laid them on the front lawn, but one of them died.' Two children who had been playing in the garden were also killed.

On 16 January over 550 heavies bombed oil plant and engineering centres in the Reich. The 448th BG was among those Units which bombed a synthetic oil plant at Dresden from 22,000 ft. Dick Dugger, the top turret gunner in *Rose's Rivets*, who was flying his second mission, recalls: 'We were hit over the target area and began to lose gasoline. The bomber had been hit in the tanks. We made it to Lille,

B-24H Ronnie, *41-29144 of the 704th Bomb Squadron, 446th BG, named in memory of S/Sgt Ronald Gannon, a waist gunner who died of paralysis during the Group's training programme in the USA. M/Sgt Michael P. Zyne in the 704th Squadron took charge of the B-24 after it had been plagued by mechanical difficulties on its first four missions with another squadron. Zyne's crew despatched* Ronnie *on its first successful mission on 5 January 1944. It flew its 100th mission on 30 December 1944, and its 105th mission in January 1945, finishing the war with an ETO record of 79 consecutive missions without a turn back. (USAF.)*

but could not cross the Channel. Finally, the fuel gave out, the engines quit and we had to land in a park just outside Lille.'

When the crew returned to Seething they were given a new B-24, which they christened *Windy Winnie*. On 28 January *Windy Winnie* was hit on the bomb run over Dortmnd, when the bad weather of the past few days had improved enough to allow almost 900 heavies to attack oil and communications' targets in western Germany. *Winnie's* pilot nursed the bomber back across Germany and France as the crew threw out everything that was not screwed down. Dugger recalls: 'We were hit many times. *Winnie* had so many holes in her, it was like flying outdoors. A Liberator does not fly well with three engines at tree-top level, but we kept in the air by throwing out everything we could – radio equipment, supplies, and even the guns.' *Winnie* finally crash-landed in Luxembourg. Dugger concludes: 'Small trees were cut

E-RAT-ICATOR *returns to Deopham Green after completing its 100th mission. This aircraft was destined to be the only original aircraft in the 452nd BG to survive the war, completing 125 missions. (Sam Young.)*

down, and with her wheels up *Winnie* did some skating. I thought she would never stop, but finally she hit a ditch. Then it was very quiet. I thought for a moment I was dead. I crawled out of the bomber on the side where it had split open. None of the ten aboard was hurt, just bruised very badly – but no blood or anything. Later, the RAF flew us to London and we made our way back to Seething and yet another new bomber.'

At this time the 2nd Air Division began receiving B-24Ls and B-24Ms. These were the same as the earlier models, but had lighter tail turrets. The B-24L sported a hand operated turret, 300 lb lighter than the conventional unit. The 'L' was soon supplemented by the improved B-24M, which had been introduced in October and reached the Liberator bases in early 1945.

On 3 February 1945 Maj Robert 'Rosie' Rosenthal, flying his 52nd mission, led the 100th BG and the 3rd Division to Berlin. Gen Earle E. Partridge, the 3rd Division CO, approved the selection of a squadron commander to lead the division. Marshal Zhukov's Red Army was only 35 miles from Berlin, and the capital was jammed with refugees fleeing from the advancing Russians. The raid was designed to cause the authorities as much havoc as possible. Some 1,200 B-17s and B-24s, accompanied by 900 fighters, were assembled for the raid. Although the Luftwaffe was almost on its knees, the flak defences were as strong as ever, as Abe Dolim in the 94th BG recalls: 'It was my seventh Berlin mission, and the Germans now had about 1,200 88 mm guns around Berlin. The flak seemed to be more accurate and the barrages more effective than some months ago.'

A total of 2,267 tons of bombs rained down into the 'Mitte', or central district of Berlin, killing an estimated 20,000 to 25,000 people. Reconnaissance photographs revealed that an area 1½ miles square, stretching across the southern half of the 'Mitte', had been devastated. The 8th lost 21 bombers shot down, and another six, including the one carrying Maj Rosenthal, crash-landed inside the

On 31 January 1945 the mission to Bremen was recalled owing to bad weather, and B-17G Heaven Can Wait, *43-37517, piloted by William Appleton, in the 418th Bomb Squadron, broke out of a heavy mist over Thorpe Abbotts and crash-landed after narrowly missing the tower. The crew evacuated before its load of RDX bombs exploded, sending one of its engines 300 ft into the air to land on B-17G 43-38610.* (Thorpe Abbotts Tower Museum.)

Russian lines. Maj Rosenthal was picked up by the Russians, but some crewmen were taken by the Germans and one was lynched by civilians. Of the bombers that returned, 93 suffered varying forms of major flak damage. Among the losses had been *Birmingham Jewel* in the 379th BG, which had set an 8th Air Force record of 128 missions.

On 6 February 1,300 bombers supported by 15 Mustang groups bombed marshalling yards at Chemnitz and Magdeburg. The next day 300 B-17s in the 1st Division were recalled over the North Sea when thick cloud intervened during the mission to synthetic-oil refineries at Lutzkendorf and Meresberg. A single B-17 continued to Essen and dumped its load before returning home alone, luckily without meeting any opposition. Altogether, 22 bombers were lost in crash-landings in England. A similar event occurred on 8 February. This time more than 400 bombers were recalled before leaving the coast of England.

On 10 February 150 B-17s bombed targets in Holland. This was the first raid in which 'Disney' bombs, invented by Capt Edward Terrell of the Royal Navy, were used in anger. The 4,500 lb bomb was powered by a rocket motor in the tail, and was designed to pierce 20 ft of concrete before exploding. Its length prevented carriage in the bomb bay of a B-17, so the nine B-17s in the 92nd BG which were despatched to the E-boat pens at Ijmuiden carried two 'Disneys' under each wing. Col James W. Wilson, the CO, led the raid, photographs later revealed a direct hit at the north end of the pens.

On the following day the Allies issued their Yalta declaration, and the policy of bombing German cities in the path of the Russian advance was put into operation. On the night of 13 February the old city of Dresden, in eastern Germany, was attacked by RAF Bomber Command. Two waves consisting of 800 heavy bombers produced firestorms and horrendous casualties among the civilian population. The next day 400 8th Air Force bombers headed for the devastated city and attempted to stoke up the fires created by RAF Bomber Command, while 900 more bombers attacked Chemnitz, Magdeburg and other targets. William C. Stewart, who 'had never heard of the German city before', was flying his first mission, in the ball turret of a 92nd BG B-17. He recalls: 'When we neared the IP I could see the black bursts of flak directly in front of us at our level. We flew to that place in the sky where the black was heaviest and I heard the bombardier shout: "Bombs away!" The 'plane rose in the air and settled back. We had dropped our bombs on Dresden, which from published reports was still experiencing firestorms from the RAF bombing the night before.' It was late evening before Stewart's crew returned to Podington, because they had to leave their aircraft at another base when the number one engine caught fire. 'At debriefing I learned, when the other crew members answered, that the flak was "meagre",' says Stewart. 'I was to learn later that "intense" flak really was.'

Eighth Air Force crews were to return to the pottery city of Dresden on similar raids in March and April 1945, but the Allied air forces' top priority remained the oil producing centres. On 15 February over 1,000 heavies bombed the Magdeburg synthetic-oil plant, and next

Lt A. J. Novik's B-24 Liberator '031', 'P for Peter', in the 576th Bomb Squadron, 392nd BG, lost its left stabiliser when bombs from a high squadron B-24 hit its tail on the bomb run over Salzbergen on 16 February 1945. Novik nursed P-Peter to Wendling, climbed to 10,000 ft, and ordered the crew to bale out before heading the bomber out towards the Wash. Novik extricated himself from the spinning B-24 with some difficulty and sustained some injuries bailing out. (USAF.)

day almost 1,000 B-17s and B-24s hit oil targets at Dortmünd, Saltzbergen and Gelsenkirchen. On 22 February, George Washington's birthday, the 8th launched 'Clarion', the systematic destruction of the German communications network. The strike was planned by Maj Gen Orvil Anderson, 8th Air Force Chief of Operations. More than 6,000 aircraft from seven different commands were airborne this day, including 1,359 B-17s and B-24s which struck at transportation targets throughout western Germany and northern Holland. All targets were selected with the object of preventing troops being transported to the Russian front, now only a few miles from Berlin. It was all part of a strategy worked out at Yalta by the 'Big Three' earlier that month.

Abe Dolim in the 94th recorded it thus: 'The bombing was carried out at extremely low altitudes, and our targets were secondary rail junctions and marshalling yards in smaller cities not previously bombed. Just east of Ansbach, our target, we passed an enemy airfield and I counted ten Bf 109s and other types on the field. We were only 5,500 ft above the ground, but they did not fire at us. This was the first time that I felt the concussion of our own bombs and also the first time I saw boxcars tumble through the air. I felt we were unnecessarily exposed to light flak, which can be murderous at low altitudes and slow speeds. I feel uneasy when a boxcar attains almost as much altitude as our bomber.'

A B-24 in the 707th Bomb Squadron, 446th BG, on the mission to railway marshalling yards at Aschaffenburg on 25 February 1945. (USAF.)

B-17s of the 91st BG release their bombs over Berlin on 26 February 1945. (USAF.)

B-17s in the 351st BG head for Berlin on 26 February 1945. (USAF.)

Despite the low altitudes flown, the 8th lived up to Anderson's expectations and only five bombers were lost, including one to an Me 262 jet fighter. The next day only two heavies failed to return of the 1,193 despatched. The flak batteries were being deprived of ammunition, and gunners had to conserve their meagre reserves. On 26 February even the normally notorious flak defences in Berlin could shoot down only five bombers.

'Clarion' had ripped the heart out of a crumbling Reich, and the following two months would witness the war's bitter conclusion. Even RAF Bomber Command could reduce its nocturnal rôle and join in the daylight war with the 8th Air Force. By March 1945 the Third Reich was on the brink of defeat, and the systematic destruction of German oil production plants, airfields and communications centres had virtually driven the Luftwaffe from German skies. Despite fuel and pilot shortages Me 262 jet fighters could still be expected to put in rare attacks, and during March almost all enemy fighter interceptions of American heavy bombers were made by the *Jagdevbande*. However, the German jets and rockets had arrived too late and in too few numbers to prevent the inevitable. On 2 March, when the bombers were despatched to synthetic-oil refineries at Leipzig, Me 262s attacked near Dresden.

Abe Dolim, who flew in the deputy lead ship in the 94th BG, recalls: 'One of our bombers took hits from 30 mm cannon fire. It all happened so quickly, only a few airmen saw the action.' There appeared to be no immediate counter to the jet fighters of the dying Luftwaffe, but flak batteries had lost much of their effectiveness thanks to shell shortages and extensive electronic counter measures (ECM) equipment.

On 3 March the largest formation of German jets ever seen made attacks on the bomber formations heading for Dresden and oil targets

Flak peppers the 93rd BG formation on 1 March 1945 on the mission to Augsburg. The two B-24J Liberators in the 409th Bomb Squadron are fitted with Carpet blinkers to 'snow' enemy radar screens, although the bottom aircraft has no Perspex covers over them. (USAF.)

at Ruhrland, and three bombers were shot down. The Luftwaffe seemed to have found a temporary new lease of life, for on the night of 3/4 March 30 Me 410s, which had infiltrated the stream of returning RAF bombers, attacked airfields in Norfolk and Suffolk. Six of the attackers were shot down, two of them them by RAF Mosquitoes. At Tibenham the intruders put a few holes in some buildings, and they

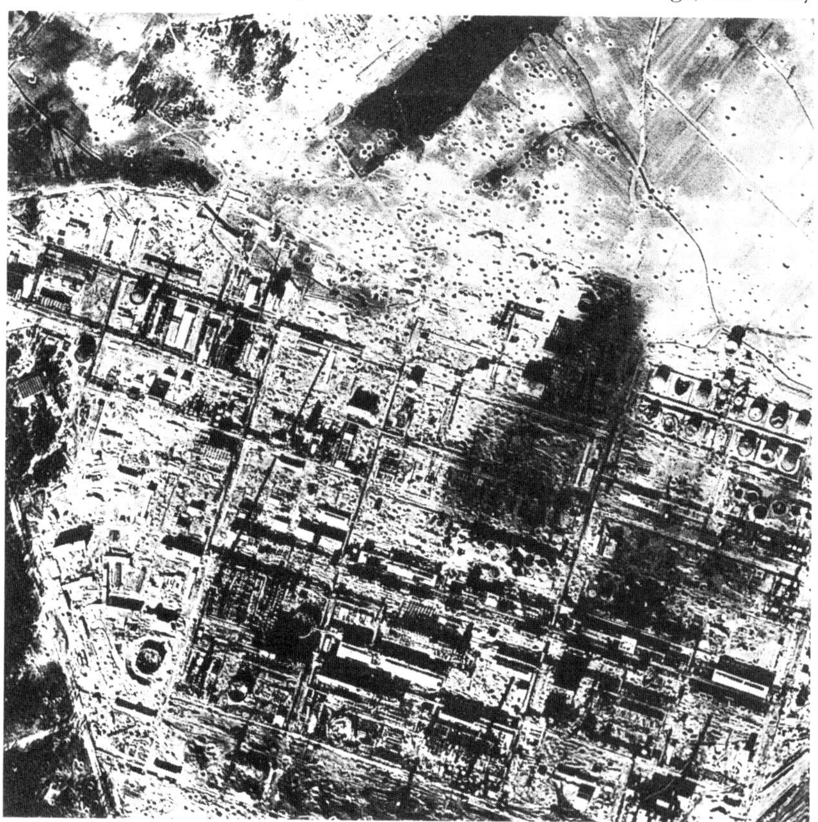

Heavy bomb damage to the oil plant at Politz can quite clearly be seen in this 544th Squadron, 384th BG strike photo taken on 3 March 1945. (USAF.)

damaged the control tower at Bury St. Edmunds. Great Ashfield was bombed and strafed, and Rattlesden, Lavenham and Sudbury were also attacked. The intruders returned again on the night of 4 March, but damage to the bases was insignificant.

On the same day B-17s and B-24s headed singly to assembly points over France, adopting a new technique aimed at conserving fuel. The Fortresses formed up at Troyes, while the Liberator groups assembled near Nancy. The 466th BG, led by Lt Col John Jacobowitz, with Col Ligon flying deputy commander in the number two aircraft, led the 96th Wing to its target at Kitzingen after assembly, but thick cloud persisted over the continent and the bomb run was scrubbed. The secondary target at Aschaffenburg was also clouded over, so the call went out to switch to the marshalling yards at Stüttgart, about 80 miles from the Swiss border. Using H2X, the 466th started a northerly bomb run on the target, but visibility was so poor that crews had difficulty seeing their wingmen. Suddenly, out of the mark roared a group of B-17s, also lost, sending the Liberators scattering wildly in an effort to avert a mid-air collision. The mission was abandoned when 20 B-24s became separated.

The remaining eight B-24s, which had retained some semblance of formation, formed up on the lead aircraft and turned for home. In the lead was an H2X ship which spotted a town through a hole in the clouds. The lead crew navigator identified it as Freiburg, a town lying a few miles from the Rhine and south-west of Stüttgart. Some navigators suspected that the town might be Basle in Switzerland, which was about 25 miles further south. Freiburg was a target of opportunity, and a bomb run was ordered. Several minutes after the bomb run word came through that Basle had been bombed. The order went out for the formation to return to Attlebridge and for crews to remain in their aircraft until they were picked up by the base vehicles. Some crews landed unaware that they had dropped their bombs on Swiss territory. Stringent interrogations by 8th Air Force Intelligence officers followed the dèbacle, and some crews had their return to the States blocked because of the six weeks' investigation into the incident.

News filtered through that the 392nd had also violated neutral territory. At the turning point south of Stüttgart the 14th Wing received a recall message. The 44th started their turn home and the 392nd followed, although it soon lost the 44th from sight. The 392nd lead squadron, led by Col Myron Keilman, made a radar bombing run on Pforzheim, but there was no sign of the second squadron. The 392nd lead squadron returned to England at 13:20. Keilman wrote: 'Shortly after landing, our second squadron returned without apparent difficulty. At their debriefing, the lead crew explained how they got on the outside of the turn and lost us in the cirrus clouds and heavy contrails; that upon breaking out of the clouds they came upon what they believed to be Freiburg, Germany, and bombed it as a target of opportunity. The debriefing was hardly finished when Col Lorin Johnson, the CO, was called to the telephone and a long conflab took place. Zurich, Switzerland, had been bombed.'

The US Ambassador had only recently attended a memorial service and visited reconstruction projects resulting from the previous bombing of Zurich on 18 September 1944. Gen Marshall urged Gen Spaatz to visit Switzerland secretly, and reparations involving many millions of dollars were made to the Swiss Government. A court martial was held at 2nd Air Division headquarters at Ketteringham Hall, with Col James M. Stewart appointed president of the court, but no further action was taken. At least one lead crew was restricted to base until April 1945.

On 15 March 1,282 bombers escorted by 14 fighter groups hit the German Army HQ at Zossen, near Berlin, and a marshalling yard at Orienburg. Two days later 1,260 B-17s and B-24s, again heavily supported by fighters, bombed areas in west and north-central Germany. On 18 March a record 1,327 bombers bombed Berlin again. Although flak was particularly hazardous, 37 Me 262s of the I and II/*Jagdverband* 7 attacked the massive bomber formation and shot down 16 bombers and five fighters for the loss of only two jets. Another 16 bombers were forced to land inside Russian territory. The 'Bloody Hundredth' lost four bombers, including one which was cleaved in two by Me 262 gunfire. The 8th was to lose 30 bombers to

Bombs drop on smoke markers released by the leading B-17Gs in the 100th BG. At top left is Lt Alfonso Guardino's B-17G, 43-37812, in the 351st Bomb Squadron, which crashed with the loss of all nine crew after it was hit by flak and then collided with Lt Laurence Lazzari's B-17 on 23 March 1945, while returning from the mission to Marburg. Lazzari's B-17 was righted and then escorted home by P-51 Mustangs to Thorpe Abbotts with 8 ft of its left wing crumpled. (Thorpe Abbotts Tower Museum.)

the German twin-engined jets by the end of the month.

The jet menace became such a problem that, beginning on 21 March, the 8th flew a series of raids on airfields used by the *Jagdverband*. The raids also coincided with the build-up for the impending crossing of the Rhine by Allied troops. Next day, at the targets of SHAEF headquarters, 1,284 B-17s and B-24s bombed targets east of Frankfürt and ten military encampments in the Ruhr, in preparation for the Allied amphibious crossing of the lower Rhine. Nine fighter groups strafed airfields. Capt Robert B. Grettum's crew in the 392nd BG returned to Wendling in their PFF Liberator, firing flares at 2,000 ft in celebration of completing their final mission. Somebody fired a flare from a gun that was probably not locked. The flare-gun probably spun round, because the aircraft caught fire. Grettum and seven others perished in the ensuing crash.

Chapter Fifteen

Visions of victory

ON 23/24 MARCH, under a 66-mile-long smoke screen and aided by 1,747 bombers from the 8th Air Force, Field Marshal Bernard Montgomery's 2nd Army crossed the Rhine at Wesel. Further south, simultaneous crossings were made by Gen Patton's 3rd Army. B-17 Groups flew two missions, hitting jet-aircraft bases in Holland and Germany, while the B-24s prepared to fly much needed supplies to the armies in the field. Liberator crews who remembered the suicidal low-level missions to Ploesti and Holland viewed their part in the crossing of the Rhine with mounting apprehension.

On 24 March 240 Liberators, loaded with 600 tons of medical supplies, food and weapons, followed in the wake of transports and gliders ferrying troops of the 1st Allied Airborne Army. The 446th, with Lt Col William A. Schmidt, Bungay's Air Executive, flying as 20th Wing Commander, led the 93rd and 448th with 27 aircraft. Flying as low as 50 ft, the Liberators droned over the dropping zone at Wesel at 145 m.p.h., using 10–15° of flap to aid accuracy in the drop. Grey-white smoke shrouded the battlefields and engulfed the city of Wesel. Smoke canisters which had blacked out over 60 miles of the front for more than two days were still burning. The Liberators passed Wesel a mile to the south and continued to the dropping zone, which was strewn with wrecked and abandoned gliders, smouldering haystacks and dead livestock.

Eight of the nine 20th Wing squadrons loosed their wicker loads with attached multi-coloured parachutes in the dropping zone. They encountered spasmodic and highly accurate small-arms fire. This and heavy 20 mm cannon fire caused the loss of six 20th Wing Liberators – three in the 446th and three in the 448th. Seventeen of the Bungay Buckeroos' B-24s sustained battle damage, while the 448th's lead ship, carrying Col Charles B. Westover, the CO, crash-landed in England with two men wounded. The deputy lead crew was forced to bale out over England. Twenty-millimetre fire pierced the armour plating and struck the control column of one of the 93rd Liberators, but the two pilots escaped injury in the subsequent explosion .

One of the B-24s despatched from Shipdham was *Southern Comfort III*. In mythology the phoenix is 'a bird which can only be reborn by dying in flames'. So it was with *Southern Comfort*, which was lost over

B-24 Flying Jackass *in the 854th Bomb Squadron, 491st BG, normally flown by Capt Wilson's crew at North Pickenham. On 24 March 1945 it was flown by 2nd Lt Rice, who landed at Manston, Kent, after the B-24 was badly shot up on the resupply mission to Holland. Next day the Liberator was destroyed in a crash when a RAF Lancaster landed on top of it. Capt Wilson and crew were lost on the 24 March mission. in another Liberator.* (Dan Winston.)

Foggia in August 1943. The ground crew had returned to England and were assigned to a fresh combat crew skippered by Lt Waters. Their brand new B-24 was promptly named *Southern Comfort III*. Their luck held through 25 missions, the crew returning to the States to participate in a Bond-raising tour.

Lt Chandler and his crew, on their fourth mission, flew the 'phoenix' on the supply mission. When the 44th arrived at the dropping zone a fierce battle was raging. The gunners of *Southern Comfort* strafed the German gun emplacements as Allied troops waded

B-24J Liberator Dorothy *in the 453rd BG at snow-covered Old Buckenham in the winter of 1944–45.* (Frank Thomas.)

B-24H Liberator of the 44th BG at dispersal at Shipdham in the winter of 1944–45. (USAF.)

across the river with their guns above their heads. The B-24s had to drop their supplies on the opposite bank. *Southern Comfort III* was less than 100 ft above the ground when, hit by German small-arms fire, it lost an engine. The aircraft rolled over and her belly struck the ground. She raised a cloud of dust, bounced into the air again to about 50 ft, and then exploded. All the crew except the two waist gunners were killed. Sgt Vance returned to Shipdham about three weeks later with both arms in plaster. He had been liberated when the British overran the German field hospital where he was being held captive.

B-17G-50-VE, 44-8183 in the 418th Bomb Squadron, 100th BG, at its snow-covered dispersal site at Thorpe Abbotts during the winter of 1944–45. (Thorpe Abbotts Tower Museum.)

B-24J-5-FO 42-50896 Southern Comfort III which was lost on the Rhine crossing mission. (Via Mike Bailey.)

Approximately 6,000 aircraft, including Liberators, gliders, transports and fighters, took part in the Wesel operation. The murderous ground fire probably accounted for the 14 B-24s which failed to return. Five of the 20 officers at 20th Wing Headquarters, including Gen Ted Timberlake, who flew in an escort aircraft, flew on the mission. Despite intense ground fire the Wing hedge-hopped to friendly territory and re-formed in the Brussels area for the return flight to England. Some 104 B-24s returned to their bases with some degree of damage.

Everywhere the Allies were victorious, but while the enemy kept fighting missions continued almost daily. Bomber crews were now hard pressed to find worthwhile targets, and the planners switched attacks from inland targets to coastal areas. On 4 April the 92nd BG dropped 'Disney' bombs on pens at Hamburg while other groups bombed Kiel. German jet activity seemed to be on the increase, and the Liberators were attacked by Me 262s. One of the jets made a pass at the 458th formation which was en route to Perleberg, but broke off the attack after being fired on by several B-24s in the formation. More Me 262s successfully intercepted the 20th Wing, which was heading for the jet airfield at Wesendorf near Dortmund, and shot down three 448th Liberators.

Col Troy Crawford, CO of the 446th BG, who was flying a blue-painted Mosquito borrowed from the 25th BG which was being used to monitor the formation, was shot down in extraordinary circumstances. Paul Surbaugh, a pilot in the 446th, explains: 'Someone announced over the radio the presence of an Me 262 and Col Crawford, unable to outfly it, moved in closer to the Group for mutual protection. His convergence was said to have been a textbook "pursuit curve", and with the Mosquito frontal view looking not unlike the Me

Lt Robert L. Mains' B-24M-10-FO, 44-50838 in the 714th Bomb Squadron, 448th BG, was cleaved in two by fire from an Me 262 SE of Hamburg on the mission to Parchim airfield (Wesendorf) on 4 April 1945. Nine of the crew were killed. The right wing burned and broke off and the weight of the left wing threw the B-24 over on its back. Charles E. Cupp Jr, the top turret gunner, was sucked out wearing a parachute a few hundred feet from the ground and he landed in a street in Ludwigslust where he was captured and made a PoW. Mains' crew were on their 28th mission. (USAF.)

262, and considering the great rapidity of events in air combat at times, plus the standing order to fire on all approaching aircraft, a hail of bullets sent the Mosquito spiralling downward.'

Col Crawford was captured and taken for interrogation near Standahl. He had to endure the interrogation knowing that Standahl was to be the 446th's next target. Crawford was later approached by some Germans who realized that Germany had lost the war. He and 40 other Americans finally escaped to the American lines, and Crawford eventually arrived back at Flixton on 25 April 1945. During his absence Lt Col Schmidt assumed command, a post he continued to hold when Crawford returned to the USA.

A 25th BG Mosquito similar to the one flown by Col Troy Crawford in the 448th BG which was shot down on 4 April, on the mission to an airfield at Perleberg, after being mistaken for an Me 262. (Via Peter Frost.)

An Me 262 stalks a solitary Liberator somewhere over Germany early in 1945. (USAF.)

On 5 April the weather over the continent improved dramatically, and the B-17s were despatched to U-boat pens on the Baltic coast. The following day the 467th flew its 200th mission of the war, a bombing raid on Halle. On this mission one B-24 was involved in a collision with an enemy fighter which was suspected of deliberately trying to ram American bombers. It tore away the starboard fin and rudder, but the crew succeeded in reaching Allied territory before they baled out. A few days earlier an Fw 190 had rammed a lead Liberator and careered into the deputy lead, resulting in all three aircraft going down.

On 7 April Lt (later Col) George Matecko was among those at the briefing at Old Buckenham, apprehensive that the Luftwaffe might be resorting to 'Kamikaze' tactics. 'However,' he states, 'Lt Col Jerry V. Davidson, CO of the 734th Squadron, opined that the pilot must have either been killed or unconscious when the collision occurred. This was later proved correct at a post-war debriefing.' In fact, the 453rd encountered only Me 262s, as Matecko recalls: 'An Me 262 climbed between the 453rd Bomb Group and the Group ahead. I called to S/Sgt Adler to swing his guns to 11 o'clock, and as he swung his turret a second Me 262 pulled up about 150 ft ahead of us. Adler fired into the Me 262, getting hits through the cockpit, left wing, and left engine. Sgt Klien observed the Me 262 continue its climb, now trailing smoke, upwards another 1,000 to 1,500 ft, when it fell off into a vertical dive. It was last seen burning, in the dive, going straight down into a cloud at 3,500 ft. Both my crew and other crew members surmised that the Me 262 could not have pulled out of the dive at that low altitude. Maj Erich Rudorffer, one of Germany's leading aces (222 kills) commanded Group II, *Jagdverbande* 7, the first true Me 262 squadron composed of famous Luftwaffe pilots, located at Kaltenkirchen airfield near Hamburg. These Me 262s were most likely from that squadron.'

Radios in the 100th BG formation also came to life with shouts of "Bandits in the area!" Griswold Smith, a pilot in the 100th recalls: 'This had been called several times on other missions, and we had begun to look upon it as calling "Wolf", but I called the gunners on interphone and told them to be on the alert anyhow. Then I heard the groups in front of us calling for P-51s as they were being hit by Bf 109s. Baugh was the first on our crew to see an enemy fighter. He reported them attacking and shooting down a straggler.

'The first pass was made from 7 o'clock low, up through "C" Squadron and then on to us. Baugh and Russo were the first in the squadron to open fire. This Bf 109 put a couple of slugs into us. One went through the nose and almost got Wilkerson and Turnipseed. When this happened Wilk' said he looked at "Turnip" and could see it dawn on "Turnip's" face that this was the "real McCoy". "Turnip" started unlatching the nose guns and firing like hell. Wilk' said that he started shooting at our P-51 escort and "Turnip" maintained he was "keeping the area clear". The fighter went past us and turned back down at us. Wilk' and Szalwinski were pouring .50s into him from their two turrets, and O'Leary got a few from the waist. I think he was diving directly for us, but he came just in front and knocked the left horizontal stabilizer off Lt Martin's ship in front of us. That Bf 109 diving into the formation spurting flames all over presented such a vivid picture that I shall never forget it. When he hit Martin's ship there must have been some sort of explosion, as the nose and cockpit of our ship were filled with black smoke and dust. The Bf 109's wing flew off and went over my wing, knocking Lt Joe King's ship in the "horizontal diamond". (Both Martin and King managed to make it back to England.) Wilk' and our crew got credit for the '109.

'Another Bf 109 came in from 5 o'clock high. Everyone said he was coming directly at us, but our gunners put out so much lead that he diverted and crashed into a ship in the lead squadron. We saw both ships explode. The reason we got so many fighter attacks directed at us was because we were the top ship and the corner ship in the group, and therefore around us was the least possible concentration of friendly fire. Ordinarily, fighters made their passes in a dive to get greater speed. The enemy fighters stayed with us for about an hour.

'We were at 15,000 ft as no flak was expected. However, there was plenty of accurate flak at the target. I never thought I would be glad to see flak, but I was this day because it meant the fighters wouldn't "come in". We started out with ten ships in our squadron, and on "bombs away" there were six ships. We were glad to return from this one. There were so many holes in the nose that Wilk' nearly froze sitting up there on the way home. There was plenty of close support by the P-51s all the way back across the North Sea. I guess they finally found us.'

On 8 April, more than 1,150 B-17s and B-24s, escorted by 14 groups of Mustangs, bombed a wide variety of targets in the Leipzig, Nürnberg and Chemnitz areas. On 10 April Griswold Smith was in the 100th BG formation which bombed the German jet airfield at Burg near Magdeburg: 'This was just about our worst mission of all. We were flying in the low squadron, which was the worst place to be when jets attacked. The jets usually made their attacks in twos and threes from 6 o'clock low or level, because from that angle they looked like P-51s with wingtip tanks and the gunners were afraid to shoot until they got in real close. They would coast in on a formation from the rear with their jets off, open fire, turn on their jets and vanish with terrific speed. They were armed with 30 mm cannon.

'They made several passes at us from 6 o'clock low. I distinctly remember two ships going down in flames. I believe a couple of others were crippled and knocked out of formation; one or two aborted earlier. Anyway, there were damned few left when we went over the target. Lt Reeve, who was on his first mission, was flying in my squadron in front of me and a little higher. He burst into flames and a wing ripped off on one of the first jet passes. They put a few holes in us, too, but no-one was hurt. I credited my life to Baugh and Russo, the tail and ball turret gunners, for putting out so much accurate fire that the jets diverted their attacks when they came in close. We were in the best position for them to attack.'

The continual pounding of German airfields reduced the threat posed by the jets. However, othe hazards sometimes caused casualities in the B-17 groups. On 13 April the 398th BG from Nuthampstead flew its 188th mission of the war, to Neumunster. Over the target a leading aircraft salvoed his RDX bombs in error. Two of them touched about 400 ft below, exploded, and brought down six Fortresses in the 601st Bomb Squadron, five of which had to be abandoned on the continent. RDX bombs were fitted with close-proximity fuses and were most unstable at all times unless handled with great care. Bombing results were later described as 'excellent', but the price had been high indeed.

On 14 April the B-17s and Liberators were once again called upon to carry out a specialist task. Their target was a pocket of German resistance (some estimates put the force at 122,000 men) holding out and manning gun batteries in the Royan area at Point de Grave. Their resistance was denying the Allies the use of the port of Bordeaux, and the bombers were called upon to help dislodge them after all appeals to surrender had proved in vain.

Conditions were perfect, and crews at briefing believed it would be a 'milk run' as the defences were neglible and the flak was unlikely to reach the high-flying bombers. However, almost from take-off things began to go wrong. At Horsham St. Faith two B-24s fell near the base shortly after take-off. *Hookem Cow* crashed at about 15:15 in the parish of Hainford which borders the airfield. The other, belonging to the 754th Squadron, crashed 15 minutes later near the base at Spixworth.

Altogether some 1,161 heavies hit 22 defensive installations along the Gironde estuary. The 467th successfully dropped all of its 2,000 bombs within 1,000 ft of the MPI, half the bombs falling within 500 ft. This was a bombing pattern unsurpassed in 8th Air Force history.

B-24H 6X-S in the 854th Bomb Squadron, 491st BG, releases its Napalm canisters over the coastal installations at Royan, France, on 15 April 1945. (USAF.)

B-24H-25-FO Hookem Cow, *42-95120, in the 458th BG, named after a club in the home town of Capt Ollum and his crew chief, Sgt James McGinn (pictured) – St Paul, Minnesota, was a major cattle centre. Ollum's wife's portrait was also painted on the starboard side, with the name* Stinky. *All of the artwork was by squadron artist Harold Johnston. On 14 April 1945, just after take-off, the No.2 engine caught fire and exploded two miles north of Horsham St. Faith airfield, killing the pilot, D. R. Totten, and four crew and injuring two men. B-24J-100-CO, piloted by R. M. Gibson, also crashed, killing six men and injuring another. (George Reynolds.)*

The view from a 487th BG bombardier's compartment during the run-in to the target at Royan on 15 April 1945. (Robert E. Foose.)

The 389th BG lost four of its Liberators when 3rd Air Division B-17s, making a second run over the target, released their fragmentation bombs through the Sky Scorpions' formation. Two Liberators plummeted to the ground, while the other two crash-landed in France. A fifth limped back to England.

On the next day nearly 850 2nd and 3rd Air Division aircraft returned to the area, and for the first time carried Napalm; 460,000 gal of it. The 1st Air Division carried 1,000 and 2,000 lb GP bombs, while three fighter groups snuffed out any gun emplacements which opened fire on the bombers. Mosquitoes were also called in to sow a cloud of chaff to snow radar screens which might be used to direct the radar-controlled flak guns. These precautions were the only protection the bombers had to prevent their lethal cargoes being exploded by German gun batteries.

The bombers released their 75–85 gal liquid-fire tanks, along with

A direct flak hit tore the nose off this 855th Bomb Squadron, 491st BG, B-24 Liberator. (Via Mike Bailey.)

A 446th B-24H Liberator drops its bombs over Salzburg during the penultimate mission of the war, on 21 April 1945. (Author's collection.)

conventional incendiaries, on the east bank of the Gironde estuary. One 458th Liberator left the formation after bomb release and headed inland with one engine feathered. A total of 1,280 heavies, supported by the French ground troops of the 6th Army group, bombed 16 defensive installations. No flak was encountered and French forces later captured the port.

On 17 April Dresden was again bombed. The German corridor was shrinking rapidly, and the American and Russian bomb lines now crossed at several points on briefing maps. During the week of 18 to 25 April, missions were brief and scrubbed almost simultaneously. General Patton's advance was so rapid that on one occasion at least crews were lining up for take-off when a message was received to say that Patton's forces had captured the target the B-17s were to bomb!

The end came on 25 April, when 275 B-17s escorted by four fighters groups bombed the Skoda armaments plants at Pilsen in Czechoslovakia and the B-24s, escorted by four fighter groups, bombed four rail complexes surrounding Hitler's mountain retreat at Berchtesgarden. Lt Lewis B. Fisher's crew were the last in the 92nd to be shot down when their aircraft was struck by a flak burst. No parachutes were seen. Next day the American and Russian armies met at Torgau and further bombing missions were cancelled.

Starting on 1 May, before the Germans surrendered, the 8th Air Force mounted 'Chowhound' missions (together with RAF 'Manna' operations, which had begun on 29 April), dropping food supplies to starving Dutch civilians. During the winter of 1944–45 15,000 Dutch civilians had died of starvation. Some of the deaths had been caused by the Germans in revenge for the help which Dutch railway workers had given the Allies at the time of the Arnhem operation. Agricultural land had been flooded as an anti-invasion measure, and the invasion of Germany from the west had also left 3½-million Dutch in western Holland living in a virtual island Fortress.

Griswold Smith recalls: 'The Germans had promised us a corridor to

B-17G-70-DL 44-6954 of the 569th Bomb Squadron, 390th BG, releases its cargo of supplies to the Dutch in May 1945. (USAF.)

fly across the country unmolested at low level. We could see German troops marching around in their black uniforms with swastikas flying. Our second mercy mission was on 5 May, the day the Germans in Holland surrendered. We went in at 200 ft, buzzing a small sail boat on the Zuider Zee and blowing it over. We had orders not to drop unless we saw crowds of civilians, but the Dutch were lined up around the edges of the field waving and cheering. They had really turned out. Flags were flying everywhere and the streets were packed with people waving and cheering. It was a great day for the Dutch. We dropped our 4,000 lb of food after trouble with the improvised "drop doors" in the bomb bay. We buzzed Amsterdam a couple of times. John O'Leary, the waist gunner, who was riding up front in the nose where he could get a better view of the town, called over the interphone: "Church steeple coming in at 12 o'clock high!"'

The B-17s headed for their drop zone at Vogelenzang, a Scout Jamboree park. The Dutch had cut out of flowers growing in a bulb field the words 'Thank You Boys' in large letters. Bill Carleton recalls: 'I remember a little Dutch boy looking up and trying to race us on his bicycle. There were 'planes ahead of us who made their drops and people were running across the target area to get the food, unmindful of the fact that they could be knocked to Kingdom Come with a can of Spam. [A German soldier threw a Dutch girl to the ground and shielded her with his own body on one such overshoot. The overshoot hit and killed him, but the Dutch girl survived.] 'Planes all around us were starting to drop their food, but our 'plane flew across the field without any salvo. The bombardier had gone to sleep! He awoke with a jerk and made the drop into the Zuider Zee. Such folly, but how typical. The best of intentions, the worst in execution. I hope the forthcoming peace would be better than that!'

On 7 May the heavies flew their sixth and final supply drop to Holland. The supply drops had already claimed two B-17s, when they collided soon after take-off. Tragically, the war was to claim its final

The Dutch show their gratitude for the 8th Air Force mercy drops by mapping out the words 'Many Thanks'. (Hans Onderwater.)

heavy bomber victims on the 7 May mission. A 95th BG B-17 with eight crew and six passengers (from the Horham photographic section), piloted by Lt Lionel N. 'Spider' Sceurman, got into difficulties over the North Sea after a food drop near Hilversum. At 1,500 ft oil was seen spurting on to the No.2 engine nacelle. Oil pressure dropped to zero and thick, acrid smoke filled the fuselage. The engine was shut down, but the fire extinguishers failed to put out the fire. Sceurman, who put the Fortress into a controlled dive to 'blow' the fire out, knew the engine was in danger of exploding, so he ordered the crew to bale out. Incredibly, six of the crew and one of the photographers got out before the engine exploded at 600 ft. The bomber's wingtip hit the surface of the sea, and the aircraft cartwheeled and sank immediately. All this happened just five miles east of Benacre Ness on the Suffolk coast.

A Lancaster of No. 550 Squadron diverted the nearest ship to the scene, and the RAF crew even dropped their own Mae Wests to crew members seen in the water. Lt James R. Schwarz, the co-pilot, and S/Sgt David C. Condon, the togglier, were picked up by an ASR

The final casualty, B-17G-75-VE 44-8640 of the 334th Bomb Squadron, 95th BG. This veteran of 58 bombing missions and six food drops was lost over the North Sea on the afternoon of 7 May 1945, only about 15 hours after the final surrender, while returning from a food drop to Holland. Ironically, this photo was taken on 20 April, from Better Duck, *by* A. N. Braidic, *the original bombardier in 1st Lt Lionel N. Sceurman's crew; the very crew that was lost in 44-8640 on the mercy mission of 7 May.* (Via Ken Wright.)

OA-10A Catalina of the 5th ERS at Halesworth. Lt Russell J. Cook, the navigator, was rescued by an RAF Walrus but died before reaching hospital. The bodies of 'Spider' Sceurman and Norbert Kuper, the armourer-gunner, and one of the six passengers, were recovered and, together with those of Cook and S/Sgt John J. Keller, the ball turret gunner, whose body was washed ashore, were interred in the US Military Cemetery at Madingley, near Cambridge. Sceurman had wanted to celebrate the final day of the war with the same crew he had trained with in Florida, and at the flight line had asked Tony Braidic, his original bombardier, if he would change places with Dave Condon. Braidic declined, and flew the last mission with Lt Paul Crider instead.

Crews who returned safely had their pistols and ammunition collected. At 21:00 the radio announced that VE (Victory in Europe) Day would be announced next afternoon, 8 May, at 15:00. When victory came the bomb groups brought Allied PoWs home from their camps in eastern Europe to France, and airlifted displaced persons from all over Europe. They transported troops from the UK to Casablanca, where they continued on to the China-Burma-India Theatre, and also acted as 'moving vans' for fighter groups to be based in Germany. 'Trolley' or 'Revival' missions in bombers crammed with ground personnel were flown at heights ranging from 1,000 to 3,000 ft over bombed-out cities. These 'Cook's Tours', as they were known, showed the 'tourists' the results of Allied bombing over the past four years.

The middle of May saw the bomb groups leaving the east of England for America or Germany. People thronged the streets of the towns and villages as the 'Yanks' marched to waiting trucks and railway stations en route to ports of embarkation. Bombers with 20-man crews left almost daily. Liberators in the 467th circled Rackheath in a farewell gesture. *Witchcraft* was flown home by Lt Fren Jansen with crew chief Joe Ramirez aboard, having completed 130 missions without a turn back. On 13 May 1945 the 467th BG led the Victory Flypast over the 8th's Headquarters at High Wycombe. It was a proud day for everyone in the group, not least Col Albert Shower, the only bomb group commander in the 8th Air Force to bring his group to England and retain command of it until the end of hostilities.

Many people, of course, were sad to see the bomb groups go, and a few Americans, married to their English wives, have remained ever since. The young, sometimes brash, Americans had become a part of everyday life, and their departure was greeted with a mixture of great sadness and joy. Almost all left their youth behind in a land they had come to love and respect. Many hundreds lie buried at Madingley, where each year a memorial service is held for those who died flying from these shores. A few miles away bomber, fighter and transport wings of the US 3rd Air Force, established in England on 7 August 1948 under the command of Maj Gen Leon Johnson, continue to maintain the peace and freedom won by units of the 8th Air Force operating from 'Little America' alongside their RAF comrades in 1942–45.

Index